The Essential
G.E.M. Skues

The Essential G.E.M. Skues

edited by Kenneth Robson

A&C Black • London

First published 1998 by
A & C Black (Publishers) Ltd
35 Bedford Row, London WC1R 4JH

ISBN 0 7136 3590 4

A CIP catalogue record for this book
is available from the British Library.

Typeset in 10 on 12pt Galliard
Printed and bound in Great Britain by
Creative Print and Design Wales
(Book Division), Ebbw Vale

Dedication

For Eileen, Graham, Jay, Daniel and Gabrielle

Publisher's note
In the preparation of this publication every effort has been made to locate the legal owner of the literary estate of G.E.M. Skues. Unfortunately, it has been impossible to do so. However, members of the Skues family, including the widow of G.E.M.'s nephew, and G.E.M.'s great nephew, have co-operated in the book's compilation.

Contents

Editor's acknowledgements

I wish to record my gratitude to a number of people who have helped me in writing and editing this volume of G.E.M. Skues's works.

Peter Lapsley suggested that I might like to edit Skues's writings, and he has read the book in manuscript and made invaluable and helpful comments throughout.

Roy Darlington has discussed Skues with me on numerous occasions, has read the manuscript, provided important background information about Abbots Barton and allowed me to fish there over many years. He also provided the transparency of the Highland Burn for the front of the dust jacket.

I have been privileged to use the fine illustrations drawn by Alex Jardine for Skues's book, *Itchen Memories*, thanks to the generosity of his son, Charles. These are entirely appropriate to this work. I should also like to thank Charles for his own equally beautiful illustration which appears on page 77.

Eric Williams provided the photograph of me on the back flap of the dust jacket.

Winifred Allen, widow of Derek Allen, Skues's nephew, and Keith Skues, his great nephew, unearthed photographs, some never seen before, of their illustrious ancestor.

I am particularly grateful to John Goddard for writing the foreword and for providing me with information and comment on Skues.

Sidney Vines, Simon Ward and Gordon Mackie have helped in various ways whilst Donald Overfield has encouraged me throughout and provided the photograph of the Nadder Vale Hotel.

Peter Williams allowed me to read his correspondence as a 16-year-old with Skues, whilst Richard Hunter obtained snippets of correspondence between Skues and W.H. Lawrie.

The Flyfishers' Club was Skues's spiritual home and houses many of his artefacts. I am indebted to the Club for the use of a great deal of original material and, especially, to John Morgan, the Club Librarian, who provided it.

My daughter, Jay, has cast an expert professional eye over the page proofs.

Finally, I wish to thank Jonathan Taylor of A & C Black, and Nick Lyons, for their support.

Editor's note

Skues used the 'New Numbers' scale which came in with the introduction of eyed hooks. I have transposed these to the 'Old Numbers'
scale, originating from the days of eyeless hooks, but now commonly used. Skues also tied flies on hooks sized 13, 15 and 17 which are
now almost unobtainable.

The present Abbotts Barton Fishery spells its name with two *t*s. I
have used one *t* throughout as this is what Skues did.

I have also endeavoured to retain some of Skues's spellings pecu-
liar to him although to be found in the Oxford English dictionary,
e.g. *recognize*.

Except in chapters 1 and 3, my comments are differentiated from
Skues's writings insomuch as they are not indented from the margin.

I have used the general convention of first letter capitals for artificial flies and lower case first letters for naturals. Skues did not always
differentiate between the two.

Editing Skues's works created a problem as to how they should be
best presented. I decided to divide the book into various aspects of
his fishing with a linking narrative to provide informed comment and
background. This enables the readers to dip into the book as they
will, and to savour the incredible versatility of Skues on virtually every
fly fishing topic known to man.

Foreword

When we look back at the history of fly fishing, two names stand out above all others. They are F.M. Halford, the father of the dry fly who during his lifetime became a living legend, and G.E.M. Skues, now regarded as the father of nymph fishing although during his lifetime he was never accorded the same adulation or following that Halford enjoyed.

I have considered Skues as my hero ever since I first learned the finer points of nymph fishing many years ago under the tutelage of my great friend, the late Major Oliver Kite, whom I consider one of the greatest exponents of the relatively modern methods of fishing the deep-sunk nymph. I was therefore greatly thrilled to be asked to write a foreword to this monumental collected volume of Skues's writings.

At one time I became completely besotted with nymph fishing and would always fish the nymph in preference to the dry fly. Today the opposite applies because, although successful nymph fishing requires a high degree of skill, once mastered I feel it offers less of a challenge than dry fly fishing where an educated trout will test your prowess to its limit.

Despite this, I still look upon Skues with considerable awe as, without doubt, the greatest thinking fly fisher ever to put pen to paper. In this respect, he was way ahead of Halford as an observant and creative angler.

Even today, Skues has a great following with fly fishers all over the world as the constant reprints of his many books prove. I am sure that his followers, myself included, will be eternally grateful to Ken Robson for providing such a splendid book on this great master of the angle.

Whether one is an avid reader, a keen fly fisher or merely a fishing book collector, this is one book that should be given a place of honour on the bookshelf. I am sure that with time it will become one of the great classics of fly fishing literature. While I found it very difficult to put down once I had started reading, I feel it should be looked upon as one of the ultimate bedside books, where it can be savoured slowly and so thoroughly absorbed.

I think the editor of this book has missed his vocation since he would have made a wonderful detective! The hours, or more probably years, of research that must have gone into *The Essential G.E.M. Skues* (much of it, incidentally, completely new) is absolutely breathtaking.

Did you know, contrary to the popular belief that Skues was a rather grim-faced, irascible martinet he was, in fact, a lovable, tolerant and generous person with a great sense of humour?

Another very interesting and illuminating fact that has now come to light is the possibility that Skues may well have been at times fishing with weighted nymphs long before they were apparently invented and perfected by Sawyer. While he never mentioned fishing with deep-sunk nymphs – probably for obvious reasons – it now transpires from the editor's research that on occasions Skues perfected and fished with a shrimp pattern which must have been fished below the surface. Apart from this, we are now told that his great friend and fishing companion, Dr. Barton, did in fact use weighted nymphs designed to sink by winding fuse wire round the hook shank. If this is correct then it would seem inconceivable that Skues was unaware of this.

Finally, the information collated on Skues's boyhood and early life, never before covered in such depth, is alone worth the price of this book.

John Goddard
Cobham, Surrey
April 1998

CHAPTER 1

The Life of G.E.M. Skues

In 1857, W.C. Stewart, one of the greatest names in the history of fly fishing, published his book, *The Practical Angler*, and converted the world to upstream wet fly fishing. The following year was born the man who would ultimately introduce the practice of fishing upstream with wet fly and nymph to the chalk streams. It was an imaginative way of modifying the system of dry fly fishing – and complementary to it – introduced by another great man, Frederic Halford, which had become elevated into a rigid cult by some of his followers.

Skues wrote more words on fly fishing than any man in history, and most of them were wise, observant, original and creative. His experience and expertise are recorded in his six books, countless articles, correspondence and an unpublished manuscript of reminiscences.

Skues explored virtually every aspect of fly fishing: trout and their behaviour, their environment, fly dressing and fly patterns, entomology, fishing tackle, tactics and strategy. Though he will be for ever associated with the development of nymph fishing, he never neglected the dry fly, and he was probably the greatest all-round fly fisherman ever to have strode the banks of a chalk stream.

George Edward Mackenzie Skues was born on the 13th August, 1858 at St. John's, Newfoundland, and was the eldest in a family of five sisters and three brothers. The Skues family were natives of Helston in Cornwall, and his father's forbears were for generations Receivers of Tin Dues for the Duchy of Cornwall. His grandmother was a Mackenzie and sister of Lord Seaforth from whence he took one of his many pen names, Seaforth and Soforth, from a nickname he was given at Winchester School. His father was William Mackenzie Skues, a Surgeon with the Newfoundland Company, and his mother, Margaret, daughter of Christopher Ayre, Clerk of the Parliament and Acting Colonial Secretary of the colony.

At the age of three, Skues was brought to his grandparents' house in Aberdeen from Newfoundland in a sailing vessel. He was never to cross the Atlantic again though he was to correspond with a number of Americans including Theodore Gordon, Edward Hewitt and James Leisenring.

The young boy was left with his grandparents and two sisters whilst his father and mother went to India on service. The grandparents moved to Langford in Somerset and then to Wrington on the River Yeo. In 1867 Skues had an operation on his left eye which permanently impaired his sight in that eye and which makes his success in later life as fly fisherman and fly dresser all the more remarkable.

In July 1872 Skues and a school fellow went up to Winchester as candidates for scholarships at Winchester College. It was thought that he might be good enough for a small scholarship at a certain other public school but that it would be worth the expense of trying the Winchester entrance to get him accustomed to the examination atmosphere. There were 150 candidates on the first day; on the second 40; on the third there were 20 candidates left for the *vive voce* examination of which he was one. He was interviewed by the Head and Dr. Spooner of Spoonerism fame. Fifteen were elected and he was one – 14th out of 15. Skues said he never understood how he was selected as his school fellow was far better than he was. He thought his performance on the Euclid paper helped. He tackled the six riders out of the 18 problems and appeared to have got them correct.

In 1877 he left Winchester. His comments on the school reflect both his loyalty and sturdy independence. He said, 'All through my five years at Winchester I was dimly conscious of a pressure to mould me to a pattern, and though I count these five years as the happiest of my life, and though I came away with a lifelong affection for my school and with a strong liking for most of my school fellows and an active dislike for only one, my instinct was to resist the pressure and to retain my individuality.'

After school he went to live for a year in the Channel Islands with his parents who had taken up residence there. Whilst there, he injured both his wrists playing football. He claimed that they were weakened permanently and this may have influenced his preference for light rods and short, accurate casting.

The following year he entered the offices of the family's solicitors as an articled clerk. The firm of James Powell was located in Essex Street, off the Strand. By 1895 Skues had become a partner and the firm subsequently became Powell, Skues and Graham Smith. He was to remain as an active partner until 1940 when he retired at the age of 81.

He was to have little time for trout angling in the next few years apart from a few expeditions to the Thames where he fished for dace and chub with the fly. However, he began to take *The Fishing Gazette*, that essential piece of Victorian fishing literature for all game, coarse and sea anglers. It cost him 2d(½p) a week. His first contributions to that journal, in 1886, were, surprisingly, letters about sea fishing. His first article to be accepted appeared in 1891 and with characteristic modesty was entitled *Some Jottings of an Amateur Fly Dresser*. He signed the article and others which followed 'Val Conson', a legal abbreviation for 'valuable consideration'. It was a pen name he used for a long time in contributions to *The Fishing Gazette* in the hope that the editor might find them worthy of cash remuneration. Skues said that it was many a long day before the hint intended to be conveyed was taken.

Throughout his life he used a large variety of pseudonyms. He said that he wrote so much and so frequently he feared that readers would tire of so much from one pen, and often used differing names for different subjects. For instance, if a paper were a bit statistical he would sign it E.O.E. Accountants used E.O.E. as an abbreviation for 'Errors and Omissions Excepted'. The pen name 'A Limity Dincombe' was used, he stated, as a man of restricted means. Others he used included 'S.A.S.', 'Simplex Mundishes', 'Spent Naturalist', 'W.A.G.', 'B. Hinde', 'Unspoiled Child', 'Captain Stoke', 'A. Fluker', 'Integer Vitae', 'I. Caunter Fordham', 'A. Butt' and 'Current Calomel'.

Skues had other interests, and London afforded him the opportunity of regularly visiting the finest theatre in the world. He saw some of the great actors and actresses of that time including Henry Irving and Ellen Terry. He recalled once visiting the theatre in the early nineteen hundreds and seeing the then King, Edward VII, seated in a box with his mistress, Lily Langtry. He was even consumed with ambitions to be a dramatic author. 'I perpetrated some appalling trash in pursuit of that ambition. I have destroyed all of it long ago being convinced that I have not the faculty for writing drama.' If he had been successful the fishing world might have been deprived of a great deal for his easy conversational style was ideally suited to the subject in which he made his name.

In later life, he may have given the impression of being somewhat of a solitary. This was certainly not the case in his younger days. His work and colleagues brought him into contact with London society, and he speaks in his reminiscences of meeting at a friend's house for dinner Oscar Wilde and the African explorer, Stanley.

1883 was a turning point in Skues's fishing life. He visited the Fisheries Exhibition of that year and saw there beautifully tied split-winged floaters which were so much better than the flies he had used before. He also fished on the Colne for dace and chub, and on the Tweed and South Esk for trout. He was then invited by Irwin B. Cox, a client of his law firm and one of the proprietors of the country magazine *The Field,* to a day's fishing on the River Itchen which Cox had recently rented at Abbots Barton. This resulted in his purchasing a decent fly rod. On the first day he met Francis Francis there and was so impressed by Francis's success in taking a leash of two pounders that it inspired in him an enthusiasm for the floating fly which was clinched when, in 1887, he was presented with Halford's *Floating Flies and How to Dress Them.* Until then his fishing had been entirely empirical and he had no idea why one fly offered a better chance than another. With the advent of *Floating Flies* he began to get ideas on the subject. In the latter part of that year he took up trout-fly dressing and read in the British Museum and elsewhere every book he could find on the subject, and analysed and recorded the dressings.

Cox, seeing his enthusiasm, gave him leave to fish the Itchen whenever he wished, and this continued until 1917 when Cox gave up the lease and Skues joined the little syndicate which took over the water. His love affair with that river was to continue until 1938 when he resigned his rod. During those years, he met most of the great fly fishers of his time.

He broadened his fishing experience by holidays on the Tweed and the South Esk in Scotland, and, in 1888, the Rivers Coquet and Wear in Northumberland. Later he fished in Bavaria, Bosnia and Norway, and on the Ure in Yorkshire. He was certainly no narrow chalk stream man, and acquired a knowledge of the upstream wet fly which was to form the basis of his later theories on the chalk streams.

In 1889, he became the happy owner of Halford's *Dry Fly Fishing in Theory and Practice* which became to him, as to many others, a sort of gospel.

In September, 1891, he met Halford during a week's fishing on the Itchen and made such a good impression that he was invited to become a member of the Flyfishers' Club which had been founded in 1884 by R.B. Marston, editor of *The Fishing Gazette*, H.S. Hall, William Senior, Francis Francis and others. It was destined to become the most famous fishing club in the world. Skues turned down the invitation because he had suffered a series of infections which he suspected might be tuberculosis, a family malady, and did not expect to live long. However, a cruise to South Africa seems to have restored him to full vigour and he joined the Club in 1893, proposed by Frederic Halford and seconded by William Senior who became a life-long friend. Skues said it was 'a fellowship which I have ever since had good reason to regard as one of the great privileges of my life.'

Meanwhile, both of Skues's parents had died in the early 1890s, and he became responsible for his four sisters and two brothers, and in 1894 he moved the family to Croydon where they lived for many years.

Though continuing to fish the Itchen with the dry fly, Skues was becoming more and more convinced that when trout were not taking the floating dun it was more profitable to use an upstream wet fly. A period of experimentation followed with articles explaining his research in *The Fishing Gazette* and *The Field*. This culminated in the publication in 1910 of his first book, *Minor Tactics of the Chalk Stream*. In a foreword, Skues made it clear that his advocacy of the upstream wet fly was to be used as a supplement to and in no way intended to 'supplant or rival the beautiful art of which Mr. Halford is the prophet.'

Interestingly, there were only five pages in the book devoted to the nymph although Skues had been using nymph imitations for some years. The dry fly lobby tended to equate this upstream wet fly fishing with an indiscriminate flogging of the water, and it was an impression that Skues fought to eradicate to the end of his life.

Skues's experiments with nymph imitations continued on the Itchen, the little River Tillingbourne, a tributary of the Wey in Surrey and on the River Test which he fished through the good offices of his friend, Dr. E.A. Barton. He wrote about this research and on many other subjects for various publications including the *Flyfishers' Club Journal* which had been founded in 1911, and to which a stream of the finest fishing writers has contributed to the present day.

In 1921, *The Way of a Trout with a Fly* was published and is the book which is known to most trout anglers. Although it had important chapters on the dressing of nymph patterns, its remit was much wider. It investigated most aspects of trout behaviour and its significance to the angler and fly dresser; a further section of minor tactical studies and some delightful fishing episodes. Written in Skues's lively prose style, it is almost entirely relevant to the modern-day angler.

In the same year as *The Way of a Trout*, Skues discovered the use of the marrow-scoop for investigating the contents of a trout's stomach. This avoided the gory business of trout autopsies thus performing a service for which all subsequent trout anglers have been grateful. It also made it easier for Skues to investigate and classify natural nymphs.

In 1932 Skues published his third book, *Side-Lines, Side-Lights and Reflections,* which was a collection of his various articles which had appeared in the usual fishing journals plus the *Salmon and Trout Magazine* and *The Bulletin of the Anglers' Club of New York*. For me, this is the most endearing of his books with more revealing glimpses of the man himself and, especially, of his sense of humour.

Clouds were beginning to appear now on Skues's horizon, and not just war clouds. He was becoming unhappy at developments in his syndicate which fished the Itchen, and heated controversy about nymph fishing appeared in the angling press culminating in a debate on the subject at the Flyfishers' Club which left Skues profoundly disillusioned. These are dealt with in detail in the body of this book.

Both of these matters, and his increasing concern over the travesty of nymph representations sold by some tackle dealers, led to Skues's decision to write a final vindication of his art of nymph fishing. This last book, appearing in 1939 when Skues was 80 years old, was entitled *Nymph Fishing for Chalk Stream Trout*. It was a clear exposition of the practice of nymph fishing, and remains the definitive work on the subject to this day.

In 1938, Skues finally and regretfully severed his connections with the Itchen syndicate and he took a rod on the River Nadder between Barford St. Martin and Wilton, near Salisbury in Wiltshire, where he fished at weekends.

In 1940, on the death of a brother who had lived with him, he retired at last from his legal practice, closed his house at Croydon, despatched his sisters from there to a place safer from Nazi bombs, and went to live at the Nadder Vale Hotel on the banks of the Nadder. Unfortunately, in 1942, the lease on the Nadder fishing changed hands, and Skues was forced to take up a rod with a small club on the Bemerton stretch of the Nadder which entailed a bus ride and a walk to the river when he was in his 84th year.

Old age was now catching up with him, and he suffered from giddiness and trouble with his feet which prevented him from standing for long. He, therefore, resigned his rod in 1945 but continued to take a keen interest in the river and its fly life.

He also had the solace of his immense correspondence with people from all over the world ranging from famous British and American angler/authors to young aspiring tyros like the 16-year-old schoolboy, Peter Williams. C.F. Walker's book, *Angling Letters of G.E.M. Skues*, contained only a fraction of the letters Skues wrote in his lifetime. The replies, good humoured, authoritative but not dogmatic, kind and courteous, were invariably sent by return of post.

Among his correspondents and visitors was Frank Sawyer, keeper of the Officers' Fishing Association water on the Upper Avon, north of Salisbury. They met through a mutual friend, Sir Grimwood Mears, who had lent Sawyer *Minor Tactics* and *The Way of a Trout*. Sawyer compiled some notes of criticism for Sir Grimwood who passed them on to Skues who, to Sawyer's surprise, replied, urging Mears to encourage Sawyer to write articles, saying he would arrange for them to be published.

Sawyer was also invited to visit Skues at the Nadder Vale Hotel. He had tea with him on his first visit and talked for more than two hours. The memory of that meeting remained very clear. 'Skues was nearly 90 years old. To me he looked a little fragile old man who wore a black skull cap to cover his extreme baldness and heavy lensed glasses to aid his sight. But though frail in body and aged in appearance I quickly found that his brain was very alert . . . I wondered then how he could have possibly constructed the most beautiful little dry flies he had in his boxes and the various nymph patterns he had evolved through the years . . . All around him in his room was an immense collection of fishing books and sporting periodicals, and apparently he had many more books in store.'

Through the agency of Skues, Sawyer got an introduction to H.D. Turing, then editor of *Salmon and Trout Magazine*, and this led to the publication of his first article on nymphs and nymph fishing. Thus it was that Skues passed on his campaign for the nymph to the man who would bring it to its logical conclusion.

In 1948, the Nadder Vale Hotel was closed and converted into flats. After a brief stay in Wilton, Skues moved to be near his brother, Charles, at Beckenham in Kent. He continued writing letters to his friends and correspondents to within a few days of his death on the 9th August, 1949 at 23, Kelsey Park Road, Beckenham. He was four days short of his 91st birthday and succumbed to myocardial degeneration and carcinoma of the colon.

Two more of his books were published after his death. *Silk, Fur and Feather* appeared in 1950, and was a collection of articles on fly tying which had appeared in the *Fishing Gazette* under his pen name of Val Conson. Skues had directed that the second, *Itchen Memories*, should not be published, to use one of his favourite phrases, 'until I am under the turf.' Despite an inordinate number of errors possibly caused by the difficulties of reading Skues's writing, it is a charming collection of his days on the river he loved so well, and was much enhanced by the fine illustrations of Alex Jardine.

A year before he died, Skues decreed in his will, 'I desire that my body shall be cremated and the ashes scattered by the River Itchen on the Abbots Barton Fishery preferably in the tussocky-paddock on the East bank of the main river adjoining the clump of trees near the Winchester Gas Works.' His brother, Charles, brought the ashes to the river in the winter following Skues's death. There they were scattered by his old friend, William Mullins, the long-serving head keeper of the syndicate which had fished the river.

The Winchester gas works are no more, but, 30 years later, in the month of his death, a handsome commemorative stone bench was installed on the west bank of the main river, approximately opposite the point at which Skues's ashes were scattered. It stands there today, in the shade of a fine weeping willow tree, providing a resting place to contemplate a lovely stretch of this most famous of rivers. The legend on the plaque says: 'In memory of G.E.M. Skues who fished these waters from 1883 to 1938. A man who had a way with a trout.'

I leave the last word with one of Skues's kindred spirits, Donald Overfield. 'The old gentleman lies beside his beloved Itchen, placed there by a friend and angling companion of many a long summer's day. To rest where trout sip down the spinners of late evening and the early night wind rustles the waterside grasses. That all flyfishers should end their days beside well-loved streams would no doubt be George Edward Mackenzie Skues's final wish, while to him we say *requiescat in pace* beside your quiet Itchen, for your immortality is assured while anglers cast the fly to chalk stream trout.'

CHAPTER 2

Boyhood Fishing Days

Not long after Skues was left with his grandparents in Aberdeen in 1861, they moved to Langford in Somerset and then to Wrington on the River Yeo just below what is now Blagdon Reservoir, which is the village where the famous Dr. Bell of Blagdon and buzzer fame had his practice years later. A tributary of the river ran across the corner of the paddock of the garden. It was full of scarlet-bellied minnows and, occasionally, the young Skues was greatly excited by seeing brown speckled fish which were trout. His grandfather neither fished nor encouraged his grandson's interest and it was not until years later, after his grandfather's death, that he learnt that the old man had been a fly fisherman on the Scottish Don and a fly dresser of some repute.

Skues was sent to a series of boarding schools dependent on the movements of his father and mother, and one of them was near the New River, a water course built by Sir Hugh Myddleton in the early seventeenth century to bring water to London from Chadwell Springs and Amwell in Hertfordshire. The fishing was free and here for the first time he saw anglers fishing with a rod and line and float.

NOT FAR FROM my Hornsey Dames School ran a short stretch of the New River where the fishing was free and on one half holiday I was taken there by a school fellow and saw a number of rods at work. Particularly successful was a middle-aged Scot who kept on catching perch. I grew wildly jealous but could do nothing about it. I invested in a cane winder with a float and a hook to gut and some shot but, before I could manage a rod, I was sent off to boarding school at Stokes Bay near Gosport. (*Trivialities of a Long Life*)

He was then sent to a private school at Alverstoke, near Stokes Bay, where he acquired a two-piece hazel rod for one shilling (5p) to fish for eels. Small perch and shoal bass and mullet were also present in a number of brackish moats with which the bay was intersected. He had only used bread paste to fish for roach and was bitterly disappointed when the eels ignored his bait. At that time he was so ignorant that he was unaware he could dig for worms. One incident stood out in his memory.

I WAS GOING home at length, rod over shoulder with my rejected bait dangling behind me when I felt a tremendous tug and found that I had hooked a hen belonging to a railway porter who kept a crossing on the Stokes Bay line. The porter and his sons waged a constant war with the boys of my school and so, more than a little scared, I played that shrieking fowl down a hundred yards or so of road and round the next corner before trying to extract the hook. She was too firmly hooked, however, and so I cut the twisted horsehair just above the beak and took to my heels. That was for the time being the end of my fishing, for funds were low and I was not able to buy another furnished line. (*Trivialities of a Long Life*)

In 1872, at the age of 14, Skues entered Winchester College. His success in gaining entrance brought him a small harvest of tips, and he bought a 1s.6d. (7½p) rod in some hard white wood which he had long coveted together with a hank of twisted silk line and a gut furnished winder. The summer holidays of 1874 and part of 1875 were spent fishing for bass in the creeks and moats around Gosport and in the Solent. In 1875, when he was 17, he was taken for a day's fishing for roach on the River Meon at Titchfield.

I USED MY two-piece ash stick costing 1s.6d. and a silk line costing 3d and no reel. I used brandling worm on a hook to gut with a single shot. I struck my first bite so hard that the three quarters pound roach shot over my shoulder and caught my adult companion in the mouth. We finished with 108 roach and 3 trout weighing 70lbs. (*Trivialities of a Long Life*)

The fabled chalk stream, the River Itchen, flows through the city of Winchester, and Skues lost no time in making its acquaintance after becoming a scholar at Winchester College.

By now, rods of greenheart, hickory, lancewood and ash had replaced the old long, two-handed rods of the mid-century. Instead of fishing downstream with lines of horse hair, the new fashion was to cast upstream with a dry fly using fly lines of silk and hair. Even so Skues, with his stiff 11-footer, found it difficult to cast such light lines which were to be replaced with the heavier oiled silk lines later in the century. His flies, with their backward-sloping wings and hackles, were more like traditional wet flies, and the new lightweight, eyed hooks pioneered by Henry Sinclair Hall and George Bankart had not yet come into general use.

Skues used to hang around Winchester's Old Barge River which ran by the school playing fields to watch any anglers fishing with a fly, but his own finances were not strong enough for a rod, reel, line, flies and a licence. When he was 16 he bought some eyed fly hooks from Hammond's shop in Winchester with which he used to catch minnows. John Hammond leased a stretch of the river known as Old Barge for which he sold day and season tickets.

Skues's first attempt at fly fishing was with a Wickham's Fancy. His first stock of flies comprised Blue Quill, Red Quill, Pale Watery Dun (with white wool body) and Wickham's Fancy. He also bought a dozen Champion Mayflies which he never used as the mayfly had disappeared from the Old Barge with the digging of gravel from the bottom by the City Fathers. He got his first rise on a Wickham's Fancy cast with a favouring wind from the bulge at the bottom of the stretch, but was so surprised that he forgot to strike. He once saw Dr. Wickham, the inventor of the fly, in Hammond's shop on a leave-out day. Skues had now acquired a fly rod.

MY OWN ROD was an awful bean pole, 11 feet long and of a paralysing stiffness and quite unsuited to carry the light silk and hair line which was in fashion at the time. Oiled silk lines had yet to come. My line had the vice of sticking in the rings and it would not carry against the wind, but it did fall with exquisite lightness on the water. It was well suited to the type of rod old Hammond sold which was whippy beyond belief. It would have seemed impossible to handle a good fish with it, but I remember seeing old John put a fly with one of them (with the wind) right across the widest part of Old Barge, hook his trout and bring it rolling across to the net at his feet. The fly was the Pale

Watery Dun which Hammond called by some name like Infallible or Irresistible – I took it out of the trout's mouth.

Finally early in that season I lost half a yard of gut in a trout. The cast was a level one. I had never heard of a tapered one. In time the cast wore out and it was some time before I could afford another. A tip on a leave-out day enabled me to buy one at Hammond's in the Square, Winchester. In July I think, I caught my first trout. It was undersize, but I carried it in triumph – curiously enough I got it with a sunk fly. I had only one other trout that season. I had no one to teach me anything of the entomology of the river, I had no idea that the flies did not visit the water from the air and no one explained to me the theory of fly fishing. It is true that a school fellow named Kensington read one evening at a meeting of 'Bug and Snail' (the Natural History Society) an article on the Ephemeridae, mugged up from some encyclopedia, but I was too stupid to connect this information with the art in which I was so keen and so incompetent a practitioner. I had no literature on the subject and no one gave me a hint – I never saw anyone catch a natural fly from the surface or observe on what the fish were feeding – I went for the Wickham, while I had any, as the most attractive-looking of my flies.

During 1876 I had a meeting on the Old Barge side with a man whom I always identify in my own mind with Carlisle (*Major Carlisle, a well-known author/angler who wrote under the pen name of South West*). I had just risen a trout and hitting him too hard had left not only my fly but the entire remnant of my cast with him. A bearded stranger fishing close by came along and inquired what was the matter. I told him I had lost all my only cast. He promptly produced a book with an array of shining new casts and gave me one with the utmost kindness. It was tapered from medium gut to quite fine gut, as usual in those days, and it had a loop at both ends. I had never, so far as I knew, seen a tapered cast or heard of one, and I fixed it to my line by the fine end, looped on the fly to the stout end and selected a rising trout. The unstraightened undamped cast fell in a coil on the water, but I think the trout must have been insane for it sailed up, picked out the fly from the middle of the coil and went under and I, taken by surprise, responded with a violent strike and left fly and cast and all but the loop with the fish. It was the biggest

trout I had ever hooked or even seen hooked. I went back to
the College on the verge of tears of disgust and chagrin.
(*Trivialities of a Long Life*)

This was the end of Skues's boyhood fishing as, after leaving
Winchester, he went to Jersey for a year to join his parents, and
thence to London to take up articles as a solicitor's clerk.

CHAPTER 3

Fishing with Skues

There are probably few anglers – if any – alive today who actually fished with Skues. Fortunately, there are fishermen who recorded their impressions of fishing with the great man, and none more so than Dr. E.A. Barton, a physician, surgeon and paediatric specialist at the University College Hospital, London where he was known affectionately as 'Daddy' Barton. Barton is particularly qualified to comment on Skues as he fished with him on the River Itchen from 1922 to 1938, and throughout this time kept a detailed fishing diary, not only of his excursions with Skues but also of his fishing days on the Test, Anton, Kennet and other chalk streams. Barton was a fine fisherman himself, an author and artist, and we are indebted to him for taking most of the photographs of Skues which are in existence.

Through his shrewd and sometimes humorous observations, we can get a glimpse of Skues the man as opposed to the myth, both in respect of his fishing skills and as a social being. Barton quickly learnt from his very first outing that Skues could be critical, especially of his friends' fishing rods, even of a Leonard, that mould-breaking American make of rod which Skues had championed as the finest in the world earlier in the century.

'Skues disliked my brand new 9.6 Leonard, but the one I have today is the 9.4 of two years ago. This he thought a very nice rod, the only criticism – for he rarely praises a rod – being that the whippings were too dark for his taste! So it *must* be a good rod.'

Several people who fished with Skues commented on his idiosyncratic style of casting. 'When we fished together Skues declaimed as to the strength of my wrist in casting almost entirely from the wrist, but I like his casting much better than my own. His line was much straighter and more wire-like than mine, and he made it run along the water uncurling as it went, the fly falling last at the end of quite a straight gut. It was very pretty. Whereas I make my fly, gut and line fall at one moment and never like a wire. I must practise his method and see if it is easier and better. He cuts into the wind better than I do, bringing his rod point in vertical plane down almost to the water at the end of the cast. All this was interesting to watch.'

Another of Skues's friends and fishing colleagues, Douglas Goodbody, describes Skues's casting in this way: 'When he saw a fish rising he would drop on one knee behind the grass or reeds and give his rod a series of short sharp flicks with no preliminary false casting or waving. He held the line in his left hand in some quantity and appeared to feed it through the rings, after which the cast shot out very straight and low along the top of the river so that the fly did not drop on to the water from a height.'

Barton and Skues often travelled down together to Winchester, catching the 5.10 evening train from Waterloo, Skues arranging for them to stay at the Corner House in Winchester. Barton placed great store on good accommodation and food to which Skues was largely indifferent. 'Now I can never sleep at the Corner House as it is at the junction of five roads, four of which are main arteries of Winchester. To hear conversation in the front room is impossible with the window open as the kerb is only two feet from the hotel wall. The lorries roar and rumble by, shaking the very house; every car hoots at each corner and changes gear. The noise is deafening, and the garages at the back keep the racket going all night. Never was such a row . . . I bargained for a room right at the back but on arrival I found that I was put at the side. The consequence was that I got sleep only between 2.30 and 6 at which time the garages began to churn up their engines.' Roy Darlington who now leases Abbots Barton, tells me that the Corner House still survives, but ceased to be a hotel many years ago. It is now used as offices which the agents have great trouble in tenanting due to lack of parking and noise.

Skues, on the other hand, slept like a log. 'I am sure that he will sleep soundly through the last trump,' records Barton who usually drank cocoa before bed. Skues said on one occasion, 'Those who drink cocoa think cocoa; I prefer something for the good of the house.'

Skues ate a huge breakfast consisting, among other things, of a huge chop, sometimes tying flies before it was served. However, he took only two or three sandwiches to last him all day on the river and sometimes no drink. Eating wasted good fishing time.

There is an image of Skues as a crusty old bachelor, and there is some evidence for this. His brother, Charles, records that his wife was under the impression – a mistaken one – that George did not like her, she being at times overawed by his caustic wit. Talking to Winifred, the widow of Derek, Skues's nephew, she told me, 'Uncle George was a grumpy old man.' We must remember that by then he was near the end of his life and had ceased to fish and tie flies. On the other hand, Sheila, the daughter of his brother Charles, who left thumbnail sketches of all the Skues brothers and sisters, reveals a hitherto unknown aspect of her uncle. 'As young children we were rather in awe of him – but grew out of it! He was very kind and generous, and I shall always remember his Strawberry Tea Parties in the garden of a country inn at Shalford, near Guildford, when he invited his relatives and fishing friends to join him every Summer.' Douglas Goodbody, in his memoir of Skues in an anthology compiled to celebrate the hundredth anniversary of the Flyfishers' Club, wrote: 'He was human and enjoyed the face of a good looking woman and his whiskies in the evening.'

Barton records in his earliest visit to Abbots Barton that Skues went off on the first day to watch his old school, Winchester, play Eton at cricket, leaving Barton to get on with it. This was probably a regular part of Skues's social calendar as he records that many years previously he saw the great George Selwyn Marryat at the cricket match but was too shy to introduce himself. In 1931, when the 'talkies' were coming into vogue, he took Barton to the cinema in Winchester. Barton comments, 'We went to the cinema at Skues's suggestion and saw some wretched stuff with American talk which I could not understand.'

Skues would accept invitations to tea at Abbots Barton Farm and to stay on to dinner. Barton's reaction: 'The idea of tea at 4, talk on farm subjects till 8 and dinner, and more talk after a day on the meadows had a horror to it that I could not endure. He was a bit hurt and said he would not go if I didn't. This was silly and he finally said he would go alone. So that was another trouble avoided.'

Skues certainly liked to chat. Barton records in his diary, 'My dear friend has one drawback – only one. One can never read in his presence. He disturbs one every few minutes about something, so I put my book aside till I was on the train.'

Once, however, Skues was down on the river, his pursuit of fish was relentless. Barton describes his fishing outfit in the era long before commercialised clothing. One could never imagine Skues in a fishing waistcoat plastered with garish fishing logos. 'He carries *always* besides his white canvas bag and shoulder strap containing macintosh, lunch and odds and ends, a long wooden-handled net about 6 foot long, very heavy with a big round net, casting with this long thing sticking out under his left arm. Then a shooting stick to sit on is always carried so that he is fairly loaded up. His fly box or boxes are tin matchboxes about 4 x 2 inches in which are flies stuck through bits of paper to prevent flying off in a wind. Another, 1 x 1 inches, has loose flies in it. A tobacco pouch is his damper, and he makes me angry by using Vaseline for his floating line grease, dissolving off the varnish of his line, and also because he lets his line sink without it worrying him, so that at the end of the day his line fountains the water as it comes through it. He dries his fly in the air very little.'

Another thing that surprised Barton was the way that Skues felt quite safe casting at right angles to a fish across the stream whereas he always got some way below, casting a long line diagonally to it. 'Yet it seemed all right and the fish did not mind.' Discussing this with Roy Darlington, he told me that casting to a trout virtually opposite is still frequently possible on the Itchen if the angler keeps low, and in numerous places on the fishery the surrounding meadow is quite a bit lower than the river which assists this approach. In any case, it does seem that Skues rarely used a long cast partly because of the weak wrists which he sustained in an accident playing football in his youth. However, his casting was extremely accurate.

As already mentioned, one of the reasons that there are comparatively few photographs of Skues is that he strongly disliked being photographed though this was not for the want of Barton trying. 'When I was on the Test a week ago I had my small camera and on the bridge said, "Let me have a picture of you as you are." He was kneeling at the end casting to a fish in the right hand bank looking upstream. He paused and then said, "I am not in love with the idea! So I shall not try any more." He is peculiarly sensitive and I am sorry for there is no picture of him in my copy of his book.' However, Barton made that good later on, and his copies of Skues's first three books are now all in the Flyfishers' Club library and contain a number of photographs of his friend. He also had the happy, bad habit of writing comments in the margins of the books: that is, bad for the book but happy for us. In a passage where Skues mentions his dislike of cut hackles, Barton writes in the margin that Skues once said to him, 'A man who would cut hackles would cut a throat.'!

On one occasion when they met at Waterloo to go down to Winchester, Skues said, 'I seem to be giving pleasure to others. People are laughing at me' – and no wonder. 'To describe his getup would want a pen of Kipling and a pencil of Hogarth. My attempt at a back view is in no way exaggerated. His hat, originally a homburg, battered and twisted, was jammed over his eyes, his mac – a wading cape mac – was stiff with age and want of use, it stuck out like a crinoline in transverse curves across the back and rigid creases behind which made it stick out like a tail. Thin legs in tight breeches in gaping gum boots. His bag was a white one with a brace (*words not decipherable*) to button it torn to ribbons and held together with a safety pin. The whole turnout would have got the gods in a roar at any theatre. No wonder the small boys nudged one another and fell in shrieks of joy as he passed, no wonder discreet ladies raised their eyebrows and glanced at one another when he went by. I would not have missed it for pounds.'

His outfit, however, was no joke for the fish. On the last weekend of the year in 1924, Barton saw Skues coming downstream on the Test. He had a bag full and had caught ten brace, returning half of them. 'Skues thoughtfully put all his fish into my bag – the brute – almost 12lb and I puffed down to the 'Seven Stars', our inn.'

One rainy day in 1933, with a bitter north wind, Barton records that nothing was moving and that it got colder and colder. Skues went upstream after crossing in the boat. Barton remained on the other side to seek what shelter he could. The cold was so bad that his feet and hands lost all feeling and he could not tie a fly on. So he sheltered in a small boathouse for two and a half hours. Meanwhile, Skues sat on his seat-stick by the very exposed upper stream. He waited two hours for one particular fish to rise. When it did, he hooked and landed it. At the end of the day all Barton had was a one pound grayling, but Skues came in with four large trout. Barton comments, 'What a man!'.

Barton was, of course, a first class fisherman, and there were times when he caught fish when his friend came in with an empty creel. In fact, for us ordinary mortals it is cheering to know that even 'the master', as Barton called him, had days without fish. The first time he fished with Skues on the 2nd July, 1922, he had a nice two pounder whereas Skues had touched nothing all day. He later confessed to Barton that since the 18th June he had caught no fish.

Nevertheless, one of the things that stands out from Barton's diaries is Skues's sheer persistence and stamina. On one day on the Itchen in 1931, Barton finished with no keepable fish. Skues had two and a half brace mostly about one and three quarter pounds besides some hefty grayling. 'He walks all day (his age is 73) up and down his two miles of water, tireless over the awful walking. I am dead beat after two hours, but at 5 p.m. he suggests "one more look round about the hut" which means the top of the water again – not me! I said to the keeper I would give him all I possessed for a bath chair home: my legs were done to a turn. When we got home Skues said – to my immense relief – that he thought there would be nothing doing in the evening, so I was spared another tramp in the wind and the rain.'

On another occasion Barton comments, 'He is a tireless man – five years older than I am, and strides along all day on his long legs and small body like a kindly spider, he takes two sandwiches to last him all day – nothing to drink and says he has paid 5/- (five shillings) in doctor's fees in ten years.'

There were times when Barton regarded Skues's invitations as a mixed blessing. There was no doubting his affection for his old friend, but he regarded his outings to the Itchen as very exhausting. 'The walk to the river all but if not well over a mile. Also the going is very bad, over water meadows where the cows have trampled the field into deep holes. There are no seats and no shade except at Duck's Nest Spinney.' Barton would find things very different now at Abbots Barton in that respect. When you had a day's fishing with Skues it meant *all* day from early morning until 10.30 in the evening!

In 1925, Barton did not go out in the evening with Skues, saying that his lumbago was bad. Skues went off at 7.30 and did not return until 10.50. Just as Barton was about to organise a search party to look for his friend he turned up after a most unsuccessful time. He had broken eight feet off his tapered line; his brogue had lost its sole and he had tied it on with string. He had been chased by heifers and horses who, seeing him in the half light, had rejoiced around him kicking up their heels and alarming him.

That Skues had a certain ego and could be pernickety in his criticisms is apparent in this incident. Barton contributed to the *Journal of the Flyfishers' Club* with almost the frequency of Skues. In 1925 he had written a poem called *River of Heart's Desire* which was later reproduced in *The Fishing Gazette*. He received a letter from Skues to this effect:

My dear Barton,

Congratulations on your spring poem in the *Journal*. The only fault I have to find with it is that there are two syncopations immediately after an adjective which makes it a little gaspy just at those points. It is an unusual number in that it has no contribution from me.

    Yours sincerely

    G.E.M. Skues

Skues had a naturally enquiring mind, great gifts as an observer, and a lawyer's talent for reasoning and rationalisation. This did not prevent him on occasion from making irrational excuses for not catching fish. Barton records, 'The fish during the evening had been "coming short" or at any rate we did not get any. Skues declared it was the moon! I knew his fad and let it go at that, but it was said at 8.30 when I had to search the heavens for a thin young moon in a full daylight sky in first quarter.'

It is well known that Skues encountered much prejudiced and ignorant opposition from the dry fly disciples of Halford to his use of nymphs for subaqueous feeding fish. However, many of his fishing friends were receptive to his ideas and Barton was fishing with nymph patterns as early as 1923. The first nymph Skues gave to Barton was a Pale Watery with a dressing of yellow silk, blue squirrel for body, yellow silk rib – no gold – very blue hackle, very sparse. Apart from the colour of the tying silk, this appears to be the Pale Watery numbered XI in *Nymph Fishing for Chalk Stream Trout*. After trying his favourite Red Pheasant Tail and a Tup, Barton put on Skues's fly and rose a fish first cast. Like many a novice nymph fisher after him, he saw a big boil but missed the fish. From then on, Barton seems to have used Skues's nymphs whenever appropriate. A note on the 6th June, 1931 says, 'Below McCaskie's Corner a nymph got me a one and a quarter pound fish and a few grayling.' Unfortunately, Barton never gives the dressings of the nymphs he used but, in one respect, he carried Skues's ideas further and, as I have recorded elsewhere, in some ways anticipated Sawyer's famous Pheasant Tail Nymphs. He records that he tied nymphs with fuse wire around the hook shank and called them 'loaded' nymphs. On one occasion he refers to his nymph as 'The Rake'. It is interesting to ponder on the implications of that name.

Roy Darlington talked to Sir John McNee, an eminent surgeon and physician, not long before he died. He was a colleague and friend of Barton and fished with Skues and Barton on the Itchen. He said that a great deal of leg pulling used to go on, usually over lunch. He remembers Skues as a charming and very considerate host, always anxious that his guest did well, and he would frequently urge Barton on when his enthusiasm flagged. McNee said that Barton could lose interest quickly. John Goddard, during his long and illustrious career, met several fly fishermen who either knew Skues or had fished with him, and gained an insight into both his extraordinary ability as a trout angler and also into his behaviour on the river. Once on the water, he had little time for idle conversation, concentrating one hundred per cent on the fishing from the time he arrived until he left. He may have been a somewhat selfish fly fisher as apparently he always caught more trout than his guests, but this may have been more due to his outstanding ability than selfishness. He did not suffer fools on the river gladly, yet was very generous with help and advice to any keen and reasonably competent fly fisherman that he encountered.

By 1936, Skues's excursions to Abbots Barton with Barton were approaching their end. He told Barton on the train down to Winchester that he would have to share his rod. This was a new rule brought in by the syndicate which ran the fishery, and one which contributed in no small measure to Skues's decision to resign his rod in 1938. Barton said, 'I would rather share a rod with Skues than most men, but I loathe sharing a rod at any time.' Most of us, I am sure, would concur with that view. Barton went on, 'Anyway I went down and took a camera by which I could kill time. It was the 18th April with a perishing north wind in the coldest April for 40 years. As to sharing the rod, I did not bother and let old Skues have it. I sat about where the wind was least while he fished. In all the day, I had it for less than 20 minutes.'

1938 found Barton fishing with Skues on the Nadder, to which the latter was to transfer his affections. They stayed at the Nadder Vale Hotel, and once again, Barton was far from happy, being extremely critical of the hotel food. This did not augur well for Skues who was eventually to live at the hotel!

However, the pattern of fishing was just the same and Skues's advancing years did nothing to impair his dedication and application. 'The rain came down in sheets, slanting in the gale, and I got under the lee of a big tree and had my lunch with the rain dripping off my hat on to my sandwiches. The rain let up at last, and there was old Skues hard at it and in the open. I asked if he found shelter and he seemed quite surprised. "No," he said, "I fished all the time." And he is in his *eightieth year*.'

In fact, he fished on into his 88th year!

The friendship of Barton and Skues continued up to Skues's death, and Barton wrote his obituary in the *Flyfishers' Journal*. They were certainly prime examples of the adage that none of your fishing days counts against your age. Barton lived to be 89 whilst Skues was almost 91 when he died.

CHAPTER 4

Skues and the Trout

In 1921, Skues produced the book which is considered his finest work, *The Way of a Trout with a Fly*. His original intention was to write a work on trout-fly dressing which would exceed in scope all previous books on the art. His decision to give up this ambitious project was based on the fact that there was one governing factor in the treatment of the subject which he considered vital yet which was lacking, namely scientific knowledge on the vision of trout. He decided, instead, to collect in book form his reflections on a number of considerations leading up to an understanding of the true nature of trout-fly fishing, in the hope that future generations would take up the problems and solve them.

Commenting on *The Way of a Trout with a Fly* in his own book, *The Way of a Man with a Trout*, Donald Overfield said that 'never before had I seemed to be so in tune with an author; witty, gentle, observant, inventive, never dogmatic, aye, here was a man with whom I would have loved to wander the banks of the River Itchen.' Sir Grimwood Mears, a friend of Skues to whom he had introduced Frank Sawyer, in a letter to Skues, said of *The Way of a Trout with a Fly*, 'It will be being read three hundred years from now – indeed as long as trout exist and man exists to catch them – and read with delight.'

So what are his considerations which will lead us to the true nature of trout fishing?

The why

To Skues, the prime attraction of trout fishing was that it was an intellectual exercise designed to outwit the trout.

WHY DOES THE trout take the natural fly? Undoubtedly, as the contents of his stomach prove, as food. Why does he take the artificial fly? In my opinion, in the vast majority of cases, because he supposes it to be his food. On occasion the motive may be curiosity, jealousy, pugnacity or sheer excess of high spirits. But if I did not believe that the trout took the artificial fly not only as food but as food of the kind on which he is feeding, the real interest of trout fishing would be gone, so far as I am concerned. That is the reason why, for me, trout fishing on chalk streams transcends in interest any other kind of trout fishing, for on streams where the fly is comparatively scarce trout are more apt to take any kind of insect that may be on the menu, and are to be taken freely on patterns which do not represent the fly on the water. But chalk streams are rich in insect food. The duns come out in droves, and the fish show a discriminating determination to take only one pattern at a time, which convinces me that they mean to have nothing which does not satisfy them as being that on which they are feeding. Even on chalk streams there are occasions when there are exceptions to this rule, but in my experience, stretching over thirty five years, these occasions are few. (*The Way of a Trout with a Fly*)

Colour

One of Skues's theories was that trout may not see colour in precisely the same way as man does. This apart, his theories on the sensitivity of trout to various colours have largely been confirmed by later research which has shown that they can even distinguish gradations of colour.

CAN IT BE doubted that if the fly dresser knew exactly the degree of the trout's sensitiveness to different colours, and also knew the combinations of colour producing any particular shade for the trout, he would have gone a very long way towards solving the secrets of fatally successful trout-fly dressing?

It is, I think, beyond dispute that trout are extremely sensitive to red and are greatly attracted by it. Witness the value of a red tag to a fly. Living as so many do among surroundings of green weed with a diet of insects in so many shades of green, it seems unlikely that they are insensitive to green, but there are practically no blues in the trout's habitat unless you count the blue of the sky seen through the circle of vision above him. And it would not surprise me if it were proved that trout are comparatively insensitive to blues.

At no point is there greater divergence of opinion among anglers than on this of the power of the trout to distinguish colour; but it is only possible to reason from one's own experience, and to appeal to that of others. For the moment we are dealing with the colours suggesting current daily food, and setting aside the colours of lures which excite tyranny, rapacity or curiosity. These latter are usually bright and stimulating, and they are rather beside the point of our argument. The colours of the nymphs, duns and other insects which form the daily menu are in general sober, and if trout were incapable of making fairly fine distinctions of colour, it is hard to account for those frequent occasions when fly after fly is tried, seemingly like enough to the fly on the water, in vain, and finally a pattern is found which kills fish after fish. Again, on wet-fly waters, where the angler is laying a team of flies across the stream, one fly out of the three or four will be persistently selected by the trout, and if two or more anglers are using the same pattern on diverse casts they all find the same pattern selected. My own belief, for what it is worth, is that where the supply of food is moderate or small and the fish is hungry, his taste is apt to be far more catholic than on those occasions when there is a strong hatch of one or more varieties, one of which appeals most strongly to the trout. There must have been days within the experience of most of us when the water has been covered with yellow duns and small pale olives, with a sprinkling of iron-blue duns among them, and all else has been neglected in favour of the iron blue. Here it is true that the fly is quite distinctive in colouring from the others on the water at the same time; but on similar occasions, when the iron blue is not to the fore, the trout will as a rule not be mixing their diet, but confining themselves to fly of one kind, and sticking to that, and that only, and letting all else go by.

So far, we have been dealing with surface feeding mainly, but where the trout are bulging it is not so easy to ascertain what they are feeding on. It involves an autopsy – a messy and uncertain business at best (*written before Skues discovered the marrow scoop*) – for it is impossible to say when and where the nymphs in the gullet were taken; one can only make an approximate guess. It is true that one generally finds one type of nymph predominating, but one often finds odd specimens of other kinds, and it may be suspected that the trout, accustomed where no rise is on to forage among celery beds and other vegetation in search of nymph and larva, shrimp and snail, is then much more catholic in his tastes than when he is busy gathering in the surface duns. If one puts down a soft muslin net among celery beds just before the rise is expected one will bring it up wriggling with larvae and nymphs of very varying dimensions and colouring, from darkest olive to something like bright dandelion and primrose. So it may easily be true that the trout when nymphing may more readily be induced to make a mistake than when feeding steadily on the surface.

There it is much more important to get the right fly. And the right fly is that which the trout finds to be the right colour. It does not always seem the right colour to the angler, and so it may fairly be questioned whether the trout sees colour just as man sees it. (*The Way of a Trout with a Fly*)

The vision of trout

Despite the lack of scientific data available to him, Skues was largely correct in his assumption that trout do not see precisely as we do. We now know that the shape of a trout's lenses and its means of focussing are different from man's. He was also correct in saying that trout had both binocular and monocular vision, and the exact parameters of this vision have since been explained to us by Clarke and Goddard in *The Trout and the Fly*. Even his speculation that a trout may be able to focus simultaneously on more than one object has been proved correct.

THE NATURE AND the needs of trout differ greatly from those of man, and it need not therefore surprise us if examination should lead us eventually to the conclusion that his perception by eyesight differs materially from that of man. Indeed, I think it would be remarkable if, living in a different medium that is subject to certain optical laws from which the air is free, and having different needs and modes of being from man, the trout were to see things in all respects as man sees them – even after making all allowance for the correcting and coordinating effects of tactile experience.

To begin with, while man's eyes are placed in front of his head and operate together so that his vision is stereoscopic, the trout's eyes are on the sides of his head, slanting slightly forward and operating separately, so that it may be inferred that in most cases his vision of an object is monocular. It may be that in the act of taking a fly, whether on the surface or below it, both eyes may be trained forward upon the object, or, alternatively, that one eye only may be on the object and the other attending to business in another direction. (*The Way of a Trout with a Fly*)

Looking upwards

Dr. Francis Ward was the pioneer in experiments to look upwards through water, and his *Animal Life Under Water*, published in 1919, had a chapter entitled 'The Angler and his Lures'. It is typical of Skues that he should have arranged a visit to Ward's observation chamber. His observations on the window and mirror are years ahead of their time, and have been confirmed in more scientific detail recently by Clarke and Goddard. The fine circle separating the window from the mirror where the colours of the fly can be clearly seen is called Snell's Circle. Clarke and Goddard say, however, that the nearer the fly gets to the centre of the window, the darker it becomes, which is contrary to Skues's observations.

I WAS GIVEN the privilege, some few years ago, by Dr. Francis Ward, the author of *Marvels of Fish Life*, of spending some hours in his underground observation chamber built below water level on the side of an artificial pond with plate-glass sides cutting off the water from the chamber. I made some brief experiments in the direction of trying to divine how trout see the fly, whether floating or sunk.

The pond was a cement construction, lined at bottom with rock and pebble, but showing from the darkened observation chamber in one side a far side of bare cement. The water came flush with the top of the glass window. The first thing that struck me was that the whole cup of the pond seemed reflected upside down. Except for a little semi-circle of light it seemed as if one were gazing into a big ball of water with a little round hole of rainbow light at the top, and except at this hole the sky was cut off by a sort of mirror, like plate glass. But the tank was full of light, reflected from the bottom and no doubt back again from the mirror made by the underside of the surface. The semi-circle, of course, indicated by its edge the margin beyond which rays falling upon the water surface are so deflected by refraction that they do not reach the observer's eye. Outside the semi-circle I could only see the bottom of the tank reflected on the surface, except so far as any object such as a hook or hackles penetrated the surface or made some impression upon it; and it seemed to me, no doubt wrongly, that such an impression might be the only indication which the fish received that some floating object which might be fly food were approaching.

But inside the semi-circle, within the angle of 48 degrees, everything floating on the surface was not only visible, it was extremely clearly visible, and was surrounded by a prismatic radiance which was more specially in evidence the nearer the fly was to the outer edge of the semi-circle. There was no difficulty about distinguishing the colours of flies on the underside or on the sides. Indeed, the effects produced were all much what I have suggested above may be the light effects where the light is behind, or at any rate not directly shining into the eye of the trout.

I blame myself for not having ascertained and recorded precisely the position of the pond and the observation chamber in relation to the points of the compass, and the relative position of the sun at the time of observation, so that I might be able to deduce with more certainty the difference in appearance of a fly with the light between it and the fish and a fly between the fish and the light. The day, however, was very overcast.

A May fly was the first subject – one tied with summer duck wings, red hackle and tail, and a brown dappled pseudo-natural body. The first thing we noticed was that, when thrown on the surface dry, the gut was not noticeable from underneath, except in the semi-circle of light, and not very noticeable there. In the rainbow semi-circle of light above the observer's head in the pond the whole artificial May fly became not only clearly visible, but extraordinarily and brilliantly so. The wings seemed coated with a spun-glass brilliance which was most attractive. It may have been all in the observer's eye, because it is quite conceivable that, looking up through a triangular wedge of water, one may have been looking through a sort of prism, which perhaps gave the rainbow effects above referred to.

With the May fly sunk below the surface, much of the brilliance was lost, and the gut became obvious at once. But whether the fly was outside or within the rainbow hole at the top, it was extremely difficult for the observer to say that it was not on the surface. A sunken fly, however, was readily visible at quite a distance through the water. The insistence of the dry-fly angler on extreme accuracy of casting and absolute dryness of gut and fly seems, from these observations, so far as they go, to be thoroughly justified. It is also obvious why a trout which will move a long way to intercept a nymph or sunken fly is not to be tempted by a dry fly that does not come accurately over him into the circle of light above his head. (*The Way of a Trout with a Fly*)

The sense of form and definition

Skues expands on his theory that the predominantly important factors for an artificial fly are its colour and size.

THE TROUT IS credited on authority with being the keenest eyed of animals, and doubtless most of us have too frequently found him keener of sight than we have cared about. Yet the nature and limitations of that keenness are well worth examining if we are to get a working grip of the principle which should underlie the art of trout fly dressing.

Let us grant, then, that the trout's sight is quick; let us concede him a strong sense of colour or texture or both; but is that sight clear? Has the trout even a rudimentary sense of form? There are grounds for doubting it. I am going to get into hot water with the apostles of the 'precise imitation' school, but I am not going to dogmatize, but to call attention to facts.

If we take the most exquisitely dressed Olive Quill or Iron Blue Dun and compare them with their prototypes in nature, can we honestly say that the resemblance of form or attitude is marked? We know it is not. We are satisfied if in colour and size the imitation is approximate. If the fly be tied with rolled wings reversed, it is frequently as good a killer as, or even better than, the ordinary pattern. Yet the fly with dense, stiff wings thrown forward is really not, in shape at any rate, a striking likeness of the natural insect, with its wings sloping just the other way. A good instance of this is the Mole Fly – a sedge; instead of having its wings laid back over the body, it presents them flung forward in the opposite direction, yet it is indubitably a successful pattern. Then, does the trout pay much attention to the fact that the floating fly of commerce is generally able to give the centipede fifty legs and a beating? There are times when he does not. Does he even mind where the legs occur in the anatomy of the artificial fly? They may, as in the Wickham or any other sedges, be in spirals all down the body but what does he care?

Let us turn to the Iron Blue Dun. The natural insect has lead-coloured wings and red feet, and the artificial may be dressed either winged or hackled. If hackled, a dark blue dun feather with copper-red points is an admirable feather to use. But the trout does not mind a bit that your Iron Blue Dun has a mop of blue wing all round its head, with a little red foot at the end of each fibre. It is a commonplace of fly dressing that, in translating a winged pattern into its hackled correlative, you select a hackle combining as far as possible the colour of wings and legs, and, so long as you kept the colours, their relative position is of little consequence.

Taking it by and large, the fact is indisputable that the shabbiest, roughest, most dilapidated, most broken-winged fly is as likely to kill as the newest and freshest of the fly-tier's confections – provided size and colour be right. What is 'right' must be the subject of further discussion. Meanwhile, I think I have established this, that in appreciation of form and proportion and detail the sight sense of the trout is defective. (*The Way of a Trout with a Fly*)

The sense of size

Skues puts forward the hypothesis that size and colour are more important than shape.

'THE FULLER THE water the larger the fly' is a good general working rule, and so it follows that where, as in the chalk streams, the flow is steady and constant, there is seldom any occasion to increase the size of the artificial fly above the normal size of the natural. And on these streams one is liable to find that the presentation of a fly above the normal size is apt to be resented, and many experienced anglers advise a size smaller than the natural fly rather than an imitation of equal size. What, then, is the ground for the use of a fly larger than the natural upon rougher and less constant streams? The only one which suggests itself is that a full water (once it clears enough for the fly) stimulates the fish to such high spirits and such extremity of hunger, that the added size of the angler's lure, so far from giving rise to suspicion (as it would in more normal circumstances), becomes an added attraction in its promise of satisfaction of an oppressively vigorous appetite. The angler therefore may be sure that he will be wise to pay attention to this matter of size, as it is one of which, for good or for ill, the trout takes notice. It is a curious point that the wet fly may be fished a size larger than the dry representing the same insect. I record this as a matter of experience without being able to give, off my own bat, even a guess at a reason. A very skilful and observant wet-fly angler of my acquaintance says that the nymph and the creeper are larger than the winged insect.

The conclusions which I venture to submit as the sum of the foregoing arguments and inferences are that in flies purporting or intended to imitate natural insects, size and colour are the matters of consequence, and that, apart from mechanical considerations as to the structure and wearing power of the fly, shape is of very secondary consequence. (*The Way of a Trout with a Fly*)

The invisibility of hooks

Few would disagree with Skues's assessment of why trout take a fly apparently containing a large piece of ironmongery. It also accounts for the fact that upside-down flies created by various anglers such as Joscelyn Lane and Clarke and Goddard have never 'caught on' as it were.

THERE IS ANOTHER matter in which the trout's eyesight sometimes serves him ill. A wise old mother trout was portrayed as assuring her too ardent offspring that 'that horrid fly is meant to hide the sharpness of the hook.' It may be so, but performance, alas, often falls short of intention, and the instances are few in which the horrid fly does anything of the sort. Indeed, a very competent school of Scottish fly dressers is all for minimum of wing and body, so that the fly is the merest sketch, and the hook is the prominent thing. Therefore, in speculating on the vision of the trout, we have to make our account with the fact that, whether the hook be blued or brown, it does not deter trout from frequently seeking to make a meal of the artificial fly. The trout, therefore, must either fail to see the hook, or, seeing it, must ignore it. If he sees it and realizes that it is an unnatural appendage to the artificial fly, he could hardly ignore it. He must therefore either take it for a natural appendage, or for some casual, but quite irrelevant, attachment, or be so obsessed by his intentness on his food as to see only what he wants to see – namely, that combination of colour which seems to him to correspond with the natural insect in favour for the moment. It is impossible to say that he does not take the hook for some casual attachment, for all sorts of odd things float down the water with the natural fly. Yet he will not as a rule take fly to which a weed attaches. The balance of probability, I think, leans to the theory that the trout is so obsessed by the pressure of appetite that he only sees what he wants to see – his supposed insect prey – and ignores the hook as an irrelevant detail, all of which goes to prove that the wily trout of the poets and journalists is – may Providence be devoutly thanked for it – really rather a stupid person. (*The Way of a Trout with a Fly*)

The rise

Clarke and Goddard described Skues as 'The greatest liberator of the human mind in fly-fishing this century.' They have produced their own analysis of rise forms which differ in few respects from Skues's produced 60 years previously. They do, however, point out that the association of 'kidney-shaped whorl' with the blue-winged olive and large dark olive is probably mistaken, but has become a lore to English and other anglers. Skues also omitted to mention the audible kissing noise associated with the sip or kiss rise, but as he became increasingly deaf as he grew older, this is not surprising.

WHEN THE ANGLER sees a tell-tale ring upon the surface of river or lake, he is apt to say, 'There is a rise'. But if, when fishing, he should have his fly taken by a trout, whether under the water or at the surface, he would in recounting the incident say, if he were a Briton, 'I had a rise'. If an American, he would say, 'I had a strike.'

A close study of the form of the rise may often give the observant angler a clue, otherwise lacking, to the type of fly which the trout is taking, and to the stage and condition in which he is taking it. The chalk streams and rivers of quiet and even flow obviously afford greater facilities for observing the phenomena of rises than do streams less clear or of more turbulent habit, and it is from the chalk streams that one can most easily acquire the bulk of the data which may be applied, with the necessary qualifications, to the solution of similar questions on other streams.

Every chalk stream fisherman, however much or little he may have thought about the subject, will recognize that there are a great many forms of rise. It is now proposed to consider some of these, and to try and ascertain what clue they severally give to the food the fish is taking.

Analyzing broadly, the insect taken will be either (1) poised on the surface; (2) flush with the surface, as being either spent or entangled by wetting of the wings, or in the earlier stage of the process of hatching; or (3) subaqueous.

The best known and the most obvious rise is that in which the trout takes the floating dun or upwinged spinner. It is the foundation rise of dry-fly theory and practice, and it is to this, with the spent spinner rise thrown in, that the dry-fly purist would, in theory at any rate, confine the angler. But, as a matter of fact, this super-surface taking forms only a small part of the evidence of a trout's feeding known as the rise, and it is often supremely difficult to determine whether a given rise or series of rises be at food superaqueous, flush or subaqueous. Much of the floating fly food of the trout is very small and hard to detect on the surface, and it requires some close watching to say whether it be sipped from above, or at, or just under, the surface. Thus it comes about that many a would-be dry-fly enthusiast has spent busy hours presenting a floating fly to trout which are taking subaqueous food.

Assuming, however, that the insect be seen coming down to where the fish is seen or known to be lying in wait, the trout comes up from a greater or less depth, with more or less diversion to right or left, and with more or less confidence or eagerness, and, with a smack, a suck, or a sip, takes down the fly. The smack involves some exposure of the neb and a considerable ring in the water which never ceases to cover the fish. The sip does not expose the neb at all. A fish coming from a depth and turning down again makes more of a swirl, from the energy expended in the movement of turning down again, than does a fish hovering just below the surface and merely putting up a nose. The size of the fly also makes a difference. The tiniest insects are sipped, the larger ones are taken down with much more of a swirl. The rise to the blue-winged olive is indicated by quite a large kidney-shaped whorl; and the large dark olive of spring and late autumn is taken in a similar way. The degree of eagerness of the fish also has an effect on the size of the swirl he makes in taking. The fondness of the trout for the iron-blue dun, for instance, leads him to take it with an agitation which betrays him to the observant angler as feeding on the iron-blue dun or its nymph, though no iron-blue may have been observed on the surface or in the air.

Where duns are floating in eddies one often sees trout sailing gently under and sipping them softly. Occasionally in these positions one sees a succession of head-and-tail rises – first the neb appears and descends, then the back fin, and then the upper portion of the tail fin. It is my belief that this in general indicates that the trout are taking duns which through accident or defective hatching are lying spent or on their sides on the surface. The same type of rise in the open stream may generally, especially in the morning, before the dun hatch, and in the evening, be taken to indicate that the trout are taking spent spinners. In the eddies and over weed beds, however, when no fly is visible on the surface, it may mean that the trout is taking nymphs, just in the film of the surface, about to hatch, or, it may be, swarming from refuge in eddies after a weed cutting.

In these circumstances nymphs seem to be taken with a quiet deliberation very different from the swashing eagerness with which the bulger swirls to meet his underwater prey. Very often, however, in streams the trout will be nymphing for hours together with just the same quiet deliberation and with just as little excitement as when taking floating duns; and, as on these occasions there is no head-and-tail rise, the angler is usually immensely puzzled to make out on what they are feeding. The writer does not profess to have worked out any reason why nymphs should be taken on one occasion with the head-and-tail rise and on another with an action apparently differing in no appreciable respect from the ordinary rise to floating duns. The nearest thing to a clue he has been able to observe is that while spent spinners are taken with the head-and-tail rise, floating upwinged spinners are absorbed, especially if small, with a soft suck which spreads a ring so thin and creating so little disturbance as to be scarcely visible in the dusk or the moonlight, while within its circle the water looks like a little pool of fine creaming lines whorling towards a pinhead hole in its centre.

Then there is bulging properly, so called, where the fish move to and fro to intercept the nymphs carried down by the current. Here in general the indication of the rise is the swirl of the fish as it turns after capturing its prey. There is also the rise to hatching sedge – having an appearance much like bulging; the rise to the running sedge – something of a slash.

Summarizing briefly the types of rise, we appear to have at least the following:

Over-surface Rises
Ordinary rise to floating dun or upwinged spinner and its variants, namely:

Big rise with kidney-shaped double whorl to large floating dun (such as blue-winged olive or its spinner)
Sucking rise to medium-sized floating flies
Sipping rise to smallest floating duns, spinners and midges
The slash – most commonly to running sedge or to flies on slow water

In addition to which there is the plunge where an eager fish comes almost entirely out of the water and takes the fly either as he leaves the water or as his head re-enters.

On the Surface or Flush Rises
Head-and-tail rises to wet duns or spent spinners or nymphs of duns or gnats suspended inert in the surface film.

Subaqueous Rises
Bulging to nymphs
Bulging to hatching sedge flies such as the grannom
Nymphing in eddies – to mobile
Nymphing in streams – nymphs

(*The Way of a Trout with a Fly*)

A problem for the optician

Skues comments on the extraordinary way that trout preoccupied in feeding may lose their shyness whilst at other times the angler cannot even get within casting distance before they dart upstream. Skues's fishing guests often commented on the fact that they regularly saw him casting directly across to fish without seeming to scare them.

I WAS CASTING a fly one sunny July day upon a shallow Berkshire brook, which, cutting its way through a boggy surface soil, babbled gaily, seldom more than eighteen inches deep, over a hard-core bed of chalk and gravel. The brook swarmed with trout, few apparently under the half pound, and very few over the pound; and when first I arrived at the waterside the only fish taking were a few casual feeders, which picked up a miscellaneous hors d'oeuvres under the bushes which lined a part of one bank where the stream, being deeper, was also slower. But as I moved upstream, at every bend I came upon a new group of trout, which darted upstream and down in a great state of agitation, long before I could come within casting distance of them. After I had walked up three or four of these groups, and could see that the character of the stream for some distance ahead differed in no material wise from that part under my elbow, I returned to my starting point and sat down on a stile to give the trout time to settle. In less than half an hour dimples here and there in the runs between the cress beds a little way up encouraged me to try again. What a change! Fish, that half an hour before had scuttled desperately while I was yet a long way off, took no notice of me now, went on feeding gaily, and did not disdain my Olive Quill on those occasions when it was put to them right. To cut a long story short, I landed during the daytime twelve brace, retaining two over the pound limit; and going out again in the evening I landed another five brace, of which one was over the pound, and was retained.

Next day was similar in conditions, and I fished for a couple of hours in the morning, catching five brace, of which one was one and a quarter pounds, one a safe pound, and the rest went back. All the while that the fish were feeding they took no notice of me – comparatively speaking, of course – until they were hooked, when they made a fierce resistance. When they were not feeding they were wild as hawks, and scuttled over the shallows in droves while I was yet a great way off. Nothing remarkable in all this, of course – nothing that is not within the experience of all anglers for trout. The experience, I admit, is quite commonplace. It is only because of a train of thought that I mention it, and mention it in detail. Were the trout so infatuated with their food that they did not care about me during the rise, or was it that, with their eyes concentrated on the nymphs and duns coming down to them, they could not see me without a special effort, or without some special cause attracting attention? If one supposed that for some reasons of self protection, or for some other sound natural cause, the eye of the trout had a wide range of focus, so that he could see – even behind him – to quite a distance out of water when not intent on his food, and that when food was toward that focus shortened to a few – perhaps a very few – inches to deal with the business in hand, would not that explain his comparative unconsciousness of the angler's presence far better than the supposition that appetite was so strong upon him as, without diminishing the acuteness of his vision, to cast out fear? It is worth thinking about. (*The Way of a Trout with a Fly*)

Exact imitation

In this extract, Skues appears to be arguing against exact imitation in favour of appropriate representation. On the other hand, he contends that minute variations in fly dressing can make the difference between success and failure. He admits that the Itchen on which he based much of his experience is a river of profuse fly hatches, and that on waters where fly life is scarce fish may be much less choosy. An interesting thought is that Skues's final list of nymph dressings would seem to me to be as near as can be to exact imitation.

IT IS VERY usual to find writers declaring that to attempt to represent or suggest the natural fly with sufficient exactness to deceive the fish is absurd, and that one fly will do as well as another, provided the size and something of the modesty of nature be observed. I can only say that thirty-seven years of fishing of chalk streams have convinced me that this is not true of them, and that the trout will, more frequently than not, refuse any but one pattern which for the time being appears to them (though it is not always obvious to the angler why it does so) to be the natural fly on which for the moment they are feeding. For instance, it is not very clear why, when the blue-winged olive is rising at night, and the trout are taking it on the surface, a large Orange Quill on a No.14 or even a No.13 hook is accepted readily by them, but a large Red Quill of the same size, dyed or undyed, will either be utterly ignored or will put down the trout. The only difference is the colour of the quill. Other instances of unlike likenesses being taken are the taking of the Blue Quill when the pale watery dun is on, the Gold-Ribbed Hare's Ear when the large spring medium olive dun is hatching, and the Whirling Blue dun for the big autumn olive.

Often, of course, the insistence of the fish is upon closer likenesses. Yet it is my constant experience that on such waters a minute variation makes the difference between failure and success.

For instance, in July 1919, the July dun was coming up freely on the Itchen, and I was introducing a guest to the water. He put up a fly which to all appearance was a close imitation. Dark starling wings, yellow silk body ribbed with fine gold wire, and greenish-yellow olive hackle and whisk. He was an excellent fisherman, and he spent a full quarter of an hour over a vigorous trout, never putting him down or scaring him. Out of my experience I had made him tender of a pattern of July dun which differed from his only in having the body silk clothed with pale blue heron herl, dyed the same colour as the silk, a dirty greenish-yellow olive, but he had refused with the remark that his fly was 'near enough'. After a while he said to me: 'Well, give him a chance at your fly, since you think it better'. The first time my fly covered the trout he had it, and my friend netted out a nice two pound six ounce trout. He then accepted another fly similarly tied, and putting it on got the next two fish he tried directly he covered them.

I have had too many similar experiences to have any doubt about the matter.

Of course, the Itchen is a river which breeds and maintains a large quantity of fly food. In rough rivers where fly food is scarce I can understand that the fish will often rise at any fly or any suggestion of a fly which comes over them. But even there, when there is a rise or fall of an acceptable species of fly, I have known occasions when the trout refused everything but a fairly satisfactory representation of that fly. For instance, on the Coquet one afternoon, seeing that there was a heavy fall of small spinners, I put on a solitary fly which I had dressed the previous day to imitate the same spinner, and I caught no less than eight-and-thirty trout with it, while a much more experienced fisherman, fishing with me on the other side of the same water and using three or four flies, one of them a wool-bodied Red Spinner, but not true to shade, took three trout only. I am therefore convinced that what I call *appropriate representation* rather than exact imitation is seldom thrown away.

Every rule has its exception, and the exception is the occasion when the hatch or fall of natural fly is so copious that unless your fly has the luck to fall so near to the trout as to be the absolute next to be taken it is in competition with too many natural flies to invite selection. On such an occasion there should be something special about your fly to attract the trout's attention from the stream of natural insects. (*The Way of a Trout with a Fly*)

CHAPTER 5

Fly Dressing

The Flyfishers' Club of London possesses a unique work entitled *Nymph Dressings* which was edited by a Colonel Pack Beresford and presented to the Club as a one-off copy in 1936. It contains 13 of Skues's nymphs tied by him, Pale Wateries, Iron Blue, Medium Olive and July dun among them, set in sunk mounts with the dressings on the opposite page. Each one is exquisitely and delicately tied, and the flies look even smaller than the size of hook given in the dressing. Yet Skues operated under several handicaps. He had very large hands and clumsy-looking fingers, and he never had a fly dressing lesson in his life. Furthermore, he had very little sight in one of his eyes as a result of an operation at the age of nine. This necessitated his use of a jeweller's eye glass when he was dressing flies.

Skues's first successful fly dressings

Skues began to tie his own flies in 1887, inspired by the acquisition of Halford's *Floating Flies and How to Dress Them*, and his first successes are recorded on a visit with a friend to the River Coquet in Northumberland in 1887. From the beginning, he strove to achieve translucency in his flies by various dubbings of hare's ear, seal fur and heron and peacock quill.

I SUCCESSFULLY IMITATED the spinner of the august dun with flat gut dyed bright orange wound on a bare hook. It killed well in the evenings when I saw the spinners like red-hot needles dancing in the dying sunset. (Letter to J.J. Evans, 21st December, 1938)

THERE WAS A fair sprinkling of august dun on the water and among the flies bought were a number of imitations of that fly and of its spinner. The latter did fairly well, but not as well as a pattern I evolved tied with flat tawsy gut body dyed a bright orange and wound, with no silk underneath it, over a bare eyed hook, thus ensuring the maximum of transparency. (*Side-Lines, Side-Lights and Reflections*)

Fly dressing equipment

Surprisingly, bearing in mind that he must have accumulated a huge stock of fly dressing materials, Skues never had a fly dressing cabinet, but preferred to keep his stock in several elephant files and a ready-use supply in a wallet for ease of transport.

FOR A NUMBER of years I have kept a large supply of fly dressing materials at my fishing headquarters together with the necessary tools. The materials in a large Elephant file and the tools in a small bag with the silks, the wax and a small bottle of celluloid varnish, and I have only used the wallet to which you refer to amuse myself by tying a few flies on train journeys and on visits to other waters.

The wallet in question was not bought by me. It was the property of my Father's Father who fished the Don from Aberdeen in his youth and middle age, so the wallet may be for all I know a hundred years old. It is nothing but an old fashioned fly book constructed to carry flies tied to gut in the usual compartments with a parchment addition which I got my women-kind to stitch for me. This consisted of three sheets of parchment sewn together at the edges, down the middle and across three times, dividing it into sixteen compartments with a round hole in the middle of each into which was tucked a small supply of dubbing, mole, water rat, hare's ear, hare's poll, rabbit's poll (plain), rabbit's poll dyed hot orange, Tup's Indispensable materials, English blue squirrel, opossum, black rabbit's blue belly fur and a selection of seals' fur.

A small supply of the more useful hackles was placed in little packets tucked into the divisions constructed to take flies tied to gut. The pockets, of which there were two, held some peacock's herl and eyes, some floss silks wound on small cards, tying silks in skeins cut into lengths and threaded into channels in a silk container and other oddments. A leather band on the side of one of the pockets took scissors, pliers and old fashioned hackle pliers until I replaced the latter with artery forceps which I kept in a waistcoat pocket with a tiny hand vice. If I wanted any other material the change presented no difficulty. At my fishing headquarters I had little occasion to resort to the wallet as my Elephant file supplied all my needs. Wings when I wanted them on railway journeys I put in separate envelopes in my handbag.

It was, of course, a very makeshift arrangement, but it often served to while away a tedious hour on a railway journey. (Letter to Sir George Eastham, President of the Flyfishers' Club, November, 1942)

The travelling companion

The little hand vice was invented by an American friend, George Benson Stewart, a dentist who practised in Harley Street. He and Skues fished together and he helped Skues with his early nymph patterns. Skues tells a charming story of his use of the vice and travelling wallet on one of his train journeys. It is also a model lesson on how to dress a spinner.

I HAD SECURED a window seat, back to engine, on the sunny side of the two o'clock train for Winchester, had extracted from my kit-bag my little travelling wallet of fly-dressing materials, and had settled into my corner, when I became aware that I was not to travel alone. A passenger who had already come up from somewhere down the line – Winchfield or Old Basing, or farther south – was to go down with me. It was a mid-July day, and my companion was no less a personage than a dark sherry spinner. He had placed himself obligingly on the lower ledge of my window-pane, and had disabled himself from flight by the loss of his setae. He therefore offered himself most conveniently as a model for imitation, and as soon as the other companions of my journey were seated, and the train moving out of the station, I fixed a Limerick hook of the correct length in my

little hand-vice, selected a little batch of ruddy-brown seal's fur
dubbing, matched it against the model in the sunlight, waxed a
length of hot orange tying silk, selected a rusty blue-dun cock's
hackle of appropriate size, and whipped it on to the hook,
broke off the waste end, whipped to the tail, tied in three
bright honey-dun whisks and a length of gold wire, spun on a
tapered length of the dubbing, wound it to the shoulder,
wound on the wire at nice intervals, secured it at the shoulder,
broke off the waste end, nipped hackle-point in the pliers,
wound the hackle some six turns, wound the tying silk through
it, pushed back the hackle fibres, and finished with a whip finish
on the neck of the hook. Twice the process was repeated before
the train ran through Farnborough, when the wallet was tucked
away. (*The Way of a Trout with a Fly*)

Quality of hackles

Skues was particularly knowledgeable on the subject of hackles,
having at one time bred his own birds, though this is not mentioned
in any of his books. However, in a letter to John Evans who himself
became famous for his pen of game birds, he reveals a disaster.

GRAHAM CLARKE (*a well-known amateur fly dresser in his day*)
bred his own hackles. I started my lot with a few of his birds.
When I gave up I had some birds with lovely necks, and the
keeper to whom I gave them promptly killed the lot and
replaced them with White Dorkings and Rhode Island Reds. It
was infuriating. (Letter to Evans, 12th March, 1947)

In *Silk, Fur and Feather* he has this to say about hackles.

AS WE HAVE been collecting our hackles, we have, of course,
been picking them, clearing the roots of fluff, and rejecting the
proportion of useless or inferior feathers which are to be found
in the best of necks. Then the feathers move easily on one
another, in their envelopes, and are able to keep their shapes.
   A good cock's hackle is bright, active, sharp and full of
sparkle when held to the light. It should recover with a spring
when the point is pressed spear-wise against the hand or sleeve.
A young cockerel's hackle is much softer than that of an older
bird, and, for that reason, it is more suitable for wet fly dressing, as the older cock's hackle is more suitable for dry fly work.

A good hen's hackle is clean, but much woollier and softer in the texture than a cock's. It is by no means every hen's neck which has really shapely hackles suitable for fly dressing; and almost as few are to be found combining colour and condition. A great many more hens than cocks seem to be hatched, so that the choice of hen's hackles is much larger than the choice of cocks.

Tying in hackles

Skues had his own way of tying in hackles which has been emulated by generations of fly dressers.

MY PRACTICE IS probably unorthodox and might be condemned by professional tyers. I have never liked and never preached the practice of tying in a hackle by the tip. I strongly suspect that it is used by professionals to enable them (1) to use poor hackles and (2) to use larger hackles than if they tied in by the stalk. Even in the poorest cocks' hackles the fibres are shortest and brightest at the tip. Amateurs who take pains to secure hackles of high quality can afford to tie in by the stalk. I always do. It secures the hackle more soundly and helps to taper the body of the fly.

For a hackled floater without wings I tie in at the eye with the stump towards the bend of the hook, winding over the stump halfway to the bend, then break off the stalk, wind to near the tail, tie in whisks, ribbing and quill (if any) at that point and in that order. I then wind tying silk back to foot of hackle, wind and secure quill (body material) and then ribbing. I then wind the hackle backwards from the eye, wind the silk (held taut for that purpose) through the hackle (2 or 3 turns) and finish with whip finish or two or three half hitches at the eye. If there be dubbing I spin it on with the silk at the tail after tying in ribbing if any and wind it to the root of the hackle. I find that flies tied in my way are hard wearing and keep their shape. (Letter to Eastham, 23rd March, 1943)

Winging flies

When Peter Williams was a schoolboy of 16, having read all of Skues's books from his angling father's extensive fishing library, he took his courage in his hands and wrote to the great man, who was in his mid-

80s, asking advice on winging flies. Much to his surprise, he received a reply by return of post and thus ensued a correspondence only ended when Peter joined the navy during the war. Typically, Skues, after warning his young protégé for calling him an 'authority', went on to establish his credentials.

> IT IS ALWAYS a pleasure to do what I can to help any brother angler, but if you have read my second book, *The Way of a Trout with a Fly*, you will have seen that if there is one thing I object to more than any other it is being called an authority.
>
> It would assist me to help you if you could tell me:
>
> (1) What books you have read on fly dressing.
> (2) Whether you use a vice and if so what kind.
> (3) What bend and types of hook you use and whether the eye be upturned or down bend.
>
> I cannot recommend the use of celluloid varnish on winging material – Messrs Ogden Smith's fly tying girls varnish the tips of the wings of their Split winged floaters – but after a little while the wings tend to split up and to shred in a number of streamy fibres right and left.
>
> I think you will find that it is a matter of practice to hold the wing material so firmly and so upright on the hook that, when tied down, there is no bind in the material. (Letter to Peter Williams, 8th February, 1944)

Young Williams sent the details he had been asked for and submitted samples of his work for Skues's critical scrutiny. Skues, as usual, replied by return of post with detailed instructions on winging and an admission.

> I THINK YOU are a lucky young man to have such a selection of books on fly dressing. I began on Halford's *Floating Flies and How to Dress Them* and Ogden's little book at the age of 29, and I never had a lesson from a professional which would probably have saved me from much stumbling. As it is I never could make a success of tying in a hackle by the point which is the method of most professionals.
>
> The pattern you sent me looks to me as if you had taken both wings from the same wing of a starling instead of corresponding feathers from opposite wings of the same bird. It has not the fault of which you complained in your letter of the 2nd inst. The

wings are not split on the flue. Getting them to sit down right without splitting is largely a matter of practice. If as you hold the pair of wing feathers to be tied down you bring up your silk perpendicularly on the inside of the hook (i.e. the near side) and bring it down between your forefinger and the hook on the far side before pulling it down, and then pull down perpendicularly with the silk held close against the hook, the wings should not split, and with practice you will get your wings much wider.

The Way of a Trout with a Fly and *Minor Tactics of the Chalk Stream* are both out of print but are selling second hand at 21/- each as against the published price of 7/6d.

I return your specimen fly and hope you may find something to help you in this long letter. (Letter to Peter Williams, 15th February, 1944)

It is an interesting thought that by 1944 Skues's first editions were selling at about three times their original value. If you wished to purchase either of them today they would cost you around £150, some 450 times their original price.

Rolling wings for the Little Red Sedge

One of Skues's favourite flies was the Little Red Sedge which he claimed would sometimes take fish in the most unpropitious circumstances, and even when there was no fly on the water. His method of rolling the wing for the fly has been used by generations of fly dressers. Landrail is now on the protected list, but lapwing or mavis thrush can be used as substitutes.

TAKE ONE PRIMARY feather of the landrail, straighten the web of the feather for about an inch to an inch and a quarter, being careful not to break the fibre. Twitch off the whole width thus straightened, in one movement, holding it firmly between finger and thumb so as to prevent the fibre from breaking. Cut away all adhesions from the quill at the root of the web thus detached. Take the upper end of the web in a pair of pliers and turn over three or four fibres. Then take the fold thus made again between the jaws of the pliers, and turn over the fold. The double fold thus made is then turned again and again until the whole of the web is exhausted. Care should be taken to flatten the bunch as each fold is taken. When the web is exhausted the rolled feather is ready to be tied on his wings.

It is placed on its edge with the cut side downwards, and is whipped on to the hook immediately in front of the ribbing hackle, tied down with three or four turns. The tying silk is then brought behind the wing thus tied on, and round again under the waste end of the wings and the pliers hung on to it. The waste end can then be cut away in a single cut of the scissors, and the roots left are drenched with celluloid varnish. The front hackle can then be tied on and wound five or six turns to the root of the wing. Tying silk is then whipped through the hackle to the head and the fly finished with the whip finish. (*Side-Lines, Side-Lights and Reflections*)

The importance of the colour of tying silk in dubbed flies

From his earliest fly dressing days, Skues placed the greatest importance on translucency to be achieved by dubbing and the colour of the tying silk, and the realisation that trout could see flies in the water either by reflected or transmitted light.

YEARS AGO I spent a week upon the Teme, fishing wet, and I remember looking down one sunny morning upon my cast in shallow water, and being struck by the appearance of my Yellow Dun. The body was dubbed with primrose wool, but though, while dry or in the air, every turn of the tying silk was completely hidden, yet, looking down upon the fly in the water, I could see every turn distinctly, and the dubbing was scarcely noticeable, and I was glad that the tying silk harmonised so perfectly with the hue of the dubbing.

The importance of the base colour of the tying silk was still more strongly brought home to me a day or two later. I had tied some imitations of a pale watery dun which was on the water with a pale starling wing, light ginger hackle and whisk, and a mixture of opossum and hare's poll for dubbing; but some I had tied with pale orange silk, and some with that rich maroon colour called Red Ant in Mr. Aldam's series of silks. The grayling took those tied with pale orange freely, but would not look at those tied with Red Ant.

It may be less material in floating flies, but for wet flies I have since always been careful to have the tying silk either harmonious with the colour of the natural subimago or corresponding to the spinner. For instance, for an Iron Blue Dun I should use claret silk dubbed with mole's fur or water rat; for the old fashioned Mole's Fur Blue Dun, primrose to heighten the olive effect in the dark blue; primrose silk also for a Hare's Ear; in the Willow Fly, orange silk under the mole's fur or water rat; in the Grannom, green very darkly waxed, or black; and so on. The fact is that the transparency of fur and feather is marvellous. (*Minor Tactics of the Chalk Stream*)

Joost boughten flees

Skues was particularly caustic on the subject of shop-bought flies, of which more later regarding his nymphs, and it might well be that even today, despite the efforts of some talented professional fly dressers, the following remarks still apply.

A CASUAL PHRASE in a recent newspaper recalled to my mind a visit which I paid in the Spring of 1897 to Lyme Regis where the kind offices of my host secured for me from the owner of the little stream which finds its way to the sea through the gravel of the Lyme Regis beach liberty to fish that stream. As I was not familiar with the water in question and had grounds for believing that it was one of the waters fished by G.P.R. Pulman, the author of the *Vade Mecum*, which was the first, or almost the first, book to recommend the use of the dry fly, I made some enquiries and came across a local man who claimed to have known Pulman. I accordingly grasped the opportunity to enquire of him what sort of flies Pulman used. I gasped at the incredible answer he gave me: 'Joost boughten flees.' It was, of course, not possibly true. Pulman was himself a flydresser, as his book shows; though he did not dress the split wing floater so far as we know. But of how many an angler's equipment is it true. 'Joost boughten flees.' And lucky are those few of us, who not only can dress our own flies, but have enough of entomological knowledge to realise what they mean. Lucky also those of us whose flies are supplied by makers who are themselves flyfishers, entomologists and artists in the production of flies. Such a one was R.S. Austin who was not only an angler and entomologist but used to dress, often on fine gut, the most exquisite winged floaters rivalling in delicacy the little miracles of C.A. Hassam.

In contrast how many professional tyers there are whose work, mechanically exact and rather wonderful, is yet so often all wrong. Duns built with squat bodies, short squat double-dressed wings twice the width of the wing of the natural fly which they profess to be representing, and two or even three hackles, often not of first rate quality. Sedges dressed exactly in the same way as the duns with upright outspread split wings instead of the penthouse laid wings of the natural fly. I might enumerate many more divergences from the delicate simplicity of nature – but these are enough: 'Joost Boughten Flees.' (*Flyfishers' Journal*)

Buzz

A perusal of Skues's books reveals many useful hints for tyro fly dressers. The first reminds me of Richard Walker's dictum in the dressing of crane flies to tie more than the regulation six legs on the basis that trout cannot count.

A GOOD DEAL of scorn has been wasted upon the excessive number of legs given by fly dressers to the artificial fly to ensure flotation, particularly to the Sedges. I would ask, how often is it that the hackles of flies are taken for legs? Many of the sedges flutter upon the surface; and may not the saying that they are dressed 'buzz' be wiser than it looks? The effect of fluttering and the effect of a bush of hackles may not look so dissimilar to the trout. Palmers, I have no doubt, are as often taken for struggling sedge flies as for the woolly bears and other caterpillars they are fancifully supposed to represent.

Then from certain points of view a good sharp cock's hackle with the light through it is nothing but sheer sparkle. It has no appearance of solidity at all, and it may be doubted whether the fish sees much of it as leg at all. It may merely give an effect of translucency to the wings. This is, no doubt, one reason why high quality in hackles is so desirable. (*The Way of a Trout with a Fly*)

Kick

Although Skues fished the Itchen for 56 years, he had extensive experience of other rivers, including northern ones such as the Coquet and the Ure. He met the renowned Ure fisherman and fly dresser, James Blades, and, no doubt, this tip comes from such meetings.

This is a quality which every hackled wet fly, for use in rough water, would invariably have. Without it, it is a dead thing; with it, it is alive and struggling; and the fly which is alive and struggling has a fascination for the trout which no dead thing has. How is this quality to be attained? It is a very simple matter. Finish behind the hackle.

Suppose you are tying an Orange Partridge. You have whipped on the gut, tied in the floss, whipped to the shoulder, wound on the orange floss, whipped down the end, cut away the waste. You then take your brown partridge hackle, and placing it face downwards on top of the hook, with the stump towards the bend, you whip it down with two turns toward the head; then, whipping over the hook and back to the feather, you form the head. Then you take two turns over the butt, and, taking the centre of the hackle in your pliers, you wind at most two turns of the hackle and secure the end with one turn of the silk. Then you pull all the fibres forward over the head, and finish with a whip finish tight up behind the hackle, and break off the waste. You then soak the whip finish with celluloid varnish (or similar), push back the hackle over the bend and varnish the head, and your fly is complete. The turns of silk behind the hackle makes each fibre sit up and stand out, the fly has kick, and it will improve rather than deteriorate with use. Hackles with good natural resilience are, of course, essential.
(*The Way of a Trout with a Fly*)

Tips

Skues's correspondence was extensive over many years, and became even more important to him when he gave up fishing in 1945 at the age of 87. Some of those who wrote to him wanted his advice on several aspects of fly fishing. This letter takes up several queries from his correspondent.

I HAVE NEVER but once had a lesson in fly dressing and have only my own amateur methods to rely on.

I cannot see why you cut up the fur for dubbing. You lose the entire advantage of the length of the fibres. (*This refers to the hare's flax used for the body of the Gold-Ribbed Hare's Ear.*)

I have used squirrel tail to *wing* a pattern of Sedge fly, adapting an American method, and it is quite a success. For dubbing bodies with squirrel use the back and *do not cut it up.*

Hare's ear and cow hair are both difficult but cutting them up makes them well nigh impossible.

I never mastered or indeed seriously tried tying in hackles by the point. *If you use good hackles* you can make a better job by tying in by the butt.

For spent spinners a hackle tied in by the stalk and wound and then bound right and left by figure of eight laps of the silk, the tips of the wings being humoured to shape, makes a good representation. For transparent wings I am content with a hackle of good quality, not tightly wound. I never cared for bundles of fibre tied upright.

The hare's ear pattern is very ancient. I am away from my books and cannot say how ancient. Like you I do not see the object of the red whisk. No doubt it does not look very red to the trout viewing it from below. Anyhow red does not attract trout. The pattern Halford favoured in his early days had not gold wire but flat gold tinsel. No hackle but tips of fur from hare's face inserted between strands of tying silk and spun. To my mind that is still the best pattern both at the beginning and end of the season.

I do not use an oil bottle but have a pad of spongiopiline in a small box or a sovereign purse and saturate that with ordinary paraffin before starting and find it quite effective. (Letter to H. Andrews of Saffron Walden, 6th February, 1946)

Renovating dry flies

Skues numbered many Americans amongst his correspondents including famous fishermen like Gordon and Leisenring, father of the American nymph. He also kept in close touch with the Anglers' Club of New York, contributing articles to its *Bulletin*.

A CONTRIBUTOR TO the New York *Anglers' Club Bulletin* of December 1928, contributes over the signature G.P.H. (which I suspect stands for George Parker Holden) a tip which might well be worth following over here. Sorting out from his dry flies all that from use were matted down or presented a dishevelled appearance and holding them in a thumb forceps he subjects them to the steam at the spout of a kettle of boiling water. This was followed by brushing wings and hackle over the forefinger with a soft tooth brush. And he says, 'The fresh groomed flies could barely be distinguished from those that were new and unused.'

I imagine this method might prove more suitable for May flies and Sedges than for small flies – but in any case it looks worth a trial. (1929)

Lost flies

A letter written in Skues's later years as a fly dresser will strike a chord with all fly tyers. The fly he refers to is now commonly known as the small spurwing.

I HOPE I am not too late to save your Itchen fishing. A letter from Barton reminded me of a September afternoon he got me years ago on the Leckford Abbas length of the Test when there was a strong hatch of that feeble little insect the autumn little pale blue and between 4.30 and 7 I got five trout weighing 10lb 5ozs on a home-made representation tied as follows:

Hook: No.16
Silk: Yellow
Hackle: Pale blue
Body: Yellow tying silk dubbed lightly with rabbit's poll
Rib: Yellow tying silk unwaxed
Wing: Pale blue from wing of black-headed gull

I have had, while the light lasted, three shots at reproducing the pattern, but one (of course the best) fell on the floor and though I searched hard with the aid of a powerful magnet, I failed to recover it. Here are the other two. I am sorry to say my celluloid varnish had petered out and the local chemist could not replace it, so the tying may be none too secure. If you have any and could give a dab on the heads of the flies it would make them safer. (Letter to to D.M. Goodbody, 21st September, 1941)

Two of the flies were enclosed in the letter, and Goodbody kept them there. C.F. Walker, editor of Skues's letters, commenting on the fate of the third fly, said that it would surely strike a sympathetic chord in the hearts of all fly dressers, though it seemed almost irreverent to think of Skues, at the age of 84, grovelling on the floor with a magnet in the posture so familiar to the rest of us. John Evans, who visited Skues at the Nadder Vale Hotel where he spent some of his last years, remembers an occasion when he helped Skues to collect at least four dozen flies which had fallen from the great man's table. As Walker said, the law of gravity was no respecter of persons, and Evans informs us that some of the flies had apparently been there for at least a year and were so deeply embedded in the carpet that no magnet would ever have lifted them.

Concluding advice to fly dressers

Skues concluded the articles gathered in his book, *Silk, Fur and Feather*, with the following wise words of advice to any aspiring fly dresser:

> I HAVE NOW taken the novice through the feather and material collecting year – and through the trout season – and there is nothing left but a few concluding observations.
>
> Of those who have read these pages and take up fly dressing it is probable that the majority will not go very far. They will content themselves with securing a small stock of material and mastering one or two of the simpler methods of dressing.
>
> Those who are more ambitious will no doubt wish to go much further. To them I would say read, and read freely, all the works on trout fly dressing on which they can lay hand, but, for goodness sake, read with wisdom and judgment. Do not be magnetised by names and reputations, however great. Learn all the methods of tying. It will be seen that I have only touched upon a few of the simpler. The subject is so extensive that I have merely scratched the surface. The methods are innumerable, and each has some merit of its own. Therefore it is well to master all, so as to be able to apply to any problems the most appropriate method. But do not take anything for gospel. The amount of error disseminated by men who have passed as authorities, and were doubtless often most successful fishermen, passes belief. Read then, to master method and the handling of material; and then, when you are competent, you can discard all the nostrums and take the natural insects you want to portray, and you can go to your task with a prospect of making as good a job of it as any of the authorities you have read.
>
> You will find that many of these authorities have blandly copied from predecessors, and where you find them doing this you may infer that they are not necessarily very reliable.
>
> In the patterns which I have described I have been giving you the best I know. But so probably were these others. Don't, for goodness sake, make a fetish of these patterns, either mine

or others. Tie to satisfy yourself, not to imitate me or another. And never rest satisfied – always try to be improving. So with practice you may gain for yourself a power which will add enormously to the delights of your fly fishing days. (*Silk, Fur and Feather*)

1945 saw the end of the Second World War; it also saw the end, not only of Skues's active life as a fly fisherman but also as a fly dresser. On the 24th September, 1945, he wrote to his friend, Sir Tom Eastham, the following:

FLY DRESSING HAS practically given me up as my hands have become so shaky this year as to render good winging almost impossible. I thank you for your offer to buy some of my materials and will bear it in mind. I have a number of friends in like case.

Few fly dressers have based so many of their patterns on a study of the natural insect.

CHAPTER 6

Fly Patterns

Skues's fly dressings and fly patterns were based on an ency-
clopaedic knowledge of the subject. From 1887 onwards, he often
spent his afternoons in the British Museum, studying every possible
book on the subject, analysing and digesting works new and old.
Anyone merely associating Skues with nymph fishing will be surprised
at the number of dry flies in which he was interested. He strove
always to devise his own patterns based on the natural flies, but he
never scorned the use of good imitations invented by others.

The bodies of many of his dry flies were mainly dressed with heron
herl, often dyed, and various seals' furs. In his wet flies and nymphs,
Skues showed a strong preference for different furs, above all, hare,
but also rat, squirrel, opossum, rabbit, mole, seal and, occasionally,
peacock quill. The patterns given here feature not only his own
patterns but others in which he was interested.

The Blue-Winged Olive

This was probably Skues's favourite fly, and it hatched out in some
quantity on the Itchen. Even so, he emphasised that one had to
divine whether the trout were feeding on the nymph, dun or spinner.
He always claimed when rising fish were making large and kidney-
shaped whorls they were coming up for the blue-winged olive.

Although Frank Sawyer, the famous Avon river-keeper, disagreed
with Skues on the point, stating that in his experience that type of rise
was made to many other kinds of insect, he did say that, of all the
nymphs of the ephemeroptera, he believed that the blue-winged olive
nymphs incited a trout most urgently.

Skues refers below to the Orange Quill, and later in this chapter he
describes how he first discovered the fly.

I WANT TO sing the praises of the blue-winged olive. As a sport-
providing fly it can give the May fly several stone and a beating.
From mid-June to the end of the season there is scarcely an
evening when it may not put in an appearance. When it does
put in an appearance there is always a chance of a big fish.
When it puts in an appearance in quantity there is the chance of
a big basket, and all the fish in the basket big.

The hour of the hatch is usually late. A sprinkling of blue-
winged olives will go down almost unregarded while the light
lasts, but in the gloaming, after a pause, the fly will sometimes
hatch out in quantity, and at once every big fish in the river will
be busy gulping them down.

It is at this point the angler needs to be careful about his fly.
He must be sure what the trout are doing. At one time the
trout will be nymphing, and the only way to take them will be
with a sunk, sparsely-hackled, dark brown olive pattern. At
another time, maybe later in the same rise, the trout will be
taking the subimago. Then, according to my experience, a large
Orange Quill, No.14 size, is fatal. At times, however, I have
killed well with a fly of the same size dressed thus:

Wings: Darkest starling or medium coot
Body: Greenish-olive seal's fur
Tag: Flat gold
Whisk: Pale dun cock
Hackle: Medium olive
Hook: No.14

Another pattern which occasionally kills well is dressed in the
same way except that the body is of heron herl dyed a greenish-
yellow olive, and there is a rib of fine gold and no tag.

But at times the trout will concentrate on the spinner. It may
be, and generally is, the male spinner – of a dark, rich brown
sherry colour. On such occasions I have found a fly dressed as
follows deadly:

Hook: No.14, round bend or equivalent in Limerick shape
Body: Dark sherry-brown seal's fur
Rib: Fine gold wire
Whisk: Honey dun cock
Hackle: Six or seven turns of dark, rusty dun cock

As an illustration of a correct diagnosis, let me quote a recent experience on the Itchen.

On June 21, 1919, the small fly evening rise was over, and I judged from the large and violent kidney-shaped whorls made by the rising trout that they had come on to the blue-winged olive. I offered a big fish under my own bank an Orange Quill with some confidence. He took no notice at first, but presently stopped, and I moved on to another fish. He was taking just above a large clump of a big umbelliferous plant, and I had to throw over it and recover my fly through it or not at all. So I calculated I had just one chuck, and if that did not come off I might as well move on, for I should not have another chance. I watched the fish for a minute or two, and concluded he was not taking subimagines. I had seen no spinner going down, so I knotted on a nymph, wetted it thoroughly in my mouth, judged my distance, and dropped the fly a foot in front of the fish and outside him. The fly went under, and instantly there was a telltale hint on the surface which made me pull home. I netted the fish out eventually at the place where I had put down the first fish, and the scales said two and three quarter pounds. The next stretch was barren, but when I found another riser the evening had moved on, and the trout would have nothing to say to the nymph. I tied on an Orange Quill, and the next fish had it at the first offer. He scaled two pounds five ounces. I got one other of one and a half pounds, and then all was suddenly over for the evening.

The following weekend a friend got the fish I had begun on. He scaled three pounds two ounces. If only I—!

July 6 was another blue-winged olive evening, but as there had been a sprinkle of the subimagines coming up all day, and I had seen none on the water for half an hour, I divined, when the trout began to rise madly about 9.30, that it was spinner that was doing the trick. There were two big fish rising within ten feet of one another in a favourite bend where the current ran deep and strong under my bank, the left. I therefore tied on a hackled Ruddy Spinner, and laid it across the lower fish. He had it immediately and tore off up the stream, half out of water, for some twenty yards or more. Then I turned him down but the mischief was done; the upper fish was scared and had gone. The hooked fish made a gallant fight, but the keeper weighed him a little later – two and a half pounds good. It was some way up to the next riser, and when I had put him down with a bad cast I thought all was over for the evening, and was making for the bridge to cross the river and so home-along, when I saw a fish rise under a tussock by my bank. I gave him the fly, and he took it gaily, and presently joined the fish in my bag – a comparatively small fish, one pound nine ounces, and not a very good colour. Then, as I came to the spot from which I had cast to him, I saw, three or four yards higher up, a series of spreading rings which called for the administration of the Spinner. Again, the first chuck was all that was necessary. At the movement of the neb I pulled in, and the line was torn off the reel as the fish raced madly diagonally across the river, and ended with a wild fling in the air that revealed his solid proportions. He put up a gorgeous fight, but came to the net at last – two pounds twelve ounces exactly. That was really the end of the evening.

The following weekend I was down again. It had rained hard in the afternoon and evening, and I did not get into position till 9.15. I was clad in a mackintosh, which covered me down to the tops of my waders, to preserve me from getting soaked by the dripping herbage, in places nearly man high. I began at the choice corner above-mentioned. There were two fish busy in it, both good ones, and I made the mistake of giving them the Spinner which had been successful on the previous occasion. I had seen a good hatch of subimago on the surface, and if I had only exercised ordinary common sense I would have put on an Orange Quill, and I should probably have had one and possibly both. As it was, I put both down. I then moved quietly up to get to the fish I had put down by a bad cast the previous weekend. I found him busy, but not too busy to attend to my Orange Quill. He weighed two pounds two ounces. Next I cast right across to a fish taking steadily in the shadow under the far bank. He soon stopped; probably it was drag. I felt sure he was a good fish, and I got to the bridge and down to him as quickly as I could. I was afraid the rise might be over, but he was still taking at intervals sufficiently close to enable me to cover him precisely enough, and he had the Orange Quill at the first offer. At first I thought I had misjudged his weight, his movements were so slow, but presently he became scared and showed his mettle, and during the latter stages of the battle he was half out of the water, and lashing the surface and churning it into foam. But the little nine-footer guided him to the net, and he lay on the bank in the moonlight, a perfect picture of what a chalk stream trout should be – deep, solid, short and thick, in the pink of condition, three pounds two ounces.

I have given these three evening experiences just as illustrations of the varying ways in which trout must be approached under differing conditions, even when rising at the same fly. It is often very difficult to judge which is the right or best course to adopt, and much valuable time may be lost by an error in judgment

It may be asked why the Orange Quill is taken at night for the blue-winged olive. I answer frankly I don't know. I only know that it is. I discovered it by accident in the early nineties, and it was a lucky accident, for it has been worth many a good fish to me. In one season I remember five successive Saturday evenings in June and July, each of which yielded three and a half brace to the Orange Quill. That experience led me astray at first, and I had some disappointments before I worked back to the full appreciation of the fact that blue-winged olive fishing has three phases – nymph, subimago and spinner.

To fish the nymph at night is even more fascinating than to do so by day. In order to divine the rise and the right moment to strike it is essential to choose a stretch where you look up into the light under your own bank. Then, when the fly is taken under water, there is the faintest little heave of the silver of the surface, but as the hook goes home the resistance is apt to be magnificent.

The may fly has gone from my stretch of Itchen; but if I had to choose whether I would exchange for its return the blue-winged olive, my answer would, without hesitation, be 'Not at any price.' (*The Way of a Trout with a Fly*)

The Hare's Ear puzzle

There are few flies in the fly fishers' pantheon which have killed more fish down to this very day than the Gold-Ribbed Hare's Ear. Halford included it in *Floating Flies and How to Dress Them*, acknowledging that it best imitated a hatching nymph, later gave it a wing to comply with his conventional dry fly theory and finally, as Skues says, excluded it altogether.

THE LATTER DAYS of April, with their outstanding hatch of large
medium olive duns, bring back this recurring problem for the
colourist. In a sense I am a colourist. That is, I recognize – I
am forced by the logic of facts to realize – that the trout take
certain artificial patterns for certain natural flies. I admit the
likeness is often not obvious, and infer from that – to the great
indignation of 'Jim-Jam' and others – that the trout do not, in
all probability, see colour as we see it.

For it is the fact that whenever I see the greenish olive body
of this spring dun I know that the season of the Hare's Ear –
the Gold-Ribbed Hare's Ear – has come; and I put up the
Gold-Ribbed Hare's Ear with the utmost confidence, and I find
it more certainly and infallibly right that any other dressing I
know, unless I except the large Orange Quill when the blue-
winged olive is on. But that is in the evenings, in the dusk,
while the Gold-Ribbed Hare's Ear kills in the full light of day.

Why, then, should a pattern dressed with a body of a dusty
grey-brown, ribbed with flat gold and extremely rough, be
taken by the trout for a smooth-bodied fly with an olive-green
body?

It is true that fur, when wet, is extraordinarily translucent. It
is probable that the gold catches some of the green of the
under-water weeds reflected upward from below. But still the
facts as known to us suggest some problem of the eyesight of
the trout which requires solution if we are to arrive at a true
theory of the art of fly dressing.

It has been suggested that the artificial is taken in this case
for the natural fly, either just hatching out of its shuck and not
entirely extricated, or else standing on its shuck. But if that is
so, why should not all the upwinged duns be represented upon
similar principles?

At one time the late Mr. F.M. Halford was a great advocate
of the Gold-Ribbed Hare's Ear, but I believe that latterly his
enthusiasm for precise imitation induced him to give it up,
successful pattern though he knew it to be, because he could
not explain its success to his satisfaction.

I confess I do not take it to be a lure. The trout do not take
it like a lure. I believe they take it for a natural insect – the
medium olive dun – which is on at the time. But why?

Still, the Hare's Ear kills. And I should like to know who was
the genius who first conceived its possibilities and how he got
at his theory.

If we had that information progress might be possible. (*The Way of a Trout with a Fly*)

'Jim-Jam' was the pen name of Dr. James Mottram, a fellow member of the Flyfishers' Club and author of *Flyfishing: some New Arts and Mysteries*, who had carried out some interesting research on nymphs largely in line with Skues's theories, and later on had recanted, as it were, and rejoined the dry fly lobby. He had also carried out experiments to prove that trout could differentiate colour in the way that we do.

The Orange Quill and the blue-winged olive

We have already seen that Skues was fond of using the Orange Quill at night to take the blue-winged olive, and how he was puzzled by it. His theory was that it was taken for the blue-winged olive spinner, i.e. the sherry spinner. Here, he relates how he first came to use the Orange Quill.

'ON CHALK STREAMS of the South, the Orange Quill is used almost universally, and this discovery made by Mr. Skues in the nineties, has turned a hatch of blue-winged olive, formerly an event always incalculable, and often baffling, into a most lucrative one.'

The above paragraph is quoted from pages 226–227 of Major J. Waller Hills' delightful volume, *A Summer on the Test*, and the reading of it suggested to me that it might be of interest to anglers to be told how the discovery of the value of the Orange Quill as medicine when the blue-winged olive is on came about.

This sent me back to F.M. Halford's *Floating Flies and How to Dress Them* to refresh my memory on the question whether there was an Orange Quill in that volume. I felt pretty sure that there was none, but, after ascertaining that was so, I referred to the dressing of the Red Quill, and I found there, to my surprise, that there was no dressing of the Red Quill with the plain undyed peacock's quill body, but that the only dressing given is as follows:

Wings:	Pale or Medium Starling
Body:	Peacock quill dyed on No.IX
Hackle & Whisk:	Red Game Cock
Hook:	No.15, 16 or 17

No.IX in Halford's table of dyes stands for a brownish red which Halford termed 'Red Spinner.'

To the dressing the author appended the following note: 'A larger size dressed on a No.15 hook is found very killing just after dusk'.

So it will be seen that Halford had discovered or been taught, perhaps by G.S. Marryat, the value after dusk of a large Red Quill with a body quill not differing greatly save in tone of red and in having a dark rib, from the Orange Quill. But though he included a Blue-Winged Olive among his patterns, Halford did not appear to have associated the killing quality of the large Red Quill with the appearances of the blue-winged olive.

In the early nineties I was saturated with knowledge of all the dressings in *Floating Flies*, and it was probably on account of the note quoted above that, finding a solitary large fly with an orange quill body among the stock of James Currell, the fishing tackle dealer in Parchment Street, Winchester, I took it among other purchases and put it with the Red Quills in my Hardy fly box.

It must, I think, have been in 1894 – I knew it was in September – that I was on the Itchen at dusk, just about thirty yards below a certain spinney, when I noted a procession of rather large dark olives coming down under my own bank (the right) and being greedily absorbed by a string of three trout.

Looking through my fly box for a dun of suitable size, I had the luck to find the solitary Orange Quill as the only fly that was big enough and knotting it on to my gossamer point I delivered it to the lowest of the three trout. He took it in without hesitation and proved to be one and three quarter pounds, a good fish for that part of the water. Each of the others took the fly at the first offer, and each proved to be of the same weight – one and three quarter pounds.

This proved to me that in the Orange Quill I had found a good fly to offer to trout taking duns at dusk. But at that time I had not identified the dun as the blue-winged olive. I dressed, however, a number of Orange Quills and in a season or two I made the discovery that it was when the blue-winged olive was on that the Orange Quill was great medicine. I found George Holland tied the pattern so much better than I did that for many years, till he gave up, I got my Orange Quills tied by him. Afterwards his son and later his best tier, who had set up on her own account, tied them for me. Both have gone, however, and I now find it very difficult to get the pattern dressed as it should be and I have gone back in my old age to dressing it for myself.

In none of his other works did Halford give any evidence of having given a trial to the Orange Quill. He thus deprived himself of a very useful pattern, very fatal to big fish. (*Flyfishers' Journal*, Summer 1931)

Strangely enough, although he gives Halford's dressing of the Red Quill, described by him as the sheet anchor on an unfamiliar river, Skues does not give that of the Orange Quill, and neither did he in any of his books. Halford, incidentally, did mention the Orange Quill in *Dry Fly Entomology*, though he used peacock quill for the body and not the usual condor quill. Skues makes clear in his other writings that the Orange Quill was not always the universal panacea at dusk for the blue-winged olive, and Frank Sawyer said that it was rarely successful on the Avon. The dressing of the Orange Quill is as follows:

Hook: No.14
Silk: Hot orange
Wings: Pale starling, rather full, as the natural insect has wings
          longer than the ordinary olive duns
Hackle: Bright red cock
Whisks: Same colour or paler, from the spade feather of cock
Body: Pale condor quill, stripped, so as to show no dark edge,
          and dyed hot orange

The Rusty Spinner

Though Skues made no claim to having invented the Orange Quill, he did design one of the best imitations of the little sherry spinner, the male spinner of the blue-winged olive, known nowadays as the jenny spinner, which he called the Rusty Spinner. Courtney Williams, in his *Dictionary of Trout Flies*, says that in a smaller size it often proves deadly during a fall of female pale watery spinners and was also a good pattern with which to imitate the spinners of the July dun and the iron blue dun.

FROM THE TIME when the pale watery dun first puts in an appearance to the end of the season, one of the most useful of

chalk stream patterns for evening use is the little Rusty Spinner.
Tied on a square-bent, slightly snecked, down-eyed hook of
No.14 size with hot orange silk dubbed with a fine pig's wool
or seal's fur of red-ant colour – a deep rich mahogany red –
ribbed with fine gold wire and hackled with a rusty dun cock's
hackle, sharp and bright, and with whisks of three fibres of a
honey-dun cock's shoulder hackle, it proves extraordinarily
attractive at the time when small spinners come on the water,
and according to my experience it fishes as well slightly
submerged as floating. Dressed on No.14 or even No.15 hook
it is an excellent representation of the male spinner of the blue-
winged olive. No angler should be without it at the appropriate
season of the year. (*The Way of a Trout with a Fly*)

The Alder

The Alder is a Jekyll and Hyde sort of fly, killing well on some rivers
and ineffective on others; a favourite fly of Charles Kingsley whilst
others have never caught a fish on it, and trout rarely seem to take the
naturals. Skues postulates why the winged fly takes fish below the
surface. Incidentally, his bags in Bavaria (249 in 14 days; 265 in 14
days); 20 brace in two days on the Kennet; 44 brace out of 54 brace
in three days on the Nadder may raise a few eyebrows. And he didn't
even eat trout!

FOR MANY YEARS after I had become a fly-fisherman I never did
any good with the Alder. I first owned a fly rod (of a sort) in
1874, but although I had read and loved Charles Kingsley's
Chalk-Stream Studies, it was not till 1904 that I had any success
with his favourite fly. It is true that my May and June-time fishing had been almost exclusively on the Itchen (which seldom
yields any results to the Alder) and on the lower Kennet, when
the May fly alone brought up the trout. But in 1904 I took a
holiday in Bavaria which covered the first eighteen days of June,
and for some reason which I do not quite recall I took with me
a small stock of Black Alders purchased of Messrs. Peek and Son
of 40, Gray's Inn Road which appealed to me as being of the
genuine Kingsley tie. Kingsley, it will be remembered, fished his
Alder (and his Caperer or Sedge) well sunk. These Alders,
therefore, were tied with long wings of a soppy game hen's
wing, tied slanting well back from the shoulders over a
peacock's herl body, and there was a soft black hen's hackle tied

in front of the wings. The hooks were Nos.12 and 13 eyed
Snecky Limericks.

The May fly was not well on when I arrived, though it had
begun to hatch; but at a little distance the waterside bushes
looked as if they wore plummy-dun haloes, which on approach
disclosed themselves as clouds of humming alder flies. I began
fishing on the afternoon of my arrival, and tied on an Alder. I
caught a big grayling with it at first cast, and soon after, with
the sodden fly, I hooked a trout under the far bank which,
judging from the distance between the tip of his tail and the
place where my line was cutting the water, I put down at five
pounds. I fought him down a couple of hundred yards, he
boring all the time under his own bank. Then he turned and
forced his way irresistibly, still under his own bank, right back
to the cut-weed pile close to which I had hooked him, and of
which I had steered him clear and there he came unstuck.

As I subsequently killed another trout of four pounds six
ounces on the same stream, on the same rod with 3x gut on an
Alder, and that between two trees which would not let me
move up or down, I do not think my estimate of five pounds
for that lost fish was excessive. At any rate, the incident encouraged me to persevere with the Alder, and next day I took
eighteen brace nearly all with the same pattern of Alder. I was
fishing not many yards behind my companion, who had therefore put down everything on our side of the water, and I got
nearly all my trout under the opposite bank with a sunk Alder.
Two only were under one pound weight. Next day, on another
length, I had sixteen and a half brace, nearly all with the wet
Alder fished up or across. Next day the May fly came on nicely,
but in the morning before it did so I had three brace of
pounders in fifty yards with the wet Alder. Towards the end of
our stay the heat became very oppressive and the water ran low
and stale, but in sixteen days' fishing, some days only partially
occupied, I had two hundred and forty nine trout, of which
fully half were taken with the wet Alder.

In the following season (May 22 to June 4) on the same
river, I had two hundred and sixty five in fourteen days, and
again the wet Alder scored heavily. From that time on I have
given the Alder a trial in its season in various water, including
the upper Kennet (twenty brace in two days), the Nadder (forty
four brace out of fifty four brace taken in three days), and have
always found that it fished better sunk than dry.

The wet pattern sinks readily and sinks deep. It is not in the least like the nymph of the alder. The trout undoubtedly never sees the natural alder as a perfect insect at a depth below the surface. Yet the successful period for the wet Alder is when the natural fly is out. It will take at other periods, but nothing like so well. I know of no beetle out at that time for which the wet Alder would be taken. I have heard it suggested that it may be taken for a tadpole, but I cannot say I have ever seen trout feeding on tadpoles.

The thing is an insoluble puzzle to me. The pattern is too successful to be readily surrendered. It is obviously accepted gleefully as food, but what does it represent? (*The Way of a Trout with a Fly*)

The Iron Blue

Skues considered the Iron Blue a deadly fly as May approached, noting that the natural was more prolific on the Test than the Itchen. He described it as 'a little inky-looking insect'.

THE IRON BLUE rises occur in flushes, succeeding one another until well into the afternoon. The fly appears through May and June and again in September. If the trout are taking it on the surface we should have some floaters ready. Here is a useful dressing:

Hook: No.16 Hall's Snecky Limerick (upturned eye)
Silk: Crimson or claret
Wings: Starling dyed an inky blue
Whisks: White or palest blue cock
Body: Peacock's quill from the eye, dyed inky blue, or darkest heron herl from a big secondary, ribbed with fine gold wire
Hackle: Rusty blue dun cock (darkish)

(*Silk, Fur and Feather*)

Iron Blue Nymph

Skues found his nymph pattern far more effective, and, as the iron blue nymph is an agile darter, it was ideally suited to his nymph fishing techniques.

IF I HAD postponed the publication of *Minor Tactics of the Chalk Stream* for a year or two there is one dressing, that of the iron blue dun, given as a winged fly, for which I could have substituted a far better dressing of the nymph type. Here it is:

Hook: No.16 round bend
Body: Mole's fur on crimson tying silk, well waxed, the silk
            exposed for two or three turns at the tail end
Whisks: Two or three strands of soft, mobile, white hackle,
            quite short
Legs: The very short, nearly black, hackle from the throat of
            a cock jackdaw, not exceeding two turns

There is nothing very new in this dressing. The use of the jackdaw's throat hackle for Iron Blue has long been known in Yorkshire. The only novelty in my pattern is the use of a hackle so small as to suggest legs only. In Yorkshire it appears to be used for wings.

    I dressed a couple on gut one May afternoon going down on the train, and next morning, seeing the iron blue on but neglected, and being convinced by the character of the rises that the trout were taking it under water, I soaked my pattern, and as soon as it was soft enough I tied one on and offered it to a trout under my own bank. The cast was a bad one, and the fly went under a full yard outside the trout, but without hesitation he sailed over and gulped it. I wound up with four and a half brace averaging one and a half pounds all on the Iron Blue Nymph, and went off without waiting for the evening rise.

    After that I always made it my business to have some Iron Blue Nymphs so dressed, and they have been worth many a good trout to me. In and after May, when the iron blue comes on, it will very often be found that the floating subimago is neglected, but that there are splashy, agitated, rather violent rises occurring at some not at all obvious attractions. If the angler is wise, he will have had his Iron Blue Nymph in soak and will lose no time in attaching it, and he need not be surprised if his fish comes some way off his beat to collect it.
(*The Way of a Trout with a Fly*)

Pheasant Tail

The Pheasant Tail is one of the great all-round flies mainly suggesting a spinner, and Skues had his own version. His friend, Dr. Barton, with whom he fished for many years, successfully used a Pheasant Tail which employed a foxy red hackle and whisks. It was the subject of some ribaldry by Skues who said it was only successful when stock fed fish were introduced because it simulated a scrap of liver on which trout were fed in the stews in those days. He nicknamed it the Hepatist!

I HAVE MORE than once seen propounded an enquiry to which I have seen no reply – what fly the Pheasant Tail is supposed to represent. Well, I can answer that question on my experience. In March, 1910, a friend was visiting Cornwall, and he hoped to get some fishing, and just by way of getting my hand in I sent him some flies of my own tying, with some priceless hackles. Among these flies were three or four Pheasant Tails tied on No.15 hooks. 'Ridiculously small for the water,' my friend declared; the theory being the smaller the fish the bigger the fly. The Cornish streams were in flood, and he got no chance of using my flies. But he announced his intention of using the Pheasant Tails in the Itchen a little later, when the sherry spinner of the blue-winged olive was on. So to prevent him from making an example of himself, I tied him one or two more on something nearer life-size – namely No.14 – and the result pleased me so much that I tied two or three more for my own use. This is the tie:

Silk:	Hot orange
Whisks:	Honey-dun cock's shoulder hackle, three strands
Rib:	Fine bright gold wire, several turns, to secure the herls from being broken by the teeth of the trout
Body:	Three or four strands of herl from the ruddy part of the centre feather of a cock pheasant's tail
Wings/: Hackle	A sharp sparkling golden-dun cock's hackle of high quality

In *Silk, Fur and Feather* Skues offers for the hackle 'sharp bright blue or honey or rusty dun cock'.

THE SIZE OF hook may, of course, be varied to suit the spinner which is on at the time. On May 11, I found my friend on the water, not exactly displeased with himself over a basket of two and a half brace, all of them victims of the Pheasant Tail. That night I dressed some more of them for my friend and for a guest I had brought down with me, and one for myself. I spent the following morning without using the pattern for some time. Then it occurred to me to try it, and I got a trout of two pounds two ounces. A bit later my guest got a perfect picture of a trout of two pounds with his example, and before I left at 4.30 I got another trout of one pound nine ounces with the same pattern, while my friend added to it his brace of trout.

I left him attempting to negotiate a trout of two and a half pounds or so. It was two pounds nine ounces, as a matter of fact, for I got him next weekend. There was an admirable procession of red spinners coming down the water, and, though there were few fish moving, this was one of them. He was taking with that head and back fin and tail sort of rise which, to the initiated, indicates spinner taking; and in an interval between the puffs of downstream north-wester my Pheasant Tail reached him aright, and next moment was pulled home.

Several other trout were hooked and landed, and hooked and lost, to that pattern during that weekend with red spinner on the water, and I came to the conclusion that I had long neglected a very useful pattern, in particular, in the long hot evenings of July, August and September when the blue-winged olive is on, and the deep ruddy brown sherry spinner is plentiful.

It is, however, not of an evening only that the spinner is a taking fly. It is often a tender memory to the morning trout, and a fish found feeding before the general rise begins is usually taking spinners, and is very accessible to the temptation of a good imitation. (*The Way of a Trout with a Fly*)

Little Red Sedge

The Small or Little Red Sedge was one of Skues's favourite patterns and, although he laid no claim to be its originator, it is closely associated with his name. It is a fly which will work on chalk stream and freestone river alike, and will often arouse interest when no other dry fly will persuade fish to rise.

IT IS A good many years since I first dressed the pattern of trout fly which I know by this name, and I should be sorry to say how many trout have succumbed to it in the interval. Although in dressing it I was not consciously copying any other man's pattern, I cannot pretend to any originality in its composition; but, such as it is, I have found it without exception the most killing fly I have used on chalk streams at all times when the upwinged dun was not hatching and in all sorts of places.

It is a pattern which I have found successful from May to the end of the season under a variety of conditions, but only when the up-winged dun was not present in quantity.

For instance, it is a nailer for the trout of cross-ditches and drains, however narrow. It is also very attractive to the banker that remains in position after the morning rise is over. And often one may go on securing trout with it all the afternoon and up to the edge of the evening rise, especially in places where the sedges weep over the water.

But there is one set of conditions in which I have found this pattern specially deadly. Sometimes in places where the weeds grow near the surface one may see a movement where the nose of the trout does not seem to break the water, but the back fin and the tail successively show. Just precisely what the fish is doing must be a matter of surmise. I am inclined to think he has dislodged some rather inert nymph from the weed and takes him just below the surface. If you get your Red Sedge to a trout feeding thus, and do not scare him, the odds are long that you get him, and that he will be a good one.

Skues's dressing of the fly is as follows:

Hook:	No.14 down-eyed, square bend
Silk:	Hot orange waxed with brown wax
Rib:	Fine gold wire, binding down body hackle
Body hackle:	Long deep red cock, with short fibres tied in at shoulder, and carried down to tail
Wings:	Landrail wing, bunched and rolled, and tied in sloping well back over the tail
Front hackle:	Like body hackle, but larger and long enough to tie five or six turns in front of the wing

In a letter to Peter Williams, Skues gave him a dressing which involved split wings, which he said was easier to tie but not as hard-wearing as his own dressing. This method was shown to Skues by Chaytor in 1938 when they were fishing together on the Nadder.

Chaytor was one of the sons of he of the *Letters to a Salmon Fisher's Sons*. Obviously his father's epistles had extended beyond salmon to trout fly dressing! The winging technique was as follows.

TAKE A GOOD clean landrail's primary feather, straighten the fibres so that they stand at right angles to the stem of the feather. Tear off half the effective portion of the feather. Cut away the roots. Divide the half into two and lay one neatly on top of the other. Take the doubled feathers in pliers and fold once so that the non-shiny side is outwards. Lay the quadrupled feather on edge on the wing bed so that the centre of the fold is downwards. This gives the split wings. Whip wings left to right to the front hackles. Draw the front hackle to the side and continue whipping over the roots of the wing till close to the eye of the hook. Cut away roots of the wing close to the eye. (Letter to Peter Williams, 11th April, 1944)

Tup's Indispensable

The dressing of this imitation of a pale watery was a closely guarded secret for many years between R.S. Austin, a professional fly dresser from Tiverton, Skues and C.A. Hassam, a highly skilled amateur renowned for his tiny split-winged floaters. This gave rise to many atrocious commercial dressings, and Skues finally revealed the secret after the death of Austin's daughter who had continued to dress the fly. Could the use of the tup's private parts be the earliest example of the so-called deadly effect of pheromones?

I BELIEVE THAT the late C.A. Hassam and I were the only two persons outside his own family to whom the last Mr. R.S. Austin confided the particulars of the composition of the dubbing which was the distinguishing and essential feature of that fly, and Hassam kept the secret religiously down to the day of his death, and I have kept it no less scrupulously down to the present day. I have always had it in my mind that the prescription was so valuable to anglers at large that it ought not to be lost and it was my intention, if it were not disclosed in my lifetime, to leave a record of it to be made public when the time for its disclosure came.

That time has now arrived, and I have been generously released from the moral obligation which so long bound me to keep it a secret, while fuming at the many absurd abortions which tackle dealers were selling as the real thing.

I believe I was the first angler to use the magic dubbing. I was, at the time, in constant correspondence with Mr. R.S. Austin. The date I do not exactly recall, but, from a note in Mr. Austin's handwriting describing its first use, I judge the date to have been June 1900. He sent me a sample on a broken Limerick eyed hook, telling me that with it (the actual fly) he had killed at the mouth of the Loman, where it debouches into the Exe at Tiverton, in two or three successive evenings, a number of big trout which the natives there considered uncatchable, one of them exceeding 5lb; another 3lb and half an ounce; another 2 and a half pound; and another about 2lb. Being naturally very much interested I asked Mr. Austin (in returning him the pattern) what was the nature of the dubbing, and he very generously not only gave me the prescription, but also sent me enough of the made-up material to dress a number of examples of the fly.

I told Mr. Austin that I thought the fly deserved a title, and in his reply he asked what I suggested. I replied that there was 'So and So's Infallible', 'So and So's Irresistible', and so on – 'Why not "Tup's Indispensable".' He said he did not care to name it, and for the moment the matter dropped. But that August or September I gave the pattern a trial on the Wandle (which then held trout) and from one stand I rose no fewer than 18 trout to that fly, though, fishing under a tree which prevented me from striking properly, I failed to hook many of them. But the result was enough to intrigue me, and it led me to give the pattern another trial on the Itchen at the end of the following April. I only fished about 100 yards of water all day and I killed seven brace on that difficult river, all with Tup's Indispensable, the only fly I used. The keeper Priddis ('Dabchick') reported the basket in the next week's *Field*, identifying the fly as Tup's Indispensable. The Editor was flooded with enquiries for particulars and the name of the maker. I gave him Mr. Austin's name. From that season on Tup's Indispensable had become a standard pattern.

The essential part of this dubbing is the highly translucent wool from the indispensable part of a Tup, thoroughly washed and cleansed of the natural oil of the animal. This wool would itself be, like seal's fur, somewhat intractable and difficult to spin on the tying silk, but an admixture of the pale pinkish and very filmy fur from an English hare's poll had the effect of rendering it easy to work. There was also in the original pattern an admixture of cream coloured seal's fur and combings from a lemon yellow spaniel, and the desired dominating colour was obtained by working in a small admixture of red mohair. For the mohair I generally substituted seal's fur, and I believe Mr. Austin did so himself. When wet the Tup's wool becomes somehow illuminated throughout by the colour of the seal's fur or mohair, and the entire effect of the body is extraordinarily filmy and insect-like.

My variations were made by using differing shades of seal's fur, not only in the reds but orange, yellows, cream and a range of olives, and in all shades I found the pattern useful. The reds and oranges dressed with sharp cock's hackles made a range of spinners, and a small light golden spinner may be similarly hackled. The pale yellow and the cream hackled with pale blue cock's hackles reproduce pale watery duns, while the same colour and the olive hackled with a short soft woolly hen's hackle produce a series of nymphs, which are quite attractive. Different shades were also produced by varying the quantity of seal's fur. (*Flyfishers' Journal,* 1934)

POOR MR. AUSTIN got tired of dressing the hundreds of dozens ordered of him. He told me that a Dorsetshire customer complained to him that the Frome 'stank' of T.I. from Maiden Newton to the sea. (*Itchen Memories*)

Hook: Nos14–16
Tail: Brassy or honey dun cock hackle fibres
Body: Yellow silk or floss at the tail end, tup's wool for the remainder (Variable mixtures of white, cream, yellow and crimson seal's fur are now often used)
Hackle: Brassy or honey dun cock's hackle

Shrimps

Very little escaped Skues's observant eye, and he was well aware that trout took underwater creatures other than ephemeroptera. It is, however, surprising to find him producing probably one of the earliest shrimp patterns and taking fish with it. One shudders to think what the fellow members of his little syndicate on the Itchen – who already disapproved of his nymph fishing activities – would have thought if they had found him fishing a shrimp pattern, well sunk, presumably.

IN THE YEAR 1930 the embankment which kept within it a
certain length of the Itchen at a level above that of the adjoining meadows gave way in two places on the eastern side with
the result that the meadows on that side were flooded, and
other parts of the same bank were gravely weakened. During
the Winter following the bank on that side was made up with
chalk, fortified at the places where the water had actually
broken through by bags of cement partly under and partly
above water which showed themselves rather hideously where
viewed from the western bank.

The result of the making up has been that there is little vegetation of the eastern bank under which the trout could lie and it
would not be astonishing to find that many of the larger trout
had dropped down stream to less uncomfortable quarters.
There has, however, been one very curious exception. Those
places where the cement bags expose themselves under water
have become favourite lies of the trout, two or three in a few
yards of bank, and these trout, instead of rising to the surface
fly or the hatching nymph, seem to be engaged persistently at
all times of day in the amusement of tailing.

Whether the crannies between the cement bags are the resort
of freshwater shrimp or some other, and what insect food it has,
so far, proved impossible to judge, but the activities of the fish
clearly indicate food of some kind. One of these fish, caught
with a nymph, might have yielded up its secret to the marrow
scoop, but, as ill luck would have it, that priceless weapon had
gone astray on that occasion.

A week has intervened since the above was written and I have
dressed a Palmer in shrimp colours and have cut off the hackle
fibres from the back of the hook.

Hook: No.16 Limerick, down-eyed
Hackle: Pale red dyed olive
Body: Seal's fur mixed pale orange and olive, tied to below
        the bend of the hook to suggest the curve of the
        shrimp's back
Rib: Fine gold wire

I tried this at two of the points where the cement bags showed
and collected a good fish from each. Stomach packed with
shrimp in each case. But what makes the shrimps haunt this
spot?

Yesterday's fly

In Skues's day, it may well be that the mainly wild trout were fastidious in their choice of diet, but even today with so many stew-bred fish and a sad decline in the quantity and variety of insect life, there are many occasions where the choice of fly is still important. Certainly, I have seen trout on the River Wharfe becoming fixated on minute black gnats and refusing to look at any other fly offered. So all fly fishermen will readily empathise with Skues's deliberations on the vagaries of fly selection and the choice of diet by finicky trout.

INCALCULABLE PERSON, IS good Master Trout. But at any rate we have him today. For, look you, today is the very spit and image of yesterday, with the same flies on the water and in the air, and yesterday, by luck or divination – call it divination – we did happen to hit upon the right fly, the Black Gnat, after two or three futile changes which wasted half the rise. Yet when we had hit upon it, it brought up fish after fish until the mill stopped working and the trout retired for a period of meditation and digestion. So on with the Black Gnat and have at 'em. What's this? Not taking any? Well, anyhow, four successive trout to whom we have offered it have ignored it, until one made a mistake and then incontinently ceased to feed. Divination would appear to be called for again. There was willow fly in the air just now. There goes another. Let it be Willow Fly. Same result. Well, there is a trickle of pale watery dun. Let us try Quill Marryat and Little Marryat. Same result. Was it divination yesterday? Perhaps it would be safer to call it luck. Well, then, in a spirit of resignation or exasperation or enquiry or frank guesswork, let us try the little Rusty Spinner. By George! That's done the trick. But why? Not a spinner to be seen on the surface!

On the following day we feel that the spinner would be a good fly to begin on, for – well, for the same reasons that the Black Gnat was going to be the fly for yesterday – but wasn't. Still, one's confidence is a little shaken. Yes, I thought so. That trout won't have the spinner at any price, nor the Black Gnat, nor the Willow Fly, nor the Pale Watery, nor the etc., etc., and at last we divine – no, guess is a safer word – that he is taking something just below the surface, and a pale sunk Greenwell, or an Iron Blue nymph, or a Tup's Indispensable semi-submerged may do the trick. Perhaps we fluke a sound guess, perhaps we don't. If we do not it is a blank, or near it. But if we do soon it is going to be a big day. Is it? In half an hour or ten minutes or thereabouts a change may have – did I say may have? – almost certainly will have – set in, and the whole business of divination or guessing has to be begun over again. Incalculable person, as I said, is our Good Master Trout. As for yesterday's fly – well, you know where you habitually assign yesterday's fly. (*Flyfishers' Journal*, Winter 1920)

CHAPTER 7

Skues and the Nymph

The modern angler, who habitually uses the nymph on either river or stillwater when no dun or spinner is on the water, may find it almost incomprehensible that in the early years of this century the imitation of the nymphal stage of the ephemeroptera had not been conceived. The dry fly revolution of Halford, Marryat and Hall utterly dominated fly fishing, not only in Hampshire but literally all over the world. It is a measure of the iron grip that Halford's disciples had over chalk stream fishing that when Skues tentatively put forward another method, he cautiously entitled his book in 1910 <u>Minor</u> *Tactics of the Chalk Stream.*

The first incident which made any impact on Skues's thinking came as early as 1888.

The germ of an idea

The Highland Burn, referred to here by Skues, still exists on the Abbots Barton water which Roy Darlington has miraculously resuscitated from a long period of decline and neglect. The picture on the front of the dust jacket shows the Highland Burn where Skues first encountered nymphs.

IN 1938, IN the course of turning over what I had kept of over fifty years of angling correspondence, I came across some letters

77

which brought back to my mind that in the eighties of last century I was already intrigued by the idea of representing the nymph artificially. In the spring of 1888 I had a Saturday and Monday on the Itchen, and on the Saturday, fishing up a straight stretch known as the Highland Burn, which left the west branch of the Itchen through a large sluice and ran straight across the meadows almost to the east main branch near the railway arch before turning south, I put my Pink Wickham on to the rush of water from the sluice and, rising a trout, struck too hard and left in him my fly and two strands of the gossamer's gut, then unwisely used. On the Monday, casting the same pattern to the same spot, I hooked and landed a very pretty trout a trifle over 1lb in weight (takable in those days) from which I recovered the Pink Wickham and the two strands of gut I had lost on the Saturday, but in extracting the recovered fly I found that the mouth of the fish was dotted with a number of tiny pea-green creatures, which I later learnt were nymphs. (*Itchen Memories*)

Of the beginning of things

This was Skues's first experience of the killing properties of the wet fly on the Itchen and, though it made no impact on him at the time, by 1899 he had written an article for *The Field* putting forward the idea that anglers should fish wet flies upstream when trout were not feeding on the surface.

I LOOK BACK upon many years when it was my sole ambition to follow in the steps of the masters of chalk stream angling, and to do what was laid down for me – that, and no other; and I look back with some shame at the slowness to take a hint from experience which has marked my angling career.

It was in the year 1892, after some patient years of dry-fly practice, that I had my first experience of the efficacy of the wet fly on the Itchen. It was a September day, at once blazing and muggy. Black gnats were thick upon the water, and from 9.30 a.m. or so the trout were smutting freely. In those days, with *Dry-Fly Fishing in Theory and Practice* at my fingers' ends, I began with the prescription, Pink Wickham on 16 hook, followed it with Silver Sedge on 16 hook, Red Quill on 16 hook, Orange Bumble and Furnace. I also tried two or three varieties of smut, and I rang the changes more than once.

My gut was gossamer, and, honestly, I don't think I made more mistakes than usual; but three o'clock arrived, and my creel was still 'clean', when I came to a bend from which ran, through a hatch, a small current of water which fed a carrier. Against the grating which protected the hatch hole was generally a large pile of weed, and today was no exception. Against it collected a film of scum, alive with black gnats, and among them I saw a single dark olive dun lying spent. I had seen no others of his kind, but I knotted on a Dark Olive Quill and laid siege to a trout which was smutting steadily in the next little bay. The fly was a shop-tied one, beautiful to look at when new, but as a floater it was no success. The hackle was a hen's, and the dye only accentuated its natural inclination to sop up water. The oil tip had not yet arrived, and so it came about that, after the wetting it got in the first recovery, it no sooner lit on the water on the second cast than it went under. A moment later I became aware of a sort of crinkling little swirl in the water, ascending from the place where I conceived my fly might be. I was somewhat too quick in putting matters to the proof, and when my line came back to me there was no fly. I mounted another, and assailed the next fish and to my delight exactly the same thing occurred, except that this time I did not strike too hard.

The trout's belly contained a solid ball of black gnats, and not a dun of any sort. The same was the case with all the four brace more which I secured in the next hour or so by precisely the same methods. Yet each took the Dark Olive at once when offered under water, while all day the trout had been steadily refusing the recognized floating flies recommended by the highest authority. It was a lesson which ought to have set me thinking and experimenting, but it didn't. I put by the experience for use on the next September smutting day, and I have never had quite such another. (*Minor Tactics of the Chalk Stream*)

Ethics of the wet fly

By the time Skues had written *Minor Tactics* in 1910, he had already been experimenting with nymph patterns for some years. Nevertheless, *Minor Tactics* was primarily concerned with the use of the wet fly on chalk streams which was considered unacceptable by the majority of fly fishermen at this time for whom the dry fly was de rigueur. It left Skues open to the suggestion by the more Luddite section of dry fly men that he was simply the advocate of wet fly fishing. Skues, therefore, felt called upon to put the case for the upstream wet fly to them.

IN DEALING WITH this subject, I am conscious that I start with a weight of opinion against me among the fishermen of chalk streams. I have known some of them say in a shocked tone, "But that is wet fly!" as if it were some high crime and misdemeanour to use a wet fly upon a chalk stream. To make my peace with such I want to argue this question out, and test and see what it is about the wet fly which has brought such discredit upon it among the best sportsmen in the world.

It is axiomatic with many that it is unsuccessful upon chalk streams. That is not my opinion, but in itself it is not an objection. If it were unfairly successful it would be another story. The object of fly-fishing, whether wet or dry, is the catching of trout, not anyhow, but by means refined, clean, delicate, artistic, and sportsmanlike in the sense that they are fair to the quarry and fair to the brother angler. There can be no doubt that the dry fly honestly fulfils all these conditions. Let us see where the wet fly fails.

It is said the wet-fly man's game is a duffer's game, which needs neither knowledge nor any skill beyond enough to cast a long line downstream or across and down; that it leads to a raking of the water, often with two or three flies; that it leads to the pricking and scaring of many fish, to the catching of many undersized trout, and to the undue disturbance of long stretches of water, to the detriment of the nerves of the fish and the sport of other anglers. All this I am quite willing to accept and to eliminate from the legitimate all wet fly fishing which could come under this description.

What is left to the wet-fly angler? I venture to say a mighty pretty, delicate and delightful art which resembles dry-fly fishing in that the fly is cast upstream or across, to individual fish, or to places where it is reasonable to expect that a fish of suitable proportions may be found, and differs from dry-fly fishing only in the amount of material used in the dressing of the fly, in the force with which that fly is cast, and in the extreme subtlety of the indications frequently attending the taking of the fly by the fish, compared to which there is a painful obviousness in the taking of the dry fly. Add to this that it provides means for the circumventing of bulgers and feeders on larvae, that it furnishes sport on those numerous occasions when trout are in position and probably feeding under water without ever breaking the surface, and generally widens the opportunities of sport for the man who cannot be always on the spot to seize the best opportunities afforded by a rise of trout to the floating fly.

Is this method open to any of the objections attending the downstream raking we concur in condemning? Is it a duffer's game? Is it easier than dry-fly fishing? Try and see. Does it lead to the pricking and scaring of many fish which follow a dragging fly? No. Does it unduly disturb long stretches of water to the detriment of the brother angler? Why, it is as easy to spend an afternoon on a hundred yards as it is on the purest cult of the dry fly.

If the trout are feeding, I for one fail to see why they may legitimately be fished for if they are taking a small proportion of their food on the surface, but not if they are taking all, or practically all, of it underneath. There is a sentence from Francis Francis quoted with approval by F.M. Halford, which runs as follows:

'The judicious and perfect application of dry, wet and midwater fly fishing stamps the finished fly fisher with the hallmark of efficiency.'

(*Minor Tactics of the Chalk Stream*)

Of the imitation of nymphs, caddis, alder larvae and shrimps

There were only five pages out of 133 in *Minor Tactics* which were devoted to the dressing and fishing of nymphs. Not only nymphs but caddis, alder larvae and shrimps! These are, undoubtedly, the most sensational pages in the book, and must have sent shock waves out to the ranks of Halford's disciples. It may also have made it more difficult for him to maintain that nymph fishing was an honourable pursuit. Regarding the nymphs, he indicates that his research is only just beginning, but for the other insects he recants from such 'blasphemies' for the benefit of both his own conscience and that of the dry fly purists.

FOR SOME TIME after my introduction to Tup's Indispensable I used it only as a dry fly, but one July I put it over a fish without avail, and cast it a second time without drying it. It was dressed with a soft hackle, and at once went under, and the trout turned at it and missed. Again I cast, and again the trout missed, to fasten soundly at the next offer. It was a discovery for me, and I tried the pattern wet over a number of fish on the same shallow with most satisfactory results. I thus satisfied myself that Tup's Indispensable could be used as a wet fly; and, indeed, when soaked its colours merge and blend so beautifully that it is hardly singular; and it was a remarkable imitation of a nymph I got from a trout's mouth.

The next step was to try it on bulging fish, and to my great delight I found it even more attractive than Greenwell's Glory. It was the foundation of a small range of nymph patterns, but for underwater feeders, whether bulging or otherwise, I seldom need anything but Tup's Indispensable, dressed with a very short, soft henny hackle in place of the bright honey or rusty dun used for the floating pattern.

The next I tried was a Blue-Winged Olive. There was a hatch of this pernicious insect one afternoon. The floating pattern is always a failure with me, and in anticipation I had tied some nymphs of appropriate colour of body, and hackled with a single turn of the tiniest blue hackle of the merlin. It enabled me to get two or three excellent trout which were taking blue-winged olive nymphs greedily under the opposite bank, and which, or rather the first of which, like their predecessors, had refused to respond to a floating imitation. The body was a mixture of medium olive seal's fur and bear's hair close to the skin, tied with primrose silk, the whisk being short and soft, from the spade-shaped feather found on the shoulder of a blue dun cock.

Another pattern, successful in the last two months of the season, is dressed with a very short palish-blue dun or honey dun hen's hackle, a body of hare's poll tied on pale primrose silk, with or without a small gold tag and palest ginger whisks. But it is evident that on this subject I am only at the beginning of the inquiry. Of course there is nothing very new in the idea of imitating nymphs. The half stone is just a nymph generally ruined by over-hackling.

In July 1908, I caught an Itchen fish one afternoon, and on examining his mouth I found a dark olive nymph. My fly dress-ing materials were with me, and I found I had a seal's fur which, with a small admixture of bear's hair, dark brown and woolly, from close to the skin, enabled me to reproduce exactly the colours of the natural insect. I dressed the imitation with short, soft, dark blue whisks, body of the mixed dubbing tied with well-waxed bright yellow silk, and bunched at the shoulder to suggest wing cases, the lower part of the body being ribbed with fine gold wire. Two turns of a very short, dark rusty dun hackle completed the imitation, much to my satisfaction.

Apparently, it was no less agreeable to the trout, for, beginning to fish next morning at ten o'clock, I found six fish rising in a shallow. I began with a small Red Sedge, as no dun was yet on the water, and missed several of them. Then, putting up Pope's Green Nondescript, I again missed three fish in succession. I then bethought myself of my nymph, and, knotting it on, in a few minutes I had five of the six fish, and had lost the other. I then found a trout feeding in a run, evidently under water. I made a miscast at him, and he came a yard across to take the nymph but did not take a good hold, for I lost him, only to secure a better fish a few moments later. It then came on to blow and pelt with rain as to render it no sort of pleasure to continue fishing, and I knocked off at eleven o'clock with three brace as the result of an hour's fishing.

But it is not only duns whose nymphal stages may be imitated. I borrowed of Mr. Martin E. Mosely of the Flyfishers' Club a tube containing some nearly full-grown larvae of the alder, and although he assured me that they were always in the mud, and never seen by the trout, I made a sort of imitation of them which rather pleased me, and I tried it in Germany in mid-May. Whether the trout saw or did not see the natural insect in that stage I don't pretend to know, but they took the imitation with such avidity that I speedily wore out my three specimens. They were only made as an experiment, and I tried no more, as I felt qualms in my mind as to whether it was quite the game to imitate this insect in this stage, any more than it would be to fish an imitation of a caddis. I am therefore not giving my recipe. Nor do I give that for making a caddis or gentle which I once tried, with mad success for a few minutes, and gave up, conscience-stricken.

I was at one time greatly interested in an attempt to imitate the freshwater shrimp, and I tied a variety of patterns, including several with backs of quill of some small bird dyed greenish-olive, and ribbed firmly while wet and impressionable with silk or gold wire; but somehow I never used or attempted to use any one of them. I, however, gave one to an acquaintance, and he tied it on, and, standing on a footbridge, cast it downstream over some trout which were reputed to be shy. At the first cast a big fish rushed at the shrimp, slashed it, and went off leaving the one-time owner lamenting. (*Minor Tactics of the Chalk Stream*)

Reaction to Minor Tactics of the Chalk Stream

Skues summarised the reaction to his book as follows.

BY THE END of 1909 H.T. Sheringham induced me to throw together a series of articles which I had contributed to *The Field* and *The Fishing Gazette* and to add some matter to link them up. The collection was illustrated by a number of my wet fly patterns, including Tup's Indispensable and one Olive Nymph. It was called *Minor Tactics of the Chalk Stream*, and, advocating as it did the use of wet flies when trout were not taking floaters, it produced a certain sensation in the angling world. But though I believe I was regarded by some of the ultra dry fly group as an exceedingly wicked man – a veritable lost soul – the storm of controversy which I had anticipated never materialised and the argument implicit in my volume evoked no solitary attempt to answer it. (*Trivialities of a Long Life*)

Basic nymph

By 1921, Skues had developed his research into nymph patterns much further, and in *The Way of a Trout with a Fly* he explains that his hackled nymph is designed to simulate a hatching nymph. He ultimately took up his own suggestion that someone should make exact reproductions of nymphs and larvae as Halford had done in the imitation of duns. He seemed unaware that his statement in the final paragraph that 'representation or suggestion rather than imitation is what the dressing of nymphs should aim at' contradicted his earlier pronouncement.

I HAVE USED imitations of nymphs of chalk streams for some fifteen seasons with a measure of success when the trout were not surface feeding, and I use them upstream to feeding fish, and it is my observation that a mere bare nymph without hackle is not so successful as one which is lightly hackled with a short hackle. It is my belief that the artificial nymph lightly hackled with a soft hackle (whether small bird's or hen's) is taken for the natural nymph in the act of hatching, and that in the case of the artificial nymph lightly dressed with a bright cock's hackle of a blue shade, the hackle, being almost water-colour, leaves the body of the artificial exposed, tends to arrest speed of sinking, and probably lends the nymph a certain degree of action in the water which suggests life.

Then in practically all my nymph patterns that are not hackled with a soft feather I use a good deal of seal's fur in the dubbing, which gives an effect of brilliance and translucency, to which again a fine gold wire ribbing in some cases lends aid.

All this is very crude, no doubt, and I can cordially concur in the often expressed wish that some wet-fly enthusiast would set to work and make exact reproductions of nymphs and larvae in the same way as Mr. F.M. Halford treated the floating fly. And these should be submitted to searching tests, not only by one angler, but by a large number of skilled men.

In shape of body the nymph may be easily imitated. Colour is difficult to set down with precision in writing so that the fly dresser can reproduce it with certainty, and the best line of attack seems to me to be suggested by one of the oldest nymph patterns, the Half-stone. Here one has a bright, almost water-coloured, outer hackle, almost invisible to a fish looking up, and a nymph-shaped body well displayed with the thorax of mole's fur spun on yellow silk, and the yellow floss lower half of the body which goes green in the water.

For colour, the angler who desires exact representation in that respect would have to go to the living nymph. A dip of a muslin net into a clump of river weed would produce a large variety of nymphs in all colours, from pale yellow to darkest olive, and even to carrot colour.

It was on a variation of the Half-stone dressed with a lower half of wool instead of floss that the famous Carrot fly was modelled. In a series of modifications it has killed for a brother angler many a good fish, fished as a nymph on crack waters on the Itchen, the Test and elsewhere. And dressed large it has served as a May-fly nymph on some bulging days on the Kennet, and has beaten the winged fly and the Straddlebug hollow.

Representation or suggestion rather than imitation is what the dresser of nymphs should aim at. That is one reason why dubbings outclass quills for bodies of nymphs. (*The Way of a Trout with a Fly*)

Evolution

In his last book, *Nymph Fishing for Chalk Stream Trout*, written in 1939, Skues traces the development of his ideas on fishing the artificial nymph, and how the discovery of the use of the marrow scoop for extracting the contents of a trout's stomach greatly aided his research.

IN THE LATER nineties the difficulty of inducing bulging trout to take the floating fly, combined with the obvious fact that they were feeding on nymphs, led me to experiment on bulgers with patterns of wet flies which were successful on rough North Country streams where trout were seldom seen to break the surface, and to cast these flies upstream to the bulging fish.

From this beginning there naturally came to my mind the question, why, if the wet fly on chalk streams had brought great baskets in the past, it should have lost its efficacy with the advent of the dry fly. I had no desire to search the water by random casting. Trout rose too freely in the chalk streams which I fished to render such searching necessary; and I soon found that there were occasions when the winged wet fly, cast upstream to feeding fish, was quite efficacious, though it was a long time before I realised that these occasions occurred nearly always when the trout were nymphing and not taking the floating fly.

I had supposed for a long time that the wet fly was taken on these occasions for a nymph in the very act of hatching. But after a while the presence in the mouths of some of my captures of nymphs with no show of wing led me to experiment with short hackled patterns dressed to imitate nymphs, and by 1910 when my first volume, *Minor Tactics of the Chalk Stream*, was published, though it dealt in the main with the use of the upstream wet fly cast to individual fish, I had dressed and tried with some success a small series of nymphal patterns, fishing them in calm and bright weather like floating flies, but under water. In the succeeding eleven years I had made other attempts to represent nymphs, but I was hampered by the need to carry out hateful and messy autopsies to ascertain on what my trout were feeding, until towards the end of that period I was struck with the idea of using a marrow scoop to extract the contents

of the trout's stomach in a single operation. The method
proved completely successful, and time after time I was amazed
to see what a huge proportion of these contents were nymphs,
and how few were the winged flies.

From this I moved on to the device of washing out these
contents into a deep heavy white china plate (a baby plate proved
ideal for the purpose); and, having it with the insects floating
therein by my side on my fly dressing table, I was able to dress
(and compare in the water by the side of the natural insects)
representations of the nymphs I had extracted, resembling them
in size, contour, proportions and colour. I did not need to use
these patterns when the trout were feeding on the surface, for
then the dry fly was at once easier and more effective, but on
those many occasions when the trout have been devoting their
attention to the nymph and neglecting the floating fly I have
found the appropriate pattern of nymph great medicine, however
bright the weather and however smooth the water.

I have not hesitated, therefore, to do my best to let others
share the benefit of my labours, being convinced that without
any challenge to the merits of dry fly fishing in its proper place
I have evolved methods which are often effective where it fails.
(*Nymph Fishing for Chalk Stream Trout*)

What is nymph fishing?

Skues now moves on to a fully fledged explanation of what he means
by nymph fishing. He contends that nymph fishing is complementary
to dry fly fishing, and in no way inferior to it.

IN THIS WORK then nymph fishing must, please, be understood
to mean the art of taking trout or grayling at or under the
surface with an artificial pattern credibly representing in colour,
dimensions and outline a natural nymph of a type being
accepted by trout and grayling on the stream.

Nymph fishing is not a sport by itself. It is auxiliary to the
floating fly. It is a method, just as was and is the use of the wet
fly on chalk streams, of taking trout and grayling which are not
rising to the floating natural insect but are feeding. It is a
method of presenting to the fish in these conditions representations of the food on which they are actually feeding far more
precise than the wet fly (which at best may be taken for a hatching nymph) and not less, but probably more, exact than floating

artificial flies are of the floating natural duns or spinners. And just as the time to present the floating fly to the fish is when they are taking natural flies on the surface – so are the times to offer the fish an artificial nymph the hours, often prolonged, in which they are feeding wholly or mainly on the natural nymph. That is my experience, resulting from years of practice of both methods.

Nymph fishing is a comparatively new art, or perhaps it would be fairer to say a new phase of an old and largely forgotten art that has developed on chalk streams during the present century. The old art was the art of the wet fly as practised on chalk streams for centuries before the advent of the dry fly led, through the work of F.M. Halford, George Selwyn Marryat and others, to the supersession on chalk streams of the older method by the new, and for a while to the complete and exclusive dominance of the latter. The dry fly became a sort of religion and any attempt to revert to the older practice was regarded as a sort of sin against the Holy Ghost for which there was no remission.

A few men, however, natural born heretics no doubt, being of the detached order of intellect, came in time to wonder why the old art which had for centuries served our forefathers so well, should have ceased to be effective and to have any merits, and they began to experiment by adapting to wet fly fishing the new dry fly method of casting the fly to individual rising fish, and they attained a degree of success which became embarrassing to the stern upholders of the strict faith of the dry fly. The practice led these heretics to enquire how it came about that trout were willing to accept winged flies under water; and, aided by autopsies as advocated by Halford, they became aware of a fact of which Halford was well aware, but the moral of which he had failed to appreciate, that rising trout fed more on nymphs than on their floating hatched-out subimagines. To this day, it is probable that comparatively few of the enormous number of fishers with the fly are aware of this fact or of its bearing on the art of fly fishing, and fewer still have any idea of what a natural nymph is like. But these wicked heretics decided that if the trout were willing, as for centuries they had proved themselves, to take winged artificial flies under water, it was not improbable that they would be still more willing in similar conditions to take underwater well conceived patterns representing as faithfully as possible the larval forms on which they

were for the time being feeding, and that these patterns, like
the wet flies with which these sinners had been previously
experimenting, could be presented to the individual trout with
all the pomp and circumstance of accuracy and avoidance of
undersized fish which had been hitherto the exclusive privilege
of the floating fly.

Much to the chagrin of the arch-purists, these heretics
proved to be right, and by degrees a small school of fishers of
chalk streams with the artificial nymph began to invade the
most sacred stretches of the Hampshire rivers and their practice
even extended to other rivers, such as the Usk, which had not
been sacred to the dry fly. But I must emphasise the fact that,
just as in *Minor Tactics of the Chalk Stream*, I did not advocate,
and indeed definitely disapproved of, what Halford termed fishing the water, but did advocate fishing the wet fly to the individual subaqueously feeding fish, in my advocacy of the use of
the nymph on appropriate occasions, I apply precisely the same
principles in practice. It is therefore out of place to cite against
me the practices of the uninitiated anglers who fish the water
with the nymph, searching it with a dragging nymph and taking
or pricking and scaring unsizable fish. (*Nymph Fishing for Chalk
Stream Trout*)

Needless to say, we do not have to look far for whom we consider to
be the leading 'natural born heretic'.

Dressing the nymph

By 1921, Skues had devised a standard procedure for dressing his
nymphs in a form readily recognisable by any modern-day fly dresser.
The key feature, apart from the sparse hackle, was a pronounced
thorax with feather fibres tied over to suggest wing cases and their
points divided to suggest legs.

VARIOUS PLANS HAVE been devised for the making of imitations
of nymphs. Years before anyone – so far as the books record –
was really aware what a large proportion of the food of trout
was taken in the nymph or larval stages, the Half-stone was a
successful fly. As I have said, I have no doubt it was meant for a
nymph.

The nymphs of Dr. Mottram ('Jim-Jam'), entirely without
dubbing or hackle, I have already referred to. I for some years

earlier had been feeling my way, via Tup's Indispensable, to the achievement of a series of nymphs. These have been hackled – mostly with cock's hackle – tied as short as possible, and the bodies have been dressed with dubbing. The dubbing has always consisted of, or contained, seal's fur, as many of the nymphs are full of lights and glistenings. Partly for the same reason, and partly to prevent the tearing out of the dubbing by the trout's teeth, a fine gold or silver wire ribbing has been generally used.

But the hackle has always been the trouble. It is extremely difficult to get hackles stout enough in the fibre to represent the legs of nymphs, yet short enough for the same purpose, whether one uses cock's or hen's hackles, or the feathers of small birds. Nipped hackles of the latter class will serve, but every self-respecting fly dresser resents nipped or cut hackles, and so I have thought out a method which is, I think, better than using a nipped hackle. Here it is:

Placing your hook – say, a Limerick No.16 in your vice – begin whipping near the eye, and whip nearly halfway down the shank. Tie in here, with point towards head of hook, a bunch of six or eight fibres of feather of suitable colour, regulating the length so that when the fibre is bent over to the eye of the hook and tied down there will be enough of the points left to be pressed out on either side to represent the legs. Then pass the silk under the ends of the fibres of feather on the side of the bend of the hook, and whip on the bare hook to the tail; tie in two short, stout, soft whisks of suitable colour, tie in gold or silver wire, twirl on dubbing thinly, and wind to the place where the fibre is tied in; wind on the wire in regular spacing to the same point, and secure on the head side of the place where the fibre is tied in; thicken the dubbing, and wind over roots of feather fibre to head. Then divide the points equally, and press backward from the eye; bring over the feather fibre to the head, tie it down with two turns, including a half-hitch, cut off the waste ends, and finish with a whip finish on the eye. Thus the legs are forced to stand out at right angles, or rather more backward, from the eye, and below the level of the hook shank, and the effect of wing cases is produced.

For nymphs with freckled legs, brown partridge hackles, brown or grey partridge hackles, dyed, summer duck hackles dyed in various shades of olives, or even undyed, make very effective legs. For self-coloured legs the fibre of the wings of a

variety of birds, such as starling, landrail, fieldfare, etc. are
excellent. It must be remembered that the legs of nymphs are
stouter in appearance than the fibre of the ordinary hackle.
Good effects may be produced with the yellow-pointed fibres of
the golden plover.

In dressing nymphs one should remember that, though they
should not fall on the water hard enough to scare the trout,
their composition should ensure prompt sinking, and if the
trout be handy I am of the opinion that they will not sink very
far. (*The Way of a Trout with a Fly*)

He also included a second method, suggested by a fishing friend,
which Donald Overfield considers superior to Skues's usual procedure. There is no need to guess just how much room to leave at the
head for the whip finish, and by placing the whip finish behind the
thorax it makes sure that the head of the fly is not made too bulky by
too many turns of silk. Skues did point out, however, that its defect
was that it does not lend itself to nymphs tied with a ribbing as it has
to be finished with an invisible whip finish in the middle of the body
just behind the wing cases. The process is as follows.

PLACING YOUR HOOK in the vice, take two turns near the eye, tie
down your bunch of fibres which are to represent legs and wing
cases, with the points towards the tail, with one firm turn, then
bring the silk under the points close up against the last turn and
pull taut. Now press back the points firmly. They can be divided
a little later. Spin your seal's fur dubbing on the silk in just
sufficient quantity to represent the thorax, and wind it on.
Then bring over the waste ends which were pointing over the
head so that they point over the tail, dividing the points, which
are to represent the legs, in equal portions to right and left. Tie
down the fibres with two turns, and break them off, either
singly or in groups. Whip to the tail, tie in the whisks as before,
roll on more dubbing, whip to the wing cases, clear the silk,
and finish close up to the wing cases with a close, hard whip
finish, into which a drop of celluloid varnish has been introduced, by placing it on the loop of the tying silk as it is being
drawn taut. (*The Way of a Trout with a Fly*)

Dressing methods

In *Nymph Fishing for Chalk Stream Trout*, written in 1939, a few months before the outbreak of World War II, Skues somewhat surprisingly altered his dressing method of the nymph. He omitted the wing cases altogether, suggesting them with a patch of darker dubbing, and wound in the hackle as the last part of the operation. He claimed that this produced a far more delicate nymph-like effect.

He prefaced this new method with some excellent advice for anyone aspiring to tie nymphs. He suggested that one should always try to have an actual nymph floating in a baby plate or similar container as a model for the artificial. Translucency was vital to nymph patterns and could best be suggested by fur or wool dubbing. Tying silks should be based on the natural colour of the spinner, and will show through the dubbing. The resulting artificial should be compared to the natural in the water in the plate. Whisks should be kept short as should the hackle which must be sparsely tied. The new tying method was as follows.

FIX A DOWN-EYED hook of appropriate size and length in the vice. Select tying silk of appropriate colour for the body and wax with colourless wax. Take the short end of the waxed silk between left forefinger and thumb and lay it over the hook and against the eye. Whip three turns from right to left over the short end and twitch or cut off the short waste end. Whip on the selected hackle for the legs with the stalk towards the tail and wind silk to middle of the body. Snap or cut off the stalk of the hackle and wind silk to within three or four turns of the bend. Pick two or three fibres of the whisk feather (Gallena is as good as anything, having a valuable degree of stiffness which is not excessive) and pass the roots *under* the hook. The first turn of the silk should bring them neatly on top of the hook. The natural insect has short whisks and the artificial should have short whisks too. Two more turns of silk and a touch of varnish secure the whisks, and the waste ends can be cut or broken off or left to be tied in with the dubbing or floss or quill so as to assist the taper of the body. If gold or silver wire is to be used as ribbing, it should be bound in at this stage, lying along the body and pointing over the whisks. Next, if the body is to be quill or herl or floss silk, it is bound in similarly. The tying silk is then wound to the shoulder and the quill or herl or floss is wound on and secured at the shoulder and followed by the ribbing, and the excess cut away. If the body is to be dubbing, then, instead of previous steps, the dubbing is spun on the tying silk, tapering from shoulder and wound. The ribbing, if any, is then wound on and secured. A short length of darker dubbing to match and suggest the wing cases of the natural nymph is then spun on the tying silk, wound to the root of the hackle, and secured with one half hitch. The hackle is then wound in front of the thorax, not more than two turns, the tying silk is passed twice through it and is secured by two half itches or a whip finish at the eye. A touch of varnish makes all secure and the waste end of the silk is cut away and the nymph is complete.

If care be taken not to overdress the nymph and to secure the right taper of the body and the correct bulk of the pad of dubbing which is to suggest the wing cases, it is wonderful what a lifelike representation of the nymph may be secured. (*Nymph Fishing for Chalk Stream Trout*)

The use of the nymph on chalk streams

Having explained what a nymph is and how to dress nymph patterns, Skues goes on to explain a technique which even today many good anglers have never mastered, namely, how to detect the taking of an artificial nymph. His exposition has not been bettered in the 60 years since he wrote it.

AN ENTHUSIASTIC DRY FLY fisher who was vainly endeavouring to persuade a nymph-feeding Itchen trout to accept his floater said to me the other day, 'I like to see my fly taken on the surface. That is the great attraction of trout fishing for me.' I replied, 'So do I, but I like even more to divine when my nymph has been taken under water.' 'Ah!' he said, 'that is a subtlety which is beyond me.' Yet it need not be, though F.M. Halford himself wrote in one of his volumes that the dry fly man's submerged fly was no doubt often taken by a trout while the angler remained unconscious of the fact. For in nymph fishing one has to watch not for the rise, though that is occasionally quite obvious, but for one or more of a series of other hints to which a lightning response must be made if your trout is to be hooked.

Let me give a few examples of the means of detecting an underwater taking. First there is what we may call:

The Draw
This may occur in several different conditions according to whether one be casting directly upstream, directly across, or up and across, or across and slightly down, in fast water or in slow. In every case, however, the feature of the draw is the sudden accentuation of the pace of sinking of the fine end of the cast with its attached nymph. The nymph of course is built to sink and to draw down with it the finer end of the cast while the stouter portion (oiled or vaselined maybe for rough water) remains afloat.

Just before the conversation above recorded, which took place on the banks of the Itchen in August last, I had observed a tiny dimple upstream and across under the far bank in a little bay made by and just behind a raft of cut weed which had collected in a quiet eddy. The area of the spot into which the nymph had to be delivered was not more than a square yard, and a floating fly, with the push of the stream intervening, must have begun to drag almost as it lit. I made one cast to get distance and to ensure the wetness of the nymph at the next delivery, and, standing just where the slant of the wind would give most aid to a correct delivery, at the next cast, without any intervening false cast, I dropped my nymph about three inches below the weed raft. I had just time to see the cast lie along the surface, when the fine end drew swiftly underwater. Almost quicker than thought I responded and instantly a noble two and a half pounder was thrashing madly in the bay – very soundly hooked.

A few minutes later, and a little upstream where the wind set straight across, the same nymph was offered to a trout which moved two or three times under the far bank where the set of the stream carried most food. It took several shots to get the nymph to the trout as he was cruising a yard or two up and down, but presently the fine end of the floating part of the gut went sharply out of sight and again I pulled home into a fine fighting trout.

The draw is slower if one be casting upstream to a trout moving under one's own bank. But still the hint must be promptly discerned and as promptly acted on.

Shadow and Turn
In the cases cited the trout was invisible to the angler but occasionally when fishing directly upstream on deepish water

one can detect a dim fawn coloured shadow which is a trout
busy under water intercepting nymphs and seldom breaking the
surface. Here one may detect the taking by seeing the draw, or
divine (or if you like, guess) it by seeing the fawn shadow move
towards the point of the cast and turn back into the straight,
and in either case a prompt response may be rewarded. Even if
it be not, the recovery of the line and fly is less apt to alarm the
trout than would a futile strike at a rise to a floater. In this
instance both draw and sight of the trout may be combined.

The Flash or Gleam

There are, however, too frequently, conditions of light which
prevent the angler from detecting the draw. Rough water is not
fatal, for one can oil or vaseline the cast to within three feet or
so of the nymph. But in such condition of light one may sometimes discern even through a white place some subtle shift of
colour which is caused by the flash or gleam of the trout turning to take the nymph. It is so subtle an indication that even an
eye alert to detect it may easily miss it, but it is for all that a
valuable hint to the angler.

The Shift or Turn

At times conditions of light enable one to see the fish fairly
clearly but prevent one from seeing the draw of the gut. This
may be in the open or under the far bank. There is a length of
the Itchen, perhaps eighty or a hundred yards in extent, where
from ten till two, if there be not too strong a ruffle on the
surface, one can detect under the tussocks of the eastern bank
dim forms of hovering trout even if they are not breaking the
surface to feed, and there with a westerly or north westerly trend
in the air or wind, one may drop an accurate nymph close under
the eastern bank about two feet above the trout to give it time
to sink ere it reaches him. It is most fascinating to watch the
trout shifting a few inches out or at times merely turning an inch
or two to intercept the oncoming fly and then returning, and to
find on tightening as he goes back that one has hit the psycho-
logical moment and that a good fish is on the way to be yours.

In the open, the fish being more in the stream, the turn of
the fish is apt to be more violent and rapid unless one's cast has
been, as it too seldom is, of such extreme accuracy as to drift
one's nymph into his mouth without his having to move to
meet it.

Impalpable Hints

The above are the more obvious signs. Yet I have frequently hooked my trout at some hint so impalpable that I could not tell you what bade me tighten. But there was the trout to prove that my, I must call it, intuition, for the want of a better word, was not ill-founded. Indeed I believe that the persistent study and practice of nymph fishing will tend to develop in one a sort of sixth sense which has no name, but which gives at times astonishing results. Wet fly fishermen on rough streams at times develop it to a surprising degree, but they fish with a tight line, always in touch with their fly or team of flies, so that the sense in question with them may be, in part at least, tactile, while the chalk stream angler must not avail himself of this advantage.

I think the reader will agree that the instances which I have given go far to justify the claim that nymph fishing has a charm not inferior to that of dry fly fishing. In addition to which it will often give sport on occasions when the surface fly is persistently neglected. (*Flyfishers' Journal*, Winter 1931–2)

Zeiss glass

Frank Sawyer's brilliant invention of the weighted nymph and the induced take has tended to reduce Skues's contribution almost to a single dimension, namely the taking of trout just below the surface. However, not only was that contribution a first in fly fishing, but it is also interesting to consider whether Skues fished his nymphs deeper in the water at times. One has to remember that he was always looking over his shoulder at Halford and the dry fly lobby, and may have played down any experimentation in that respect which would have been anathema to the dry fly purists. We do know, of course, that he devised a sinking shrimp pattern. There are indications that he did not always fish his nymphs just below the surface. The first involved his use of a tiny pocket spy glass which was given to him by his fishing friend, Dr. E.A. Barton. This was a little monocular Zeiss glass which stood about one inch high and had to be focused by pulling out the lower lens. How Skues would have enjoyed fishing today with polarised glasses! So Skues certainly had the means to detect deeplying trout.

I REMEMBER THE first day I used the glass – a May day with a light easterly breeze and a pleasant amount of sun. I took the left bank of a length that ran for about 300 yards north to south. So I had both sun and what little wind there was at my back. There was no sign of any hatch of fly or rise of fish when I arrived, and I walked slowly up 100 yards of the right bank without seeing any movement. All that 100 yards of the right bank was overhung with big tussocks under which the river ran 6 to 8 feet deep over a margin of yellow marsh. Then it occurred to me that I was neglecting an opportunity to test Dr. Barton's gift, and I returned to my starting point and began to re-examine the run beneath the tussocks with the aid of the little Zeiss glass. I was surprised to see how it seemed to clarify the water under the tussocks, and presently I discovered something lying deep which might be a trout. It was, and after my nymph had been down across his post several times he rose in the water and turned down again. But the hook was in his mouth. I do not recall all the detail of the ensuing two hours during which I worked slowly up to the topmost row of tussocks but it grew increasingly sunny, and, though no rise broke the surface, there were two brace of nice trout in my bag, all on the nymph *fished deep*. (*Itchen Memories*)

And again.

WHERE THE WATER was deep under the banks it was necessary to ensure the ready sinking of the nymph and the cast to attract the attention of the trout to the nymph. Then at times it was possible to glimpse, as the floating part of the line went by, the shifting across the gravel of a shadow, which was in fact a trout, and its turning back to the far bank, at which one instinctively tightened and found a good trout was fast. For such fishing naturally a sunny day with little wind presented advantages, and a bottom of light gravel was easier than a muddy or weedy one to work on. (*Itchen Memories*)

The sunk nymph

Here, Skues places great emphasis on ways of getting the fly to sink, including the interesting one of allowing the fly to brush the water on each cast. Roy Darlington has experimented with gut on the Itchen and found that when it is hydrated it sinks much more easily than nylon.

I HAVE ALREADY pointed out that in presenting an artificial nymph to a trout in position it is essential that not only should it sink on alighting, but that it should draw with it two feet or more of the cast, otherwise a fatal drag may occur. The nymph should be dressed with a short soft hackle and of material to take up water and the line should not be dried by successive casts in the air – but at each cast in letting out line to reach the fish the nymph and gut should come down on the water so that in the final cast which reaches the trout the last two feet or more of the gut shall be wet. (*Nymph Fishing for Chalk Stream Trout*)

Deep sunk nymph

Here is a reference to Skues fishing in the Itchen in 1923. I know from my research into Dr. Barton's diaries that not only did Skues introduce him to the skill of nymph fishing, but that Dr. Barton used weighted nymphs designed to sink by winding fuse wire around the hook shank. Whether Skues was aware of this, frustratingly we do not know, but, from our own experience, we know that when fishing with our friends it is most unusual for us not to be aware of the flies they are using. Incidentally, this was long before Sawyer's Pheasant Tail Nymph but, unfortunately, Barton does not tell us how he fished his weighted nymphs.

THE GRAYLING SEEMED to be looking up and one August after-noon I caught six and a half brace in one and a half hours with a *deep sunk nymph*. (*Side-Lines, Side-Lights and Reflections*)

Discussing Sawyer's nymphs with Sir Tom Eastham, Skues wrote somewhat clumsily:

OF COURSE SAWYER'S brown nymph would sink at once, dressed as you describe. I always used a *nymph that would sink*, knowing that the trout I see several under water for one on the surface. (Letter to Sir Tom Eastham, 19th September, 1946)

Exceptions

Skues said that there were three floating flies which at times attracted nymph-taking trout. The modern angler would have no difficulty in accepting the first one, the Gold-Ribbed Hare's Ear, and would

probably classify it as an emerger. Pope's Nondescript, which was tied
on a very small hook using light green floss silk ribbed with broad flat
gold, with light starling wings and bright red cock hackle and whisks,
has disappeared from the modern fly fisher's repertoire.

I DO NOT wish to be less than entirely candid with my readers
and I therefore feel bound to mention that there are three
upwinged floating fly patterns which will on occasion attract a
nymph-taking trout to the surface.

The first is the Gold-Ribbed Hare's Ear, a pattern extolled by
F.M. Halford in his earlier books and later on abandoned. He
claimed that it would take trout throughout the season. My
own experience is that it is specially successful in the season of
the large medium olive dun of spring. There is little doubt that
this pattern must be taken for a hatching nymph standing on its
partially discarded shuck. Indeed this was substantially Halford's
own opinion.

Another gold-ribbed pattern which I have found specially
attractive to tailing trout (which are, of course, often nymphing) is Pope's Green Nondescript – the invention of Mr. W.H.
Pope – which the late George Holland used to dress beautifully
and correctly, but which is now practically unobtainable, as
none of the dressers seem to use the right coloured bright but
palish-green floss for the body.

The third is the Red Quill with a ribbed body of strapped
undyed peacock herl and a sharp, bright red cock's hackle. The
reason why this is occasionally taken by nymphing fish I have
never been able to fathom.

Apart from these three patterns I know of none which attract
the nymphing trout. I have long discarded both Wickham's
Fancy and the Pink Wickham, with the latter of which I had
some success with tailing trout.

The Gold-Ribbed Hare's Ear appears to me to be a fair fly to
use as it suggests something definite which the trout may be
taking. The attraction of Pope's Nondescript I confess myself
unable to explain – the Red Quill may be taken for a spinner
which a trout taking nymphs as they arrive at the surface might
be occasionally tempted to accept – but this is a mere guess.
(*Nymph Fishing for Chalk Stream Trout*)

Skues's nymph patterns

Skues devised at least 44 nymph patterns in his lifetime, some of which were not named. In his definitive work on the nymph, *Nymph Fishing for Chalk Stream Trout*, there were 19 patterns. They included imitations of the large dark olive, medium olive dun, (seven patterns for different months of the season), July dun (small dark olive), iron blue dun, pale watery (six patterns as he said the colours varied) and blue-winged olive.

Despite his criticisms of Halford's exact imitation of dry flies, he seems to have constructed his own collection of 'exact imitation' nymphs. Skues, no doubt, would have called it representation or suggestion. It would be boring to include all these patterns here and, in any case, some of the materials in the dressings are either exotic or unobtainable now. I am, therefore, giving four patterns, three of which are recommended by Roy Darlington, who has fished them successfully at Abbots Barton. The fourth is one that I have dressed and which took a number of fish on the Itchen at Martyr Worthy in the past season.

(1) Medium Olive

Hook: No.14 down-eyed
Silk: Grey brown waxed with colourless wax
Hackle: Light medium honey dun hen, short in fibre – two turns
Whisks: Two strands pale-brownish blue cock guinea fowl's neck – short
Rib: Fine silver wire or none
Body: Abdomen: pale-brown peacock's quill, stripped
Thorax: Hare's poll

Roy Darlington modifies this dressing by using blue dun hackle fibres for whisks, and either jackdaw or soft dark blue dun for hackles. This pattern was suggested by Skues for early season. The one I have used was designated by Skues for fishing in May, June and July.

(2) Medium Olive

Hook: No.15 or 16 down-eyed
Silk: Primrose, waxed with dark wax
Hackle: Dark-blue hen or cockerel, to extend slightly beyond the dubbing of thorax
Whisks: Two strands of dark unspeckled neck feathers of cock guinea fowl
Rib: Optional. Silver wire
Body: Abdomen: Strand of brown quill from the stalk of the eye feather of a peacock
Thorax: A wad of dark hare's ear, close up to the hackle

I confess I used speckled guinea fowl neck feathers for whisks and replaced the brown peacock quill for the abdomen with light hare's ear. May Skues forgive me!

(3) Iron Blue

Hook: No.15 or 17 down-eyed (16 as a compromise)
Silk: Crimson, waxed with colourless wax
Hackle: Shortest hackle from throat of cock jackdaw – one turn or, at most, two
Whisks: Three strands of soft white hen hackle – quite short
Body: Mole's fur spun thinly on the tying silk exposing two turns of silk at tail, tapering to thickest at shoulder

(4) Pale Watery

Hook: No.15 or 17 (16 as a compromise)
Silk: Primrose, waxed with colourless wax
Hackle: One turn of very small darkish blue cock
Whisks: Two strands of pale unfreckled neck feather of cock guinea fowl – short
Rib: Yellow silk – five turns
Body: English squirrel's blue fur laid on thinly at tail and tapered to thickest at shoulder

Roy Darlington suggests using cream cock hackle fibres for whisks.

Little Brown Wink

Skues's advocacy of the nymph as an intrinsic and artistic form of fly fishing was a serious business, but, on this occasion, in this piece of doggerel which he wrote for the *Journal of the Flyfishers' Club* the humorous side of his nymph crusade comes to the fore, but with a valuable tip for the tyro nymph fisherman.

Oh, thrilling the rise at the lure that is dry,
When the slow trout comes up to the slaughter
    Yet rather would I
    Have the turn at my fly,
The cunning brown wink under water.

    The cute little wink under water!
    Mysterious wink under water!
        Delightful to ply
        The subaqueous fly,
    And watch for the wink under water.

Let the Purist rejoice in the fly that he dries,
And look down on my practice with hauteur,
    But for me the surprise
    Of the flash of the rise,
The rosy brown wink under water.

    The dear little wink under water.
    The yellow-brown wink under water.
        The subtle delight
        Of the line that goes tight,
    At the shy little wink under water.

Oh, give me the day when the fresh from the wold
Comes down with rich colour of porter,
    And tinges with gold
    That is flashing and bold
That yellow-green wink under water.

    That orange-brown wink under water,
    That ruddy gold wink under water,
        Oh, the glorious thrill
        That the bosom will fill
    At that rollicking wink under water.

Or a day on some smooth-flowing stream from the chalk,
When Aeolus no ruffle hath wrought her,
   The keen subtle stalk
   And the reel's sudden talk
At the rusty-brown wink under water.

   The heavy brown wink under water,
   The fatuous wink under water,
      When the bumping big trout
      That has got to come out
   Gives his solemn brown wink under water.

I care for no trout that comes up with a splash
To capture the fly that I've brought her;
   Let the trout that will dash
   At my fly with a flash
But tip me the wink under water.

   The gleaming brown wink under water,
   The golden-brown wink under water,
      When I think I descry
      The quick turn at my fly
   The fleeting brown wink under water.

When trouting is over, and autumn is here,
The days growing shorter and shorter,
   The grayling will steer
   For my fly with a mere
Little hint of a wink under water.

   A silvery wink under water
   A soft little wink under water,
      But she has it all right
      For the line has gone tight,
   At that wee little wink under water.

So plunging and rolling I lead her ashore
And as to the bank I escort her,
   She repented her sore
   That she'll never no more
Give that silver-brown wink under water.

That pinky-dun wink under water,
That shade of a wink under water,
   That raises a doubt
   Is it grayling or trout
Gave that misty brown wink under water?

So here's to the fish that is crafty and shy,
With the lore that Dame Nature has taught her,
   Yet we'll lure her to die,
   As she captures our fly
With that giddy brown wink under water.

   And here's to the wink under water,
   The wicked brown wink under water.
      And here's to the wise
      That decline to despise
   Any kind of a wink under water.

CHAPTER 8

Entomology

As can be seen throughout this book, Skues was immensely interested in aquatic life although he never made claim to be an entomologist. Whenever he had problems with the identification of flies, he sent specimens to Martin Mosely of the Natural History Museum. Mosely was the leading entomologist of his day, author of the classic *Dry Fly Fisherman's Entomology*, and nephew of Frederic Halford. Another of Skues's expert correspondents was C.A.N. Wauton, author of *The Troutfishers' Entomology*, so he was never at a loss when wishing to discuss his investigations of natural flies.

Skues's classification of aquatic flies was set out in *Nymph Fishing for Chalk Stream Trout*.

Insect food

THE INSECT FOOD of trout (apart from caterpillars, moths, crane-flies, cowdung and other land flies and ants which wind or rain or accident may precipitate upon the water) comprises:

1 Ephemeridae in their successive larval and nymphal stages and in their winged stages as dun or sub-imagines or as imagines or spinners both living and spent, or in some cases crawling under water to lay their eggs.

105

2 Phryganidae or sedge or caddis flies in the underwater stages when they inhabit cases and crawl on the bottom – stages in which they are of no use to the fly fisher – in the stage in which, leaving the shelter of their cases, they find their way to the surface to hatch out with great suddenness as winged flies and are apt to be attacked by the trout while on their way up – a phase which is seldom of much use to the fly fisher as the hatch is never (except perhaps in the case of a copious hatch of grannom) sufficiently concentrated in one place or line of places to enable the angler by their means to find a trout in position – and in the winged stage where they run on the surface or dance over it in the business of oviposition.

3 Perlidae or stone flies which are not so common on chalk streams as to provide a regular article of diet and are only of use to the angler occasionally – and that not in their underwater or creeper stage, though the representation of the hatched willow fly in autumn is often best taken as a sunk fly.

4 The alder, which passes its preliminary active stages in the river mud, then crawls ashore to bury itself in the earth for its pupal period and eventually hatches out as a terrestrial fly, seldom seen on the water and even then, on some rivers like the Itchen, seldom taken on the surface – while on other rivers such as the Kennet, the artificial representation well sunk is deadly.

5 Gnats in their underwater stages, both larval and pupal and in their winged stage.

6 Smuts.

7 Water beetles, some of which are subaqueous and others skitter about on the surface, being taken by the trout with a slash.

So far as these insects are taken on the surface they are matters of dry fly fishing. So far as they are taken subaqueously they are matters of ordinary wet fly fishing, but only the larval stages of the Ephemeridae are represented in nymph fishing. (*Nymph Fishing for Chalk Stream Trout*)

Large blue-winged pale watery or large spurwing

With his unique opportunities and acute powers of observation, it would have been surprising if Skues had not made one or two discoveries of natural flies during his long fishing lifetime. The first occurred in 1921.

I REMEMBER ONE of McCaskie's three-pounders – it was part of an historic occasion but was not caught at his corner. The year was 1921, the month June, and on two successive weekends I had been down, and at dusk had seen a tremendous hatch of a fly which I took to be the blue-winged olive, a fly in which I rather specialized. I had tried all the patterns of fly which had previously brought me success when the B.W.O. was hatching in quantity, but all in vain. On the third weekend, McCaskie was down as my guest, and there was a member of the syndicate present (*Fleur-de-Lys – Judge Lilley*). The hatch of fly was as full and as furious as ever. I asked McCaskie if he caught a fish during the hatch – sizeable or unsizeable – to bring it in. I was wholly beaten, as was the other syndicate member. McCaskie obediently, though reluctantly, brought in a three-quarter pounder. On return to the hotel we had out the contents of the poor little victim's stomach by means of my marrow scoop, and floated them in a saucer of water. Then, and then only, did we become aware that the fly the fish had been taking so furiously, though it had a blue wing, was not a blue-winged olive, but a fly since identified by Martin E. Mosely as Centroptilum pennulatum. I called it then a blue-winged pale watery. The fly has latterly been dubbed great (or large) spurwing.

Before we set out on the following day I had tied three imitations of the new fly, and gave one to McCaskie, one to the syndicate member, and kept one for myself. The evening rise was as furious as ever and still seemed to me so definitely a B.W.O. hatch that I tried fish after fish with my usual medicine for such an occasion, and was utterly defeated. I met the syndicate member and asked him if he had done any better. 'Yes,' he said, 'I got the fish you and McCaskie were hammering this morning, just above McCaskie's Corner.' 'What did you get him on?' 'Oh, that fly you gave me; he took it first chuck – 2lb 9oz.' The rise was nearly over but, cursing myself for a fool, I returned to the riser I had last left. He was still rising and took the fly – also first chuck – 2lb 6oz. Presently McCaskie came up quite pleased with himself, and a trout of 3lb 2oz – again first chuck – caught down below his corner, near where the cottages begin.

Next year (in July 1922) Mr. J.W. Dunne, a friend of McCaskie's, discovered the fly in quantity on the Kennett, and included patterns of it and its spinner (tied after his special method) in his volume *Sunshine and the Dry Fly* published in 1924.

I never saw such hatches of this fly again on the Itchen, though several smaller ones occurred at long intervals. It seemed to have intervals of years between one appearance and the next. An article of mine recording the discovery of 1921 and reappearance of the fly appeared in the *Salmon and Trout Magazine*. Mr. F.E. Sawyer, the extremely brilliant keeper of the Upper Avon, had a most interesting article in the January 1949 number of the *Salmon and Trout Magazine* disclosing his discovery of what may be two hitherto unknown species of spurwings. (Skues's introduction to Norman McCaskie's *Fishing: my Life's Hobby*.)

The fly was called the greater or larger spurwing by H.D. Turing, editor of the *Salmon and Trout Magazine*, from the characteristic spur found on the hind wings of the fly and its smaller brethren, the lesser spurwing. These, however, can only be seen under a microscope. Skues's dressing of the fly was as follows.

Hook: No.15
Silk: Cream waxed with clear wax
Hackle: Cream dun cock
Whisks: To match
Body: Finest cream-coloured fur from seal's cub, close to skin
Wings: Young starling

July dun

Although dressings of this fly had been given as early as Alfred Ronalds, it was not recognised by professional entomologists, and the natural seems to have been largely ignored before Skues. He found it on the Itchen in large numbers in July and August, sometime before 1921, and at a later date in Spring. It is smaller than the usual run of olives and is now commonly named the small dark olive. Strangely enough, although the artificial was one of his favourites, he does not seem to have endeavoured to identify it entomologically until the last year of his life when he asked Frank Sawyer if he knew its scientific name. The question was only solved three years after his death by J.R. Harris in his book *An Angler's Entomology*, when it was established to be *Baetis scambus*.

ONE JULY MORNING some few years back I was occupying a few minutes while waiting for breakfast at my Hampshire inn, by adding to my already excessive stock of trout flies, when the sight of a thin wing covert feather of a heron, dyed a medium greenish-yellow, tempted me to tie in a 16 size a sort of pale rendering of a heron herl bodied fly which, as the Rough Olive, had long served me well at the opening and close of successive trout seasons. So I varied a pattern which had served me well in a variety of shades all through the season by giving it a body dubbed with three strands of herl. Here is the dressing:

Hook:	No.16 down-eyed
Silk:	Yellow
Hackle & Whisk:	Greenish-yellow dyed cock
Body:	Three strands of thin heron herl from outer wing covert dyed greenish-yellow
Rib:	Fine gold wire
Wing:	Starling, darkish

I liked the look of the result enough to dress a second to match the first. It was a sunny morning with a fair air from the south east when I got down to the waterside, and I chose to open operations on a stretch of the east bank of the Itchen which runs for a couple of hundred yards from slightly north of west to slightly south of east. It is seldom that one gets the wind to serve that length perfectly, but if one does it is well to seize the opportunity, for the trout that haunt that bank run big for that part of the Itchen, and I knew that near the bottom of the length there was one particularly desirable trout.

He did not keep me long before disclosing his position, close up to the flags some thirty yards up. A little darkish dun came over him and was intercepted, and then another and another. I dropped down to the eddy at the bend and netted out one of these little duns, and it seemed to me that the fly which I picked from stock (dressed without the herl, but otherwise precisely like the pattern last above described) matched the natural fly with unusual precision. It was about 9.30 when I delivered my first cast. It was after eleven when, in despair after having tried at intervals a whole series of patterns without having put my fish down, I put on my herl-bodied dun of the morning. It was accepted with the utmost confidence, and in a moment I was battling with a two-pounder which in due course came to net. The only other fish which I found rising in the length, a trout of about one and three quarter pounds, followed suit, and I thought I was in for a good thing. Alas! the rise, which was never more than scanty during that morning, did not last me to the next bend.

But the pattern had made an impression on me, and each year since, as March has come round, I have tied for myself and my friends a small supply, which indeed I find difficult to keep, so well has the pattern justified itself. Here is an instance.

My friend B. was a guest on the same water in July of 1919, and we sat down to wait for the beginning of the rise a couple of hundred yards below the length above described. Presently a trout began feeding with great vigour in an eddy just off the centre of the current with occasional excursions into the current. He was taking a little dark dun, and taking it on the surface. I caught one of the flies, and my friend matched it, as he thought, perfectly from his box. 'You had better try one of my July duns,' I said, offering him one. He wouldn't have it, and I knotted it on to my own cast. For the next twenty minutes B. besieged that trout, casting to him with great skill, trotting his fly down the edge of the eddy, and never letting it get into the drag of it. The trout went on rising busily, taking flies quite close to B.'s, but never taking B.'s fly. I put my July dun to him, and the first time it covered him it was joyfully accepted, and B. presently netted out for me a beautiful fish in first-rate condition, two pounds six ounces in weight.

Then he said, 'If you don't mind, I'll reconsider my refusal of your pattern.' So I gave him the only other one I had, and we moved up to the next fish. Sure enough, the first time the fly went over him he had it, and B.'s conversion was complete.

Many angling books give dressings of the July dun, usually with bodies dubbed with a mixture of blue fur and yellow wool, or fur of sorts; Ronalds among others. Curiously enough I find no mention of the July dun in any of Mr. F.M. Halford's works. It would be strange, however, if all those who have given the July dun in the past were wrong, and I should hesitate to believe it, even if my own observation of the occurrence of a little darkish dun in July were not confirmed by the success which, from 1908 onwards, I have had in July with a little dark nymph tied to imitate a little dark olive nymph which I took from the mouth of a trout in that month in 1908. It has proved 'great medicine' when the trout are nymphing in July, when the little darkish dun is simultaneously coming down on the surface.

Hook: No.15 or 16
Silk: Bright yellow, well waxed
Whisks: Soft dark blue hen
Body: Mixed dubbing of olive seal's fur and a small amount
          of bear's hair, dark brown and woolly, taken from close
          to the skin, and bunched at the shoulder to suggest
          wing cases
Rib: Fine gold wire to lower part of the body only
Legs: A couple of turns of dark rusty dun hackle, very short

(*The Way of a Trout with a Fly*)

Semi-submerged

Although he never approached the subject of flies from a scientific
angle, Skues had exceptional powers of observation and the ability to
draw conclusions from them. Here, he gives a graphic description of
the hatching of May fly and deduces that what he saw is applicable to
all ephemerids.

ON A SUNDAY afternoon at the end of May I had an exceptional
opportunity of observing the hatch of the May fly on the
Kennet. The light, the position in which I sat, the swing of the
full current at my feet, and the clearness of the water after a
long drought, all combined to help me, and again and again I
saw that exquisite little water miracle recur.

    The dull, inert, brownish body of the nymph, swung down
by the current from the swaying tassels of the water weed,
coming slowly to the surface, till somehow its head and thorax
seemed to threaten to emerge. Then the bursting of the brown
skin of the thorax, the six pale greenish legs gripping the
surface, while the body curled tail downwards in the water, as if
to let the current get a purchase on the sheath. Then simultaneously the wings shooting up, the sheath coming away and floating far down the current, and the fairy-like creature standing
with wings erect and upturned tail to drift downstream, it may
be a few yards or only a few inches, before taking flight for the
meadows. These few inches or yards represent the one opportunity the trout, dace or chub has of taking the May fly in the
winged stage before, as spent imago, the fly goes drifting down
the stream, with wings flat on the water, dead or in the throes
of dissolution. The chances, therefore, for the fish of taking the
insect in the nymphal stage are obviously much greater, and it is

little to be wondered at that, in the inert semi-submerged nymph just about to hatch and in the spent, waterlogged, dying or dead spinner, the trout finds a far easier prey than it does in the fidgety, fluttering, newly-hatched May fly which is so apt to disappoint him by taking wing at the moment he puts it up.

If these deductions be sound in the case of the green drake and its spinners, they are probably equally sound in the cases of all the other and far smaller upwinged flies, which, in process of hatching, oviposition, and death follow the same sequence of stages as the May fly. And this probably is one good reason for the success of nymph-like, or spinner-like, flies such as Tup's Indispensable, fished semi-submerged. Dubbed with a body material which readily takes up the water and fills with light, and busked with a hackle which is enough to enable the fly to cling to the surface film, such a pattern may well be taken, at one stage of the fly's career, for the hatching nymph getting its head above water, and in a later stage for the spent spinner floating down helpless or dead. Trout rise at spent gnats and fallen spinner in a quiet, deliberate way, differing greatly from the fierce rushing motions with which they bulge at the ascending nymphs which they fear may escape them by hatching and transfer to the air. (*The Way of a Trout with a Fly*)

CHAPTER 9

Rods and Lines

The 'World's Best Rod'

Skues's American Leonard rod is famous, firstly because of its quality, secondly through its association with Skues and thirdly because of its sobriquet, 'The World's Best Rod'. Skues refers to the rod on many occasions. In *Itchen Memories* he states that the rod was so dubbed by a guest of his, C.L.C., but in a letter to Sir Tom Eastham he attributes it to Sir Grimwood Mears, an old friend who, among other things, introduced him to Frank Sawyer.

> SIR GRIMWOOD MEARS, having used my Leonard on several occasions on the Itchen when the only way one could have a guest was by sharing a rod, called mine the W.B.R. or World's Best Rod. (Letter to Sir Tom Eastham, 22nd October, 1946)

Like Donald Overfield before me, I had the opportunity to put the rod together and try out its action. Like him also, I did this with appropriate reverence. I have used carbon fibre rods for some years but, even so, W.B.R. felt relatively light to me. Where it was different from any other rod I have handled was in the action which went right down to the butt. I could imagine Skues putting out his nymphs with a slow, easy and accurate action.

When Skues ceased fishing with the rod in 1945, he passed it on to his younger brother, Charles, who ultimately presented it to the Flyfishers' Club where it resides to this day.

This is how he came to acquire the rod.

Eddie Mills, Priddis and my Leonards

IN THE YEAR 1904 at the Crystal Palace there took place a fly-casting tournament, the only one in which I ever took part as a contestant.

The year 1902 brought me the acquaintance (developing into friendship through the light rod controversy) of the American angler, Nathan Durfee Coggeshall, who invited me to see his Leonard rods. One of these was a ten footer of soft old fashioned type, quite unsuited to fishing the dry fly, but the other presented to him by the makers was a 10 foot Tournament rod in three joints weighing six and a half ounces and was probably the first to come over here to challenge the Houghtons, the Test rod and other dry fly rods of that day, and it made a large impression on us. So when about the end of that year or the beginning of the next a legacy put me in funds to acquire a replica of the 10 foot Tournament rod, one of the first things I did was to order one, and I took it out to Bavaria on my September 1903 holiday, and was so pleased with its performance that I let myself be persuaded to enter for the distance and accuracy event in the 1904 tournament. A badly damaged wrist prevented any success in the distance event, but I came second in the accuracy, only failing to win it because in the last and longest cast for accuracy a gust of wind caught my gut and fly just as they were being delivered and blew them off the marker.

Among the spectators was Mr. P.B. Mills, the senior member of the New York firm which sold the Leonard Tournament, and his son Eddie. I was introduced to them by Coggeshall, and, finding the young man anxious to try fishing on a chalk stream,

I made interest with Mr. Irwin Cox to get the young man a day on the Itchen. He brought with him two rods of the Leonard make – one, which he used, a 9 foot 5 ounce rod of fascinating action and the other a two and a half ounce piece of magic with which Priddis, the keeper, not only put out 23 yards of line, but hooked and landed from a weedy stretch without using a landing net a 2lb 2oz trout in fine condition.

I was not fishing, contenting myself with following young Mills and providing him with appropriate flies, but his 9 foot 5 ounce Leonard made such an impression on me that when next year a client wished to pay me a large sum in addition to my firm's costs, in recognition of a professional service, I declined the money as a benefit but expressed my willingness to accept as a compliment the best rod that money could buy, to be chosen by myself. He not only willingly accepted the plan but insisted on adding an appropriate reel and line to the gift.

It was a choice I never had reason to regret, and when in 1945 my trout fishing came to an end, I handed the rod and its one remaining top to my brother. The rod was as straight and as serviceable as on the day it was acquired, notwithstanding the hundreds of trout up to three and a quarter pounds and numbers of grayling it had mastered in the forty years of its service.

Leonard rods

Skues discusses with W.H. Lawrie the long-lasting qualities of the rod he used for over 40 years.

I BELIEVE THE supreme quality of the work of the two great Leonards (father and son) was due to a combination of workmanship and a saturating or impregnating cement. The rods were hexagonal but I think probably cut from the thick joints of the cane which would mean less sacrifice of enamel and less roundness. (Letter to W.H. Lawrie, 26th March, 1948)

Skues recalls the reaction to his Leonard rod by John Lock, the old keeper and inventor of the fly, Lock's Fancy.

ON THE ABBOTSWORTHY length one evening, just above the saw mill, I was accosted by the inventor of Lock's Fancy, old John Lock, ex-keeper and well-known Hampshire character. 'What

do e' call that?' he asked, referring to my nine footer. 'It's by way of being a fly rod,' I said. 'Try the heft of it.' He took the rod from my hand and began to cast with it rather scornfully, but in a few moments was delighted with it and at the accuracy with which he laid a fly time after time over a busy fish that was rising just above the mill. For over half an hour he stuck to him and eventually hooked him, and the fish went off like a steam engine up stream. It looked like a very big fish, but when netted proved to be 1lb 9oz only, but foul-hooked. The old man gave up the rod most unwillingly when I went in.
(*Flyfishers' Journal*, Summer 1917)

Skues's Leonard rods

The rod that he allowed John Lock to try is, I believe, the one in the Flyfishers' Club, stated to have been presented to the Club by Skues in 1920. The other one in the Flyfishers' is the famous World's Best Rod. A third is now residing with the Anglers' Club of New York. Donald Overfield ponders on the fate of the one called 'Matilda'. Dr. Barton, in his diary, refers to this rod as follows: 'Skues lent me a Leonard 9.6 which he said he did not like but which fitted me perfectly. It was the famous "Matilda" which later became my favourite rod. It cast nicely into the wind my ICI line and weighed only five and three quarter ounces – a lovely rod, given him by the daughter of Coggeshall.' Skues says in an article written in 1936 that he had six Leonard rods presented to him by clients, but the following reveals that he purchased two Leonards – and sold them. I wonder where they are now.

> IT WILL AMUSE you to know that I sold the 10ft Leonard split cane which I lent you for £17.10s having previously had a duplicate snapped up at £15. I daresay I could have squeezed more had I wished to – but the buyer's membership of the Flyfishers' Club weakened me. (Letter to Sir Tom Eastham, 26th January, 1945)

Qualities of a rod

Though written long before the advent of glass and carbon fibre, Skues's diagnosis of the qualities of a good rod are just as applicable today, with its emphasis on appropriateness for the type of fishing and the balance between stiffness and courage in the power of a rod. He

The Skues family had their children photographed annually.
Above left, the 5 year old Skues taken probably in the kilt of the
Mackenzie clan. *Above right*, Skues at 10.

Skues at 13   Skues at 14

The Winchester
schoolboy – 'My own
rod was an awful
bean pole, 11 feet
long and of a
paralysing stiffness.'

Right, the articled
clerk.

Far right, the
qualified solicitor.

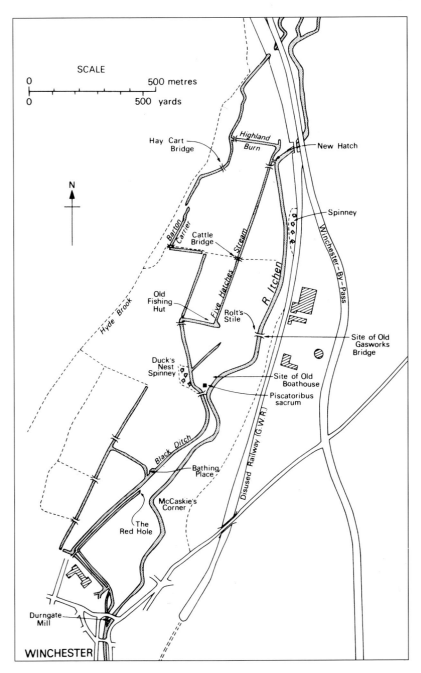

A map of Abbots Barton fishery as it was in Skues's time.

Skues at the gate between Nun's Walk and the fishery.
Abbots Barton farm is behind him.

Fishing on the Itchen by Winnal gas works, 1935. This was a favourite
reach of Skues and his ashes were scattered nearby.

Left, Skues at the top of his water. He always carried: rod, six-foot broomstick-handled landing net, seat stick, white cotton bag containing macintosh and sandwiches, big white cotton bag for fish, and fishing bag holding spare reel and gear. Hence he usually cast from the reel, not using his left hand.

Below, Dr. Barton's sketch of Skues

Three nymphs tied by Skues for Pack-Beresford's book, *Nymph Dressings. Clockwise from top left*, Medium Olive, Pale Watery, Iron Blue.

'He fished at right angles to trout across the stream, yet it seemed all right.'

Fishing the Back Stream in 1921. The bottom of Duck's Nest Spinney with aqueduct.

'Look, Barton, there's the first blue-winged olive of the season.' 1923

The Corner House, Winchester,
where Skues used to stay. It is
now no longer a hotel.

The Nadder Vale Hotel,
Wilton, where Skues spent
the last of his fishing years.

Installation of the commemorative stone bench in memory of G.E.M. Skues, August, 1979. Roy Darlington, co-lessee of Abbots Barton (3rd from left); Stuart Newell, co-lessee of Abbots Barton (4th from left); Iris Whitfield, riparian owner Abbots Barton; Donald Overfield (4th from right); Gordon Mackie, Chairman, Skues Memorial Committee (3rd from right); Keith Skues, great nephew of Skues (2nd from right).

Below, the inscription on the plaque.

also comments on the advanced quality of design in the American rods of that time.

I THINK THE chief part of the ecstasy of fishing with the fly is to be found in the qualities of the fly rod, and if I am right in this, the more exquisite the rod the keener and more perfect the pleasure to be derived from the sport, a strong argument in favour of perfection in one's weapon for the particular game in hand. It may be, indeed, it is, better to fish with any old rod than not to fish. But to fish with the most perfect of gear raises the satisfaction to the sublime – a thing of which those who have never handled a really perfect weapon can have no conception. I must, of course, predicate the use with the perfect rod of a line perfectly adjusted to its power and weight. Thus armed the angler becomes capable of a delicacy and accuracy of casting of which he had previously little notion.

There is, of course, no such thing as an absolutely perfect fly rod for all purposes. The perfection must be sought in relation to the purposes for which the rod is used, and in relation to the physique and temperament of the user. For instance, where it is necessary to swing the line over high growths behind the angler, a short rod, however intrinsically desirable, is not the weapon for the game. Nor is it desirable for wet fly work in rapid water, where little of the line beyond the cast should be in the water. The ideal solution would be a different rod with its appropriate reel and line for each type of fly fishing in which the angler engages.

But the first class rod is an expensive article, and most of us must be content with one rod (or at best a small selection) for all purposes, and such one rod, while perhaps ideal for one game, must be fairly suitable for the other kinds of fishing in which its owner engages, and thus, like too much in fly fishing, must be a compromise.

One often hears an angler handling a strange rod, or even his own, exclaim at its power, as if power in itself were a virtue. It is only a virtue to the exact extent to which it is needed for the particular game. In excess of that it is an encumbrance. Deficiency of it below that standard is a vice. If, for instance, in order to develop its power the rod requires an excessively heavy and clumsy casting line, its power is excessive. It will not serve the angler as well as a much less powerful rod which is exactly adapted to project a line of suitable weight and thickness for the

117

water. A very heavy line dries cast and fly much more rapidly than does a lighter one, and the lighter the line up to a point the better suited it is for fishing the wet fly on rough water, and, to a less extent, on smooth. The limit is to be found in the power controlling the line in casting. A certain degree of weight is necessary to carry the line accurately to its destination, and the rod must be up to this weight, must carry and project it with confident ease and precision. But in order that this may be so the line must be of a weight to develop without straining, the power of the rod. It is thus of more importance to have rod and line perfectly adapted to one another than to have the rod of exceptional power.

The extent of a rod's power is conditioned by the strength of the weakest part of the link between fish and reel, the gut. Given fine gut, a heavy rod or a rod of great power will not kill a heavy fish any more than a much less powerful one; for a wise angler will put no more strain on the gut with the powerful rod than with the weaker weapon, and the weaker has the advantage of relieving the pressure by yielding to the strain.

In speaking of the power of a rod it is necessary to distinguish between stiffness and courage. A rod of moderate strength may, if of high quality, be one of supreme courage. The resilience of such a rod is never broken. It always comes back. A rod of poor quality becomes fatigued, loses heart and shape, for it is lacking in courage. A first-rater never does. It yields to the heaviest strain, resisting all the time, and the limit of its resilience is never reached.

What is it that imparts to a rod this high quality of courage? In the first place fine quality of material, and in the second, but infinitely more important place, perfection of construction. This perfection of construction makes an ideal distribution of strain when the rod is casting or in play. There is no weak spot anywhere from butt to tip. Given homogeneous material this connotes a scientifically perfect gradation of taper from the hand to the top ring, and thus a rod made in the main by rule of thumb, though by a fluke it may be a creation, is less likely to be first rate than one designed upon scientific lines. I have handled a number of the cheaper American split cane rods which come into the English market, and I have been invariably struck by the scientific character of their taper. It is almost as conspicuous in the shoddiest of the cheap rods as it is in those of the highest quality, and thus it comes about that so many of them, though they may have little wear in them, are a pure delight to handle so long as their bindings and glue last. This is a matter in which our manufacturers of every quality of rod might with advantage take their cue from the States.

This perfection of taper involves not only the elimination of all weakness, but also the dispensing with all excess of material, whether in fittings or in the cane of the rod itself. Thus these American split canes of all classes come to a finer point in the top than do our English rods of corresponding length, and that without loss of power. And they run to less weight. Lock-fast joints are conspicuous by their absence. That joint introduces a false note into the construction of every trout fly rod of which it forms a part. It is not so secure a joint as a well-made suction joint, and has nothing like the sweetness of fitting. It is a marvel that the vogue of the suction joint could not be manufactured over here. Messrs. Ogden and Scotford have for many years past made as satisfactory a joint of that class as the best American.

The war is bringing the advantage of newer and more scientific methods home to the manufacturers of this country. Let us hope that the builders of rods will not escape its influence, and so be able to put at the disposal of the public generally rods of a perfection such as a few of the members of the Club are familiar with. Then there will be in the reach of all, weapons of seeming fragility yet of which it may be said that you cannot hurt them short of running over them with a taxi or charging a brick wall with them, and which may be used unflinchingly and unsparingly in the subjugation of big trout. (*Flyfishers' Journal*, Winter 1917–18)

The 'Coggie' line

In a later chapter mention will be made of the part that the American, Walter Durfee Coggeshall, and Skues, played in the earlier years of the century in advocating the use of shorter, light rods as opposed to the longer, heavier rods of the previous century.

Skues was also associated with Coggeshall in the development of the new silk lines, and 'Coggie' perfected the art of preparing these lines for fly fishing. His methods involved all manner of materials such as raw linseed oil, pumice, white methylated spirits, etc.

NOT LONG AFTER I acquired my first Leonard rod (a 10ft weighing 6oz) in 1903, Coggeshall presented me with two of his lines, size No.3 double tapered. One summer day not long afterwards I lent my 10ft Leonard, with one of these lines, to a guest of another rod on the Itchen, and at lunch time the guest carefully pulled out the line, laying it on the grass to dry, and after lunch he put down his lighted cigar near the middle of it, burning the line in two. I still have the second which, except for being a bit worn at the ends is as good as ever, and has never, though left on the reel, shown the slightest tendency to become sticky. It is only fair to say that except for an occasional day with the May fly I have not used the 10ft much since 1905.

When Coggeshall died in 1923 his widow put together his entire stock of eight new lines to give to me, and somewhere on the way to my office, in a bus, in a shop or in a train, the whole parcel went astray and was never recovered – a tragedy I have never forgotten. They were the greater loss inasmuch as several of them were No.2 size which suited my 9ft Leonard. But it is to the good that Coggeshall's exact method should not be lost to memory, for his lines were priceless. (*Flyfishers' Journal* Correspondence Columns, Summer 1944)

Leaders

In discussing leaders Skues is referring to gut, but it is interesting to learn that, as is the practice today, he often used leaders up to 12 feet in length as opposed to the traditional nine feet.

I IMAGINE A trout, accustomed to see the surface of the river dimpled with rain drops, or struck by some falling insect, is not too readily scared by the fall of the angler's fly, even if it hit the surface with some decision. It is another matter if the gut also hits the water with any degree of violence within the range of the trout's normal vision.

The old angling writers of Walton's day and later were, therefore, probably preaching sound doctrine when they said that the cast should be so made that the fly alone (or first) lit upon the water. This must have been a difficult job to accomplish on the smooth water of a chalk stream, even with the long rods in use in those days. Therefore, a bit of wind producing a ruffle was then almost essential to enable an angler to fish such waters with success. Today, with comparatively short rods, casting a longish line, the gut, and behind the gut the line, must hit the water – and it is therefore essential that the gut should be of such length that the casting line strikes the water at such a distance from the trout as not to come within his normal range of vision. There seems to be a consensus of opinion, based on long practice, that three yards of gut are enough for that purpose – which gives me ground for thinking that three yards is probably the outside limit of a trout's range of view of the surface in smooth water, though doubtless he can see somewhat further under the surface. Within those three yards, however, it is essential that the gut should fall so lightly on the water as not to attract the trout's attention, and I imagine (and my experience gives me grounds for thinking that I do so correctly) that if the fly hits the surface with some degree of decision, short of a scaring splash, the resulting flash not only draws the attention of the trout to the angler's fly but diverts it from any slight disturbance due to the fall of the gut.

In waters where trout nymph a great deal they are apt to cruise up and down instead of sticking closely to one spot, and on such waters it is prudent, if the wind permits it, to use a gut cast of more than nine feet. I frequently use 10, 10 and a half, 11 or even 12 feet so as not to line my fish.

It may be inferred from the above that the fly should not fall too far from the trout, or it may fail to draw attention to itself, and though this point is not quite essential if the fly be a nymph, yet even with a nymph it is as well to hit the surface within the trout's range of normal vision without gut splash, but with sufficient decision to call the trout's attention. That 'fly lighting like thistledown' theory is a very pretty theory. It involves admirably delicate casting, but it is apt not to involve the trout noticing the fly unless it pass directly over his head. (*Flyfishers' Journal*, Autumn 1932)

Nylon

In November 1938, a young and ingenious American fly fisherman, Baird C. Foster, wrote to ask Skues where he could obtain a marrow scoop and this led to extensive correspondence. Among his many accomplishments, Foster built himself a split cane rod replica of Skues's W.B.R., Skues having supplied him with the exact dimensions of the Leonard. In 1939, Foster sent him some samples of the new Dupont material for casts which later became known as nylon. Skues was soon trying it out with his usual gusto.

I FOUND, DURING the past fortnight's experience of Nylon, three faults: (1) that the points are definitely weaker than 4X gut; (2) that even with the points removed there is a tendency for flies to snap off in casting with a following wind; and (3) that the knots are difficult to tie and a bit slippery.

On the other hand, in sizes above the finest the strands are remarkably strong. I killed trout of two and a half pound and 2lb 3oz without a mark on the cast to show strain or abrasion by weeds or snags. I can see a good future for the material. (Letter to Foster, 13th June, 1939)

By October, he was describing to Foster the performance of one of his nylon casts tapered to .006 and praising its strength.

I TIED ON a grouse hackled fly with a brownish yellow seal's fur body and dibbed the fly on the water not in front of the fish but behind and to the side upstream. It immediately began to take notice and came up to the fly nearly touching it with its nose. I tried again with the same result – and again. But the third time after refusing, it must have regretted the decision, for it came up again and seized the fly. On feeling the hook it promptly bolted downstream, under the wire against which the cast was strained hard.

I dared not yield an inch expecting every moment to be broken. But after my rod had been a hoop for some time the fish bolted upstream and came down on the other side of the central post and was once more grinding the cast against the wire. Again I held on like grim death and after a while, feeling resistance slacken, I looked over and saw that I had the trout's head out of water. But I had left my landing net out of reach at the spot where I stood to dib for the fish and I had to manoeuvre the trout in front of the pile of cut weeds collected against the post to reach my landing net. This being safely accomplished I reached down with the net through the iron lattice work of the bridge and was just able to dip out the trout. It scaled 2lb 10oz. The extraordinary thing, apart from the fact that the fish did not break away, is that the cast shows no sign of wear and tear from its friction against the wire, lasting, as it did, several minutes.

I wonder whether the Y.D. (Nylon) casts may not improve with keeping. This was certainly eighteen months old and may be older. Have you any data on the subject? (Letter to Foster, 2nd October, 1940)

However, he was soon disillusioned on this latter point and discovered like many more of us since, that nylon does not improve with age especially when exposed to light.

THE OTHER DAY I used the 1939 Nylon cast on which on the 30th September last I killed a 2lb 10oz trout, fishing from a bridge and having the cast severely rubbed against a cattle wire without showing any signs of wear. I thought that that indicated that Nylon improved with keeping, but alas it was quite rotten and broke again and again. Perhaps the strain it had undergone had taken the heart out of it. (Letter to Foster, 21st July, 1941)

On the numbering of fly hooks

Skues suggests a sensible system of numbering hooks according to the length of the shank, width of gape and weight of wire.

AT INTERVALS THROUGH the ages there recurs the desperate cry of some pedantic theorist for a reform in the manufacture of fly hooks which would make all hooks the same shape and all the numberings of different manufacturers correspond. I do not agree. I think it would be a misfortune, for hooks have to fit a variety of purposes and must, therefore, vary. The utmost reform which I would like to see adopted would be the numbering of hooks in all the different shapes and bends of fly hook according to the length of that part of the hook on which the fly is to be built, with a qualification for the degree of width of gape. Thus an O hook might be classed as OA-narrow gape, OB-medium gape, or OC-wide gape. The wires might be classed as heavy, medium or light. Say H., M. or L.

Apart from such reforms as these I should be content for things to be as they are, using each type of bend for the purpose to which it is expressly adapted.

I think tackle dealers are often far too careless about the patterns of hook on which they dress flies. For instance, no wet fly or nymph should ever be dressed on a hook with an upturned eye. A good entry is essential and the fly should accordingly be dressed either on a blind hook or on a down-eyed hook.

The dresser should carefully consider for what type of fishing the fly is required. If it is to be a nymph, the body of which is relatively long and tapered, the hook for the smaller sizes should be long in the shank and not too wide in the gape. (*Flyfishers' Journal*, Summer 1938)

Dry fly hooks

In this letter Skues reveals why, in later life, he preferred to use down-eyed hooks even for dry flies.

YES, I USE down-eyed hooks for nymphs and latterly for all purposes, but that may be due to my incompetence to cut away the waste roots of the feathers used for wings on an upturned eye unless I tie the wings forward with the roots of the feather back over the shaft. (Letter to Sir Tom Eastham, 29th July, 1944)

CHAPTER 10

Skues on the River

The reason that Skues must stand very high in the pantheon of world-class fly fishermen is because his profound knowledge of the subject in all its aspects, including its literature, its tools, its fish and the medium in which they live, and its flies and how to dress them, was matched by his skill as an angler. With such resources and acute powers of observation, he was able to make decisions on the river and draw conclusions which very often led to his successful deception of trout and their downfall. Incidentally, he did not care very much for trout as a dish, and invariably gave his fish away.

Over the years, in his various writings, he gives many graphic accounts of days on the river. For someone who confessed that he had never been able to keep a diary for long, these accounts are most detailed, including the habit – which at times in reading his works I have found irritating – of giving the precise weight of every fish he caught. As he was constantly contributing articles to *The Fishing Gazette*, *The Field*, the *Flyfishers' Journal*, and the *Bulletins of the Anglers' Club of New York*, presumably many of these incidents were fresh in his mind.

Such days on the river would fill a book on their own, and I have therefore chosen a limited number of fishing episodes which illustrate some particular quality in the man and in his fishing.

Nine to one

The first extract illustrates his immense determination and patience stretched out over a period of six days involved in the capture of one fish. Where ordinary mortals would give up because of a fish's inaccessibility caused by bush and thorn and weed, Skues would attempt a solution with a fearless disregard for rod and line and fly.

THE MILL WAS a powerful one, or it would not have needed a quarter of a mile of head, generally deep, and nowhere less than five and twenty yards across to do its day's work. That there were big trout in the head I knew. I saw one a few days ago which was not an ounce under five pounds, and for some hours on each succeeding day I haunted the head in the hope of finding him again, not only in position, but in a taking mood. Once I saw a fish rise twice in a little bay above a big tussock, which, when one got near enough to cast to him, hid the rise entirely. Nevertheless, with a good heart I delivered a small floating March Brown to the spot where I imagined the trout to be, struck at the sound of the immediately succeeding rise, felt a horrid jar as if I had hit a snag, and then the still horrider sense of slackness that tells one that one has failed to fasten. The trout departed with a great wave, but he was not my five pounder.

That, however, was the only fish I saw move during the five days which followed my glimpse of Leviathan. There were other fish there I know, because on occasion I saw the wave which a trout departing leaves behind him (as the trout equivalent for 'footsteps in the sands of time'), though a most careful inspection both of surface and bottom had failed to reveal his presence alongside the sludgy, tussock-ridden bank. The opposite bank, besides being fringed with trees, often close together, and being elsewhere clad with brambles and exaggerated specimens of nettle, dock, willow-herb and what had once been meadowsweet, was anything from five feet to eight feet above the water. It did not therefore offer an ideal vantage ground for attacking the pool. Yet it was right under this far bank that on the sixth day I saw my only riser besides the one aforementioned. He was close in under the bank, almost beneath a large and bushy elm – the kind that wears a sort of hangman's fringe – and under a horrid canopy of frog-bit, deceased meadowsweet, nettle and other herbage devised for the confusion of

anglers, the profit of tackle dealers, and the despair of over-
worked recording angels.

The only redeeming features of the situation were the
direction of the wind (which was not unfavourable), and the
fact that the trout lay just where the mill-head was at its
narrowest. I calculated that with luck I might cover the fish
once in thirty or forty casts, and I stuck to him for the best
part of an hour, during which he rose perhaps twenty times. If
I covered him during that time it was not with a fly he
wanted. I must have caught up in sedges and other herbage
behind fully as many times as he rose, and my damaged wrist
waxed tired. I waded in at the top of the pool, and sought the
high strip in the middle, to see if I could get down to and
opposite the fish, but halfway down I began to ship water
over the tops of my wading stockings, and retreated to terra
firma. But I was not done yet. It was half a mile round by the
mill to the opposite side, and then the fish was quite inacces-
sible, but still I went. It was just on noon when I arrived at
the spot and began to prospect.

The fish was still there and still rising – if anything, a trifle
more freely than before. What he was taking I could not see,
but, going down to the water behind the next tree below him, I
saw some black gnat, two little pale watery duns, a blue-winged
olive, and a spent red spinner go down, and a sedge go scuttering along the water. The tree was about twenty feet from the
elm below which my trout lay, and against it, waist high, swayed
a very friendly and prehensile, bramble bush, covered with
succulent blackberries. It sufficed to hold me back some six or
seven feet from the edge, so that when my rod was held out at
right angles, some two or three feet only would project over the
stream. Then the line would have to be delivered over (1) bramble bush, (2) a thick clump of willow herb, (3) a thick clump of
meadowsweet, (4) a long and particularly offensive nettle head;
and it would have to avoid a long, trailing bramble sucker. But
before I could begin to think of casting there was the tree to
consider. Its branches hung low, and some clearance was indicated. Five minutes' faithful work with a pocket knife made just
a possible room for me to swing my Leonard horizontally, and I
calculated that I could get my line into the air under the tree at
my back without inevitably hanging up every time in the tree in
front, and could then draw it back by switching my rod
horizontally across the bushes, so that once in a while, with

luck, my line might all fall clear of the objectionable herbage, and my fly even cover the trout.

Then I put on my mackintosh, hardened my heart, and cuddled as deep as I could into the bramble bush which banked against my tree, and saw to my joy that I could spot the rise of my fish just beneath the solitary nettle head. I had quite made up my mind that if a cast failed it would be ten chances to one against my recovering my fly. I began with a Pale Watery Dun, and to my delight managed to get my line on to the water just as I had calculated. The fly, however, fell a foot short of the fish, and, though I let it drift down so as to clear most of the herbage, and pulled it very gently through the rings, the meadowsweet got it, and kept it and the point of my cast. I put on another, and this time I covered my fish nicely. But it took no notice, and the fly, after being recovered once successfully and re-presented in vain, followed its predecessor's example in yielding to the clinging affections of the meadowsweet. Then I tried a Red Quill, and after he had been rejected, I left him and more of my gut in one of the trailing brambles. Followed a home-made Red Spinner, tied with a priceless honey dun cock's hackle, a Whirling Blue Dun, and two Orange Quills on No.14 hooks. There were two of these, because the first was hung up before I got him over my trout. There were fully two yards of gut left when the first Orange Quill left me, there was but one yard when I was orphaned of the second. Then I bethought me of the scuttering sedge, and I put on a good big wholesome Red Sedge, with an orange silk body on a No.13 hook. All the time the trout had continued at intervals to take some fly or other, whose nature was not revealed to me, with a sullen, consequential 'ploop', occasionally displaying his back fin and the extreme tip of his tail as he went down. All this time he had never been scared. The Sedge went over him beautifully (I had no nerves about my casting, having not the least hope or expectation of getting my fish), there was a little hump under the surface, and the Sedge floated on undisturbed. So was the Recording Angel. Once I recovered the fly, and again put it before my fish. No notice taken, but when I tried to recover the Sedge again there was passive resistance, and I lost not only the remaining yard of gut, but the loop of my casting line.

I put a new cast into my damper to soak, emerged from my bramble bush, sat down, frayed out the end of my casting line, waxed it, waxed a doubled length of silk, and whipped a new

loop in the end. Then I put on my freshly damped cast, and as
I glanced over the fly box, looking up by chance, I saw a willow
fly on the elbow of my mackintosh. Now I pride myself on my
Willow Flies. I tie a spent Willow Fly which has a most lifelike
way of lying dead with wings outspread on the water, and I had
one left. I grudged it to the bushes, but it was almost the end
of the season. So on it went. Four or five switches through the
air to get distance, and then the Willow Fly dropped just a foot
in front, and to the outside of the spot where I imagined my
fish to be. Once again there was that solemn consequential
suck, once again the back fin and the tail tip successively
appeared and disappeared, and then, scarcely believing in what
had happened, I pulled line and raised rod together (so as not
to hit the tree above), drawing the hook gently but firmly
home. In a moment my rod and line were drawn into the
straight as the fish tore madly up under his own bank, emptying
the reel of almost all its thirty five yards of line in one streak.
Then he seemed to be seeking cover in a weed, and, forcing my
way through the bramble and other tangle, I crept up to and
close under the upper elm, and tried to pass round it to get
nearer my fish. Holding him lightly with the rod just arched, I
could feel him beating savagely in the weeds, and presently, as
he came away, I began winding him down quickly with my rod
well hooped, and butting him out of reach of several likely
looking snags on the way down, I got him at length to me in
deepish water, and more than a little tired by his exertions.
Keeping low, and as much out of sight as possible, I dipped the
net through the herbage, and a moment later I was hoisting my
fish ashore. In landing him I nearly broke my rod point
through the line catching in a bramble, but I saw what was
happening just in time. Though perfect in colour, shape and
condition, deep and thick, he was not a big fish – only two
pounds four ounces. But I do not recall many other trout the
catching of which has been a greater satisfaction to me than his.
(*The Way of a Trout with a Fly*)

'Some' shots

Skues's pleasure in the capture of that difficult fish in the previous
incident, was only matched by recollecting three of the best casts of
his life. As usual, he is not loathe to remind us of the physical handicaps under which he operated.

OCCASIONALLY IN MY not very short angling career I have stood and watched with envy a first-rate fisherman planting his fly or it may be his team of flies with seemly precision cast after cast exactly where he would have it alight, and with a softness which left nothing to be desired. Damaged wrists, defective eyesight and a natural impatience of temperament have excluded me permanently from the ranks of these for whom such consistent performances are possible, and have classed me with the rough fisherman. Yet now and again, amid such inferior casting, I have brought off a shot or two which it is a pleasure to look back to, a shot which, perhaps, I could not repeat in ten thousand attempts. Probably the same thing happens to most anglers out of the first rank who have done much fishing with the fly. Still, I hope I may be pardoned for giving myself the pleasure of recalling a few of these incidents.

On the Pang one September day in 1911, when the river was extraordinarily low, I had been getting some sport with the Whitchurch dun under difficult conditions – the river being fearfully overgrown, with rows and masses of flags above the surface and dense weed growth beneath. But there was a deep sunny pool with bottom of silver sand, and from it the stream, divided by one of these accumulations of flag, passed partly at my feet and partly out of sight but for glimpses I got through two or three narrow lanes among the flags. Two nice trout were hovering in the pool, and I put my fly over the lower of them. He came up and looked at it, backing suspiciously down with it till it dragged, then dropped back out of sight into the further channel beyond the flags. But looking down through a tiny gap between the flags I seemed to see his eye fixed on me, and hardly knowing what I was doing, I cast. By some magic the line dropped exactly in the channel, placing the fly just beyond the trout's head on the further side. I struck at the sound of a rise, and the trout, foolishly, tore back into the open pool. From thence I had no difficulty in conducting him to the landing net. I forget his exact weight. It was something over a pound.

A somewhat similar incident occurred a year or two later on the Tillingbourne. I was walking up the mill-head, rod in hand, looking out for a feeding fish, when I spied a big dark trout – big for the water, that is – resting among the flags on the far side, and protected from any rational attempt on his life by a

screen of them. I had on a Black Alder on a No.12 hook, and I
flicked it across, quite a short cast, and by some miracle it
dropped over the screen of flags and on to the trout's tail. He
whirled and seized it, and responsive to my strike leapt clear of
the flags, and we fought it out in the open. He weighed just a
pound and a half.

Not quite in the same class of experience, but one which
gave me great satisfaction, was an occurrence on the Itchen one
July not long since. It was dark and the blue-winged olives were
coming down in sufficient, yet not excessive, quantity. The
rising fish, however, were disappointingly few. But watching
carefully and keeping very low, for the moon was bright and
more behind me than I like, I made out rings emerging from
three little bays above me. I dare not stand up to see where the
trout was rising, and I cast my Orange Quill across country into
the first bay, a tiny one, very much at a venture, and probably
with no more than a foot or two of gut on the water. I struck
as the ring emerged and found myself fast in a burly fish which
took some minutes to master and eventually brought down the
scale at two pounds four ounces. Tying on a new fly to replace
my beslimed and bedraggled Orange Quill, I tackled the second
little bay. Again I laid my line across country over a mass of
tanglesome vegetation; again I struck at the emerging ring and
again was fast. This trout proved to be two pounds one ounce.
Washing the fly and drying it with amadou and re-oiling it, I
cast across country over much the same type of vegetation into
a third bay, and for the third successive time I had a two
pounder which took out of sight at the first cast.

'Shots' I called them at the head of this paper. Flukes, no
doubt justly, my readers will say, but then, I am,

A. Fluker
(*Side-Lines, Side-Lights and Reflections*)

A true tale

Skues fished from time to time with his younger brother, Charles,
with whom he had a close relationship, and they took fishing holidays
together. This is an account of an extraordinary incident which befell
his brother when they were fishing a river in Bavaria.

IN THE YEAR 1901, my brother and I were fishing a Bavarian
river, which was very heavily weeded, and it contained a large

131

stock of trout. Across the middle of the length, which was owned or rented by the Kur Hotel where we were staying, there was a wooden bridge, and against the left bank, just upstream of this wooden bridge, was a dense mass of lily pad, at one shoulder of which a trout rose persistently.

On the first day that we crossed the bridge, my brother cast a fly to this fish, which promptly took it and dived into the bed of lily pads and smashed him. The same thing occurred on the second day, on the third day and on the fourth, a different pattern of fly on each occasion, most of them dressed by me. On the fifth day my brother said, 'I will get that (qualified) fish out.' So he broke off the fine point of his cast, tied on a large Sedge fly and popped it over the fish. The fish again took it without hesitation and plunged into the lily pads. My brother pretty nearly doubled up his rather powerful rod in hauling at the fish. At last something gave way, and with a cursory remark my brother cast out his line on the water to clear it. We then observed that the fly end of the line struck the water with a splash as if something solid were attached to it. He hauled it in to look at it, and there was the right side of the upper jaw of the trout, torn away, and fixed in it not only the fly that my brother had cast to him that morning, but every one of the other four flies that he had lost on the four previous days.
(*Side-Lines, Side-Lights and Reflections*)

Two evening rises

Skues would at times brave the most appalling weather, and this is an account of an evening with such heavy rain that most of us would have headed straight home for shelter and warmth. It is also an interesting example of Skues's knowledge of English literature to which he often refers in his writings.

I HAD NOT been long by the waterside that Saturday evening in the beginning of August when I had occasion to recall the plight of Childe Roland in Browning's great poem. There had been, it is true, no 'hoary beggar with malicious eye' who had misled me, but I had been put across stream by a kindly boatman and I was just as much committed to the water meadows as Childe Roland to the grey plain. For hardly had I greased my line and attached the soaked cast when heavy drops of rain bade me turn round and look skyward to the point from which the wind came. When I had started a quarter of an hour or twenty minutes earlier, I had recognized that the S.W. wind showed no symptoms of dropping with the dipping sun, and I had gone out rather for the pleasure of being in the water meadows than with any expectation of doing much in the way of fishing unless I could find a fish or two rising in a short sheltered length. And now here I was between two branches of the river with no house, nor hut, nor boat nor trees capable of giving me shelter within half a mile, and the sky gone a sudden lowering iron blue.

Fortunately at the last moment I had decided to take my mackintosh with me, and at once I donned it. Not a moment too soon, for, as G.K. Chesterton hath it in *Wine, Woman and Song*, 'the cataract of the cliff of heaven fell blinding off the brink', and there was nothing for it but to turn up the collar of one's mackintosh, turn down the edge of one's hat over it and wait till the storm rolled by. It was then about 7.30 p.m., and from that moment until about 9.05 p.m., I stood in my waders with my back to the wind, with the rain in bucketsfull with alternating storms of hail beating on me until my mackintosh was penetrated, and I felt a cold trickle down my spine. Then, somewhat unexpectedly, the sky cleared a little and the rain let up.

I looked along the main river to see whether by any chance a stray trout were rising to any fly beaten down upon the water by the storm. There was not a sign, and I turned and crossed the drenched meadow to the side stream. Generally it is haunted by dabchicks, moorhens and coots – all of them now out with their young – and when I saw a ring under the far bank a little way up I suspected one or other of these pests or a water vole. But as I approached the ring was repeated and it indicated a decent fish. I had still attached to my cast a small home-made pale watery dun tied to fish spent which had accounted during the afternoon for a two and three quarter pound trout. It was late for such a fly, and the size of the ring rather suggested that the fish might be taking blue-winged olive. But I put it over the fish. He was, however, a cruiser, and rose a foot or so higher up, but presently he began to drop back, and I got it to him right, for he took it an inch or two from where it fell and I pulled in. It was lucky for me that the weeds had not long been cut, for the line was torn off my reel in a mad rush, and in a moment a great fish leapt five and twenty yards away and fell back with a noise like a dog being thrown into the water, and the line went slack. I was not certain, however, that he was off, and I reeled in rapidly – to find that he had got down below me and was racing for an obstacle which I could not get by. Only heroic measures could save him, so, racing down to get level with him, I put on all the side strain I dare with my rod tip almost in the meadow grasses, and succeeded in turning him and bringing him under my own bank. A premature offer of the net sent him off again at once, but fortunately up stream until he had reached the place where he was hooked. He was now beginning to tire, and presently I got him under my rod tip just off the bank, where he started lashing himself into exhaustion. When, after another run, and a second bout of lashing he was quite done, the net slid under him and drew him ashore to pull down the spring balance at three pounds four ounces. It was a strange sequel to the evening I have described, and made up for the day a brace of six pounds weight.

The wind had now dropped almost to nothing and I moved up stream in search of a companion fish, and presently saw a rise under my own bank in deep water. A creaming sort of rise indicating spinner. I offered my Spent Pale Watery with no result, and then tied on an Orange Quill on a No.14 hook. It was taken at the first offer, but the fish, which being one pound ten ounces I should, had he been first comer, have killed was spared and went back to grow bigger.

Then the sky closed in again and the rain descended in torrents. So, feeling that there was no chance of its ceasing before it was too dark to see the fly, I reeled up and waded in, grateful for the fresh proof that whatever the evening might seem there is no certainty that it may not provide you with an evening rise, or even two. (*Side-Lines, Side-Lights and Reflections*)

A fair catch

Victorian anglers were constantly concerned with the ethics of their fishing. Here, Skues tosses in a couple of posers for them to reflect upon.

SOMEWHERE IN THE later eighties of last century I was fishing the Itchen with an 11-foot split cane – a Hardy called the Test rod – on a September afternoon, and was walking down the left bank of the Hog-side stream to get the benefit of the crosswind at the next bend, when a trout rose directly below me, a longish cast downstream. Without waiting to change my fly, I made a cast which pitched it 5 or 6 feet above him and let it drift down to him. Somewhat to my surprise, he took the fly – but I tightened and had him on. He turned at once and raced downstream, with me in pursuit travelling as fast I could consistently with winding in rapidly and shortening the line between the fish and my ring. Before I reached the bend I had caught up with him and had him on a short line straight under the arch of my rod and quite close to the bank, when, to my disgust, my rod straightened as the fish kicked off.

But in doing so he lost his balance and for a fraction of a second wallowed belly upwards within reach, then I thrust the net under him and whipped him out on to the bank before he could recover. He was a nice fish somewhere about one and three quarter pound. I had knocked him on the head before I had time to consider the question: ought I to have put him back? – a question that has often recurred to me when I have recalled the incident. I felt, however, that I had risen the fish fairly, had hooked him fairly and had played him to a spot within reach of my rod, as was proved by my having netted him while off his balance; the only difference between his position and what it would have been if he had not kicked free was that the hook was no longer in his jaw. What is the verdict?

On another occasion, many years later, on the main stream of Itchen, during a hatch of black gnats, I had mounted a Black Gnat dressed on two short shanked hooks tied to gut like the late E.M. Tod's Greenwell's Glory double. With it I cast several times to trout which rose upstream of me to something tiny. Presently, when withdrawing my line to cast again, I became aware of a stout resistance. Supposing that the trout had taken my double deep, I played him downstream some way and eventually netted him out, when I discovered that the fly in his mouth was not my Black Gnat but a Red Spinner at the taper end of a rather coarse piece of gut, which in turn was hooked on to a short piece of casting line, obviously broken off either in the strike or in subsequent playing – and this piece had jammed between the two hooks of my double Black Gnat. That trout, relieved of his attachment, went free. Again – what is the verdict? (*Itchen Memories*)

Whose trout?

Skues explains how his favourite Leonard rod became known as W.B.R. or the World's Best Rod. He goes on to recount how his friend, sharing his rod, lost a big fish and contemplates whether he took it the following week.

I HAVE ALREADY expressed my views on the growing tendency in the little syndicate of four members that fished the stretch of Itchen of which I write to restrict the admission of guests to fish the water, and ultimately, in the middle thirties, much to my disgust, the only way in which it was possible to entertain a friend on it was to invite him to share one's rod. I had, and thank goodness still have, a friend (C.L.C.) to whom this restriction was not wholly a penance, because he was a devout admirer of my rod – a lovely little 9ft 5oz Leonard, dating back to 1905, which he styled W.B.R., which, being interpreted, means World's Best Rod, and so it fell to him one Saturday in June to motor over from a neighbouring valley and a village which had sheltered Izaak Walton in his old age, and to meet me on the middle of our two mile stretch. I had entered the meadows from the bottom of the length and had been detained for a while at a bend known as Mac's Corner, where the trout had the exasperating habit of proving nearly, but *very* seldom quite, 3lb – and on the occasion in question each of the brace I extracted from that curve ran true to form – 2lb 15oz.

However, that was good enough to reconcile me, when I met my friend on the middle of the stretch about eleven o'clock, to surrendering my W.B.R. to him, with the cast and the midget nymph which had done the trick with the brace – and I soon had the satisfaction of seeing my friend leading by the nose to my ready landing net a quite pleasant two pounder. Then I was able to tell him that a few yards further upstream at a bend there was suspected to be a quite impossible three pounder; and not long after I was privileged to see the W.B.R.'s top go up and the W.B.R. make the curve of beauty and to hear my friend exclaim, 'Got him!' It was some minutes before he got a glimpse of his fish and exclaimed, 'By George, I believe he's a four pounder!' It was some minutes more before he could turn the trout and persuade him to head downstream. All, however, seemed to be going well till the trout was brought close under our bank, when he took a scare and tore the line off the shrieking reel and, with a wrench under the far bank, kicked free.

Two or three weeks later I was on the river about a hundred yards below the scene of the tragedy narrated, when, near the top of a straight run of about 300 yards of river, I saw under the far bank (the left) a small raft of cut weed collected by some underwater obstruction. Watching the spot as a likely one, I presently observed the surface broken by a tiny swirl which I had no difficulty in attributing to the absorption of a nymph. Taking the hint, I dropped my nymph with a 16 Pennell sneck in it an inch or two below the raft of cut weed and had the immediate satisfaction of seeing the floating gut drawn under as by some adhesion and, on raising the tip of the W.B.R., finding that I was into something solid.

My usual experience with trout hooked under that far bank (and I had had them up to and just over 3lb) was that they could generally be persuaded to cross over and come under my bank and be played and killed there. But this fish was not having any. Nothing I could do would bring him across, and for the entire 300 yards to Mac's Corner, though he came downstream, he bored stubbornly under the left bank. At Mac's Corner, however, there is a right angled turn of the river to the east with the push of the current across to the right bank, and here, with the aid of that push, I succeeded at length in bringing that stubborn trout under my bank. But he turned upstream immediately and forced his way, still under my bank, for a hundred yards or more before I could again turn him and lead him foot by foot to a little bare patch at the top of Mac's Corner, when for the first time I got a view of his proportions. From that point I resolved that the battle *must* be finished there. But again and again, as I led him towards the waiting net, he sheered off, still keeping his balance. But at last, at the umpteenth shot, I had the net under him and drew him ashore.

Was he, could he be a four pounder? It was years since one had been taken on that stretch. The priest having performed his office, I fixed the hook of my spring balance into the trout's jaw, and was delighted to see it pull down to 4lb 3 or 4oz. But, alas, it thought better of it and reverted to 3lb 14oz, where it stayed. Still, it was the biggest trout I had ever had from the Itchen in over fifty years, though I had two or three times seen and hooked bigger. But the regretful reflection assailed me,

'Was it my friend's lost fish?' Hooked a short stretch below the spot where C.L.C.'s loss had occurred, it was unlikely that another fish of that size would have been so near. (*Itchen Memories*)

CHAPTER 11

Skues the Tactician

Skues fly fished for about 62 years on a variety of rivers and streams, and must have encountered virtually every condition of water, weather and terrain, and employed every strategy to ensnare trout. A number of the tactics he used were original, but he was always open to the advice of others. Any modern-day angler taking up and practising the hints given in the following pages will find himself a better fisherman with more trout in his bag at the end of the day.

Of courage and the jeopardising of tuppence ha'penny

My father used to say that you could buy a bread loaf for 1d before the First World War, and I found this difficult to believe. Here, we have Skues telling us that in those days you could purchase a fly for the modern day equivalent of 1p. Nowadays, they cost us at least 50 times as much, but there again, no doubt, the price of the rest of our fishing equipment has risen accordingly. Therefore, Skues's advice that we should not be put off tackling a difficult fish by the thought of losing a few flies is just as applicable today as it was then.

> THAT, MY FRIENDS, is almost the extreme price of a trout fly. Some are less. Yet how often shall you see an angler whose equipment for the taking of trout has run into pounds, and

whose railway fare and reckoning at his inn are substantial items of expenditure upon the same object, throw away most sporting occasions for the attainment of his end because, forsooth, he is sure to be hung up or weeded or smashed or something equally delightful – and bang would go tuppence ha'penny. I have no patience with this sort of thing. The more hopeless the prospect of getting out a trout from an impossible place, the more determined I am to try for him. In May 1909, just before the May fly began, I was by the riverside when I heard a loud smacking sound, and, peering through a willow bush, I saw a fine trout cruising on an eddy and sucking down flies with hearty enjoyment. If I cast over him from behind the bush, I should have to play him on a six-ounce rod with xxx gut between a thorn bush which I could touch with my right hand and a willow I could touch with my left. There were snags above and snags below. Did I hesitate? Only long enough to tie on a new Crosbie Alder, then long enough for him to reach the top of his beat, and then I dropped the fly behind him just before he turned. He was the satisfactory side of four pounds, and I got his successor next day out of the same place – three pounds six ounces. A beautiful brace! Luck! Of course it was luck, but I shouldn't have had it if I hadn't taken risks.

There was a Kennet trout under a willow in May fly time. A piled snag in the stream just below the droop of the willow made it impossible to get a fly over him by casting above the willow and floating down. There was just one possible way – to make a slanting downward cut which might bring the fly down between branches in a sort of dip in the tree, and drop it on the fish's nose. I left two flies in the tree, but I did the trick and got the fish. He was only two pounds six ounces, but I thought he was bigger. Still—

Then there was the fish which lay just above a hatch hole through which water ran into the meadows. The inevitable thing for him to do when hooked was to bolt down the hatch hole. But somehow he didn't, and I got him. There was a pound-and-a-half trout taking tiny pale duns on the edge of a small pile of weeds collected against a broken bough of a tree, into which he was sure to bolt when hooked. But somehow he didn't, and he was steered to the landing net with a No.17 dun on gossamer gut attached to his nose. Then there was that trout which I got over a barbed wire crossing the stream eight or ten yards away.

There are countless such instances, but there is one thing that may safely be deposed to, and that is, that there is no place so desperate that, with luck and management, you may not get a well-hooked trout out of it. (*Minor Tactics of the Chalk Stream*)

Lying low

As Skues says, most of us are familiar with the strategy of keeping out of sight of our quarry when casting, but not so many of us realise that if we continue to do so after we have hooked him, it makes it much easier to bring him to the net.

'Brer Fox he des' lay low and say nuffin'.' Very wise of Brer Fox. It is a commonplace among fly fishermen (though better observed in precept than in practice) to lie low when casting to a trout in position, but it is less known among them that there are frequently advantages in continuing the procedure after the trout is hooked and until he is in the net.

Let me illustrate the point by an example. One bright July day I got down on my face and wriggled serpentwise behind a screen of flags close to the edge of a bright, gravelly shallow just below a wooden carrier which conveyed another stream over that which I was fishing. It is pretty safe to say that a strong fish that got up under the carrier and into the deep, weeded pool on the far side would take more than a little dislodging. There were several nice fish out on the shallow, and though no duns were yet showing in air or on water the fish had clearly got going, for they were active in motion though not breaking the surface. Peering between the flags, I delivered a well-soaked Tup's Indispensable with a horizontal flick above the best of the nearer fish, and at the third or fourth offer he turned to it and was fast. He seemed utterly puzzled. The rod was a light one, and I did not hold him hard. He seemed only conscious of something unpleasant in his jaw. He shook his head several times and moved about uneasily. Still I kept low and out of sight.

Then, failing to dislodge the barb, he began to get a bit alarmed, and made a bee-line for a bit of rough, broken camp-sheathing on the far side. In doing so he was travelling at an angle of about 45 degrees with the stream, so that at the critical moment I had little difficulty in turning his head downstream and away from the point of danger. I did not take him far, however, but eased again. He seemed unable to make out what was the matter with him, and suffered himself to be led by easy stages and the avoidance of any serious pressure into the vicinity of the screen of flags, and into a gap in them where the landing net was in readiness to receive his one pound seven ounces. The other fish on the shallow seemed quite undisturbed, and without changing my position I realized another brace in the next half hour, and not one of the leash made a bolt for the shelter of the carrier or attempted to weed. (*The Way of a Trout with a Fly*)

The cross country cast

Here, Skues returns to the idea that too many anglers are deterred from making difficult casts by the fear of losing their flies or leaders. Having read this piece of advice before the beginning of the season, I decided to try it, where appropriate, on both my own River Lea and the Itchen. Apart from being hung up on various occasions, I found it difficult where the herbage was over knee-high continuously along the bank, to gauge with any accuracy the trout's position. However, one should bear in mind that in Skues's day, the meadows were heavily grazed by cattle, and so the bank was cropped to the water's edge.

IF QUESTIONED ON their favourite mode of approaching a trout, it is probable that nineteen out of every twenty chalk stream anglers would plump for the right bank with the rod held over the water. It is doubtless the easiest method. It has various advantages not difficult to enumerate, but it may be gravely doubted whether it is the most effective from the point of view of catching trout.

Apart from states of the wind, it must be apparent that, where the horizontal cast is used, and often where the cast is not strictly horizontal, the left bank has the advantage over the right that the rod and line are less displayed, and far less likely to alarm a wary fish under the angler's own bank than a rod held more or less over the stream; and, naturally, it is only to a fish under the angler's own bank that the cross-country cast is made.

Secondly, there is the advantage that little of the line, possibly not all of the gut, even strikes the water. It is enough if the drag and the recovery occur far enough below the fish not to disturb him; but if the fly be the right pattern the drag is a matter of no consequence, as the cross-country cast comes so lightly, so naturally, and with such concealment of its perils from the trout, that as frequently as not he takes the fly at the first offer.

Of course, the vegetation on the bank may be such as to render it almost impossible to deliver this cast without being hung up, but the angler should not be too ready to assume that this is so. It is wonderful how, with care, a light hand, and a little patience, the line may be recovered, and what risks may be taken with comparative impunity. It is often astonishing to see how anglers who pay largely for their fishing rights, own costly rods, reels and lines, and make long journeys to their fishing, will decline to tackle trout in difficult positions because it involves the possible loss of a cast or a fly, with the odds long in favour of the loss being no more than a fly, and perhaps a point. I am ever for the adventure. The certain smash does not always come off.

But after the meadows are cut, and when the sedges are low, it is often excellent sport to beat slowly up on either bank, left or right, keeping in either case well inland – especially so on the right bank – and flicking a grass moth or a small sedge dry into every little eddy and bay, and on to every likely spot under the bank, with never more than three feet – or four feet at the outside – of gut on the water (often not more than eighteen inches or a foot). Of course, a rod which will cast a short line accurately is indispensable. The fly lights like thistledown. On such days, if you work orthodoxly up your right bank, casting a longish line upstream, and covering the water with it, you shall not hook one fish for three which you shall take with the cross-country cast. Then, to recover it, you must either draw it slowly over the edge where the danger lies, or you must flick the line up so as to belly vertically away from you, and flick the gut and fly cleanly off the water or the herbage. And if occasionally one is hung up, what does it matter? If it be of service, the angler is not denied such relief as the golfer freely avails himself of when the deadly bunker has him for its own. (*Minor Tactics of the Chalk Stream*)

Picking it off – a very minor tactic

This is a different manoeuvre from the switch cast though it has affinities with it. This tactic is more concerned with placing less strain on the rod. Skues taught it to his friend, Dr. Barton, the first time he fished with him in 1920. Barton was fishing with a new 9.6 Leonard rod which Skues said he would break the heart of by his violent casting, and so he showed him this way of recovering the line from the water.

IT IS A *very* minor one.

If it had occurred to me as having any novelty in it, I should no doubt have given it a corner in a former volume dedicated to my friend the Dry-Fly Purist. But in sooth, though I had practised the device for years, it was not until the summer of 1910, after the book was on the market, that anyone ever noticed it. Since then, from time to time, men with whom I have been fishing have expressed their surprise that a plan so simple and so efficacious never occurred to them, and it therefore struck me that it might be worth while present it for what it is worth to the community of fishers with the fly. I do so with the full expectation of being told that there is no novelty in it, and that it has been practised for years. I can only say that I evolved it myself, and I never saw anyone use the plan before I did.

I put down its evolution to Mr. Walter D. Coggeshall, known to members of the Flyfishers' Club as the Member for America, and a magician in dressing casting lines.

In 1904 he gave me a priceless casting line, with a curse to follow me to the grave and blight future generations of my name, if any, if I dared to use vegetable or mineral oil or animal fat to make the line float. Having, therefore, pity upon future generations, I did not use vegetable or mineral oil or animal fat upon the line. Having also pity on my ten-foot six-ounce Leonard, I desired to save it as much as possible from the strain of picking up and lifting a heavy Halford line, partially sunk, from the surface of the water.

I accordingly sought for some method of getting the line into the air without dragging it, fly and all (especially May fly and all) through the water, and the obvious thing was to adapt a part of the switch or roll cast. I accordingly developed almost automatically the following method:

Assume that you are standing beside a stream running from your left to your right, that you have laid your cast across, and that you desire to pick it up for a new cast. You move your rod point briskly out to the right and up and round in a rapid curve to the left. This picks up the weightiest part of the line and lifts it, bellying in a corkscrew shape, into the air with an absolute minimum of strain on the rod. If the stream be running in the other direction, the loop at the beginning of the cast may be simply reversed, but this is really hardly necessary if the pace of the stream be moderate.

The method is difficult to describe clearly, but it is as easy as possible to pick up, even for an inexperienced caster. (*The Way of a Trout with a Fly*)

Side strain

Here is Skues at his best. Firstly, he goes to an enormous amount of trouble to reach his fish from a bank no one else has bothered to try. Secondly, his description of how he took the second fish is of a high order, and, finally, he explains to us a valuable tactic and why it works.

ON THE FAR side of the water, about halfway up, there is a deep muddy cross-drain unbridged, and a big willow bush on the upstream side to mark it. Just above it I had made a note of a fairly persistent banker rising. Others had found him aggravating, for he was within a longish cast and would not endure a suspicion of drag. But to go round involved something of a walk, ending in a cautious wade through a midge-ridden marsh. So I was – at least I believe I was – the first to go round to see if he were more amenable to persuasion from below than from across the river. Arrived on the spot, I could not fail to realize that if I hooked my trout he had only to go downstream fast enough and far enough to smash me infallibly. However, such a consideration never prevented me from casting to a likely trout, and I settled down to lay siege to him. This was the third weekend in July, and I had just elaborated a nice dressing of the small darkish olive that one gets at this time of year. It was tied with a body of pale blue heron herl, dyed a greenish olive, bound down with a rib of fine gold wire.

The object of my attentions was rising at intervals alongside the bank, but never twice in quite the same place, and his range brought him at times so near me that I could not have lifted my little nine-footer without scaring him, and it was only when he was at the top of his beat that I dared swing my line to him. Meanwhile I crouched low, as much hidden by a tussock as possible, and keeping the willow as a background for my willow-coloured fishing suit. Presently he was taking a fly close to another tussock not ten yards up above me (about his top limit). It happened to be my fly, and I signified the same in the usual manner by raising my hand. The little rod bowed beautifully in acknowledging the compliment to my fly dressing, and the line began to cut swiftly downstream.

Another second and the trout would have been below me, below the cross-drain, safe perhaps in a bunch of heavy weed, and it would only be a question of how much of my cast I should save. Instinctively I plunged backwards into the marsh, bending my rod almost horizontally across my body as I faced upstream, and bringing to bear on the fish's mouth every ounce of cross-stream strain I could. The effect was instantaneous. He turned and plunged desperately through the weeds upstream, and I let him go, following, however, closely, and keeping a line so short that every attempt to turn down again was met by instantaneous retreat into the marsh with rod held low and side-strain reapplied. In this way I beat him upstream until I had him almost to the place where I expected to find my next fish, and then I decided that there was room below for the normal chalk stream tactics, and I combed my fish down, and I netted him out from below the tussock from which the successful cast had been delivered. I guessed him at two pounds. The keeper's scales said two pounds exactly.

I was down again on the water on September 1, and I met one of the rods. 'By the way,' he said, 'that *qualified* trout of yours above the willow bush at the Moor drain was pegging away as hard as ever as I came down.' 'That is strange,' I said, 'I was under the impression that my family had eaten him, and I certainly knocked him on the head and brought him in. However, I will investigate the phenomenon.'

It was all right. Crouched low behind the same old tussock with same old willow as a background for the same old suit, I watched what might have been the same old trout making the same old circuit over the same old beat. And as he took a natural fly near the top limit, the same old rod delivered a little Red Sedge as if it had dropped off the tussock hard by on to the water. The greedy neb reached for it, and I responded in the same old manner. Off flashed the fish downstream. But I plunged into the marsh with rod hooped and held low. Step for step, incident for incident, the battle pursued the identical course of the just recounted fight of some weeks before, and I netted out at the same old tussock a beautiful male fish which again scaled the exact two pounds.

The point of this narrative is that a soundly hooked trout, howbeit big and powerful, need not be allowed his own way if it be inconvenient for the angler to let him go down; and that, by judicious application of strain in the right direction, he may be persuaded that he is fighting you more successfully by boring upstream at tremendous expense of energy. The time to knock it into his head that he is wrong is when he is in the landing net.

One Sunday afternoon some days later at the Flyfishers' Club I had a conversation with a guest of another member which threw some light upon this episode. The conversation led up to my recounting this episode. Of course, I had realized that I was applying side-strain to bring the fish round, but it was the guest who explained why side-strain was so immediately effective when no strain in any other direction would have availed to stop the fish. 'You see,' he said, 'the trout swims with a lateral action, moving his head from side to side, and if, as he goes downstream, you pull his head round hard sideways, half the time he must be yielding to the strain, and that makes it so hard as to be almost impossible for him to fight against it the other half of the time. So he comes round. If you applied the same amount of strain overhead it would only tend to lift him, and would have nothing like the same effect in stopping or turning him.'

Very simple and obvious when put that way. Of course, a fish forging upstream may be turned in precisely the same way if you keep opposite him or but little below. And no doubt most of us have used the method many a time. But I for one am glad to have been made aware of the cause of its efficiency, and I thank the stranger. (*The Way of a Trout with a Fly*)

Of pocket-picking

This was a strategy which Skues had evolved in the days when he was still experimenting with the wet fly, and it became even more effective when he began to use his imitative nymph patterns. He omits to tell us that once you have hooked your trout in this way, you have to haul it over the top of the weeds!

As SUMMER ADVANCES and the weeds are unusually high, there is to be found in a momentarily neglected fishery a chance of chances to find the trout in most unsuspecting humour for the fly, ofttimes for the dry, but more often for the wet. The celery beds are thrusting themselves, big and bold, out of the water, and the long sword blades of the ranunculus trail along the surface in dense masses at a little distance from the bank, coming closer at intervals and dividing the smooth run under the bank into a series of little pools. The day is perhaps hot and sunny, the wind fallen, the water smooth and glassy. Happy then is the angler of whom the phrenologist can say, in the words of the Bab Balladist, 'unusually large his bump of pocket-pickery', for the picking of these pockets in the weeds is his game.

In many of them there will be a trout, probably not taking surface food, but willing to be tempted if properly approached. If you make up your mind to offer him a dry fly, the probability is that your first offer will be your last. Either he takes it or the disturbance necessarily made in recovering your fly puts him down, but the wet fly is another story. You want your fly to sink on alighting, so it has to be sparsely dressed and well soaked, but it is wonderful what a heavy fall a fly may make without scaring your trout, provided the line falls lightly and does not drag. Indeed, the fall of the fly serves to advertise the fish of its presence, and he often takes it immediately, on its lighting, before there is time for much gut to have gone below the surface film. But assume he does not – you withdraw your fly under water at the bottom of the pocket without making any splash or drag as in lifting a dry fly, and you cast again and again to an undisturbed trout, and if he will have none of your Greenwell's Glory or Tup's Indispensable you may still try him with a floater or small Sedge, a Pink Wickham, a Red Quill or whatever you may fancy. But it is surprising how confidingly a trout lying in such a position will come to the wet fly with just enough movement of the surface of the water to give the hint that bids you fasten. (*The Way of a Trout with a Fly*)

Of baby plates and marrow spoons

Skues records in humorous fashion his discovery of the marrow spoon and baby plate. When one considers that when Halford and Marryat did their research for *Floating Flies and How to Dress Them* and following books, they had to go through the nauseous procedure of opening the trout's stomachs for their autopsies, one has to credit this as one of Skues's major achievements. It also greatly facilitated his own research into the nymph.

THE DISCOVERY OF the theory of gravity by Newton by means of the fall of an apple upon his pate is a matter of history familiar to the world at large. No doubt most, if not all, great discoveries come about more or less by accident. The discoveries, however, which I am about to narrate came about in this way, and are by no means a matter of gravity in the Newtonian sense at any rate – though their importance will be so evident to the serious flyfisher that their intrinsic gravity can be no matter of doubt.

Years ago, it befell that I found on the dressing table of my room at a fishing inn one of those solid china plates with high turned-in rims which are built for children to prevent them from spooning over their food on to the table and their pinafores, and as I used that dressing table for fly dressing as well as for personal dressing, it struck me that it might be a good tip to utilize the baby plate to prevent hooks, wax, pliers, feathers and the small impedimentia of the fly dressers' art from being swept on to the floor. It proved quite useful for the purpose, but owing to the coloured floral ornamentation with which it was decorated I often found difficulty in picking up loose hooks or particles of gold wire or tinsel. But, being a patient animal, I put up with the nuisance for two or three years until the inn changed hands, and even then I sought to buy the baby plate. Mine host's wife, however, said 'No'. It had family associations and I could not have it. So I hunted several stores and eventually found that Harrods, though they had not any in stock, were prepared to get me a couple: and then, recalling my difficulties from the floral decoration on the baby plate which was refused me, I bespoke them white – and in due course they arrived, and I took one (hereinafter referred to as 'the B.P.') down to my inn, to find that the new proprietor, finding the old B.P. in my regular room (left behind by the late hostess in despite of her professions) had assumed it was mine. However, I now had my own white B.P. and I gently but firmly discarded the decorated one and used the new white one for some years for my trout fly dressing purpose, and very useful I found it. This, however, is only by the way, and on the way.

It was some time later that I found on my home breakfast table some huge marrow bones with a long marrow spoon (hereinafter referred to as M.S.) with two ends, one containing a long bowl of about five eighths of an inch wide and the other an equally long bowl of about three eighths of an inch in width. There is no obvious connection between marrow spoons and trout, but my mind, to the lasting regrets of my women kind, runs very much on trout, and it struck me immediately, 'Here is the ideal means of extracting the contents of a trout's stomach without the nasty mess of an autopsy.'

That weekend when I sought my river, the M.S. went missing from my family plate basket and accompanied me to the river side. It was in the month of June in the year of disgrace 1921, and for two previous weekends the trout had during the evening rise, though apparently feeding greedily, entirely beaten me. I was accompanied by the owner of the celebrated Green Cat (hereinafter called McC.) and on the Friday evening the same phenomenon repeated itself. On the Saturday evening it seemed to be repeating itself once more. McC. after failing almost to the last moment to attract a trout, caught an under-sized one on an exceptionally pale Tup's Indispensable. Despite the heinous character of the act, we, recognizing that desperate cases require desperate remedies did not restore that three quarter pounder to his element, but took him back to the inn to be interviewed by M.S. before B.P.

The thin end of the M.S. wetted and introduced through the mouth of the deceased into his crop and turned round, produced a mass of semi-digested insect food which, on being floated in water in the B.P. and disintegrated by stirring, showed in the former category a number of recognizable insects and in the latter a number of specimens, some in the larval or nymphal stage and some in the imago stage, of an ephemerid then unknown to trout fishers, but since identified as the blue-winged pale watery dun and later on distinguished by being represented among the novel patterns described in *Sunshine and the Dry Fly*. The insect when viewed by daylight among others stood boldly out against the china white of the B.P., a long thin insect of a creamy white with brownish markings near the tail, and in the imago stage with a very dark blue wing, and I tied three representations (with creamy lambs' wool spun on pale orange silk and a dark blue hen hackle) which in the evening following, being tried in desperation at the last moment of a similar exasperating evening rise, McC., myself and a third rod to whom I had given one of the three, took, each time at the first cast in the dying light, trout of three pounds two ounces, two pounds six ounces and two pounds nine ounces. Similar dressings have done yeoman's service later in re-appearances of the elusive insect in question.

In view of the eminent service of the M.S. on that occasion I pass by with comparative equanimity the domestic broil which shortly afterwards led to its ignominious return to the family plate basket. I draw you on to the Jewellery Department of the Army and Navy Stores, in which appropriately enough, as all will agree, this priceless if novel weapon of the modern angler is to be obtained for the modest price of four shillings and sixpence. Thither, as soon as I had recovered my health and spirits I repaired. I parted with my four shillings and sixpence, and I became and still am the proud possessor of that indispens-able, but hitherto unknown, servant of the modern scientific angler, a M.S.

By its aid the contents of the crops of numerous trout have been floated over the milk-white floor of my B.P., the flies on which they have been feeding have been identified, and several of the nymphs so successfully represented as to lead to the premature demise of yet other trouts. And when my time comes to pass over the border and my will comes to be read, it will be found that on my tombstone is to be engraved the Inscription:

'To the memory of I.V., discoverer of the M.S. and B.P.'
INTEGER VITAE

(*Side-Lines, Side-Lights and Reflections*)

Amadou

Skues, as he makes clear here, did not discover the use of amadou to dry flies, but he certainly popularised it. Whilst the invention of better floatants has come on apace, no better way of drying a fly has been found.

WHAT IS AMADOU? Amadou is a fungoid growth which is about to settle upon the dry-fly angler. Once it settles upon him it will stick. He will be unable to free himself. Indeed, he will not want to. Ask your chemist for it. Ask your dentist.

Dentists use it for drying the hollows in teeth. Dry-fly men who know what is good for them use it for drying flies. Salmon anglers are going to find it first-rate for the purpose of drying and preserving their salmon flies. Wet and mangled May flies washed and then dried with it resume their pristine youth and beauty. Amadou quadruples the life of an ordinary May fly.

Has amadou any drawback?

Yes – one!

Amadou absorbs petroleum as readily as water. Therefore, when a fly is dried with amadou it needs to be re-paraffined.

Thus the price of petroleum is going up too.

What great events from little causes spring!

The little cause that put me on to amadou was a six-foot Berkshire parson – broad in proportion. Bless the little cause. (*The Way of a Trout with a Fly*)

CHAPTER 12

Skues the Observer

IN LOOKING BACK over the half century and more of my fly fishing experiences, it has struck me, on closer examination, that, paradoxically, such successes as I have had have been mainly drawn not from my advantages, but from my disadvantages. To begin with, at the age of nine I underwent an operation for eye trouble, which resulted in my having to rely throughout my career on my right eye only, making it do the work of two eyes. As a consequence I have had to struggle in my casting for a degree of accuracy which I might never have attempted had I been blessed with the usual complement of two eyes. And not only accuracy of casting, but also observation. (*Flyfishers' Journal*, Spring 1936)

Although Skues must have had some sight in his left eye, he obviously had good vision only in his right eye, and he wore a monocle in that one later in life. Even so, with one eye he saw more than most of us do with two. However, having made his observations, it was the originality of his conclusions which placed him above ordinary fishing mortals.

Translucency

The subject of translucency in flies has fascinated fly fishers from the days of Charles Cotton, who said in reference to body dubbing, 'Step to the door and hold it up betwixt your eye and the sun, and it will appear a shining red; let me tell you, never a man in England can discern the true colour of a dubbing any way but that.' Skues also had the benefit of reading the works of Mottram and Dunne, but here, in his book published in 1932, the subject has been treated more clearly and with more commonsense than ever before.

I AM INCLINED to think that the argument in favour of translucency or transparency of trout flies has been worked pretty nigh to death. It is assumed for the purpose of the argument that a trout rising to the fly always has the fly between itself and the light – and that therefore the artificial fly always looks black and opaque in strong contrast with the natural fly which looks transparent or translucent. If this thing were as universally sound as its advocates would have us believe, trout would rarely be caught with the artificial fly – and we know well that is not the case. That there is something in the theory cannot in honesty be denied. But it is far from universally true. One constantly finds a trout taking a fly which has covered him several times in vain. Why? Probably because he sees it on the fatal occasion at a different angle with the light upon it in such a way as to give it the appearance of a natural fly. Perhaps the fly has been passing all the time on his right side between him and the sun. It is there black and opaque and did not suggest a natural fly. But let it pass down on the opposite or left side and the sun illumines it so that it suggests by reflection the translucency which it has not in nature.

In truth there are more ways in which the fly can reach him looking to him like a natural fly than otherwise. In 1911, when looking up at flies on the surface of Dr. Ward's pond at Ipswich, from the underground glass fronted chamber in the side, I was greatly impressed by the extraordinary clearness of detail in which one saw artificial flies floating in the window of surface vision. There was then no effect of blurring or opacity. No doubt this was because the outlook through 'the window' was not into the eye of the sun.

Putting it broadly, I should say that a floating fly delivered to trout will quite as often in a day's fishing be seen in its colours as resembling a natural fly as it will be seen black and opaque against the light. In the case of a wet fly, the odds in favour of the trout seeing it as he is meant to see it are much longer. It will seldom be between his eye and the source of light. So that if the pattern be well devised to give by reflection the appearance or suggestion of translucency, it will be good enough for most practical purposes. Many dubbings and some herls suggest translucency admirably. So does the shiny surface of peacock's quill, so like the bodies of many nymphs.

The argument in favour of translucency is in truth a counsel of almost unobtainable perfection. If it were obtainable it would, I agree, be desirable, but in practice it is not obtained very often. And yet trout continue to be killed. I am not forgetting Mr. J.W. Dunne's ingenious invention for obtaining translucency – but I cannot reconcile myself to his methods of wing suggestion, and such success as I have had with flies with bodies of artificial silk tied over white enamelled hook shanks has been obtained by the use of ordinary starling wings or hen blackbird wings and silk of such colours as appeared to me to reproduce the appearance of the natural insect without paying regard to the elaborate combinations and blendings formulated in *Sunshine and the Dry Fly.* (*Side-Lines, Side-Lights and Reflections*)

The fumbling of it

Here is Skues, years before his time, making out a case for imitating the fly at its moment of eclosion; in other words, what we today would describe as an emerger.

THE UP-WINGED dun when it is once hatched out, is such a lovely, delicate, clean-cut little creature that one is apt to forget that at the moment of eclosion (which we erroneously designate 'hatching') when it emerges from the envelope which clads its nymphal form, it passes through a stage of untidy struggle not distantly resembling that which a golfer or a footballer displays in extricating himself from a tight fitting pullover or sweater or jersey. Yet from the fly fisher's point of view this is a very important stage, for it is at this that the trout, when not confining himself to duns on the surface – and he seldom confines himself strictly and exclusively to these – must be constantly seeing and absorbing the insect. Sometimes, indeed frequently, the operation of emergence is performed with neatness and despatch. Often, however, it is an awkward and fumbling occasion, affording the fish a much longer and better chance than is given by the dun which hatches neatly and quickly. At this stage the dun is something like the earth in an early stage of its creation, 'without form' if not 'void'.

The fact that the duns are accepted by the trout at this stage of fumbling may be an explanation of the acceptance by trout of artificial flies which bear little enough resemblance to the emerged subimago. It has been suggested that the Hare's Ear (with or without gold rib) may be taken for the medium Spring olive dun at this stage. It may also be that the hackled pattern, dressed with soft henny fibres closing on the body, may afford no bad suggestion of a subimago struggling, as it often does, with crumpled wing to emerge from its envelope.

Many have found difficulty in realizing why the lightly dressed Yorkshire and North Country patterns hackled with soft hackles are accepted. Yet the contents of a trout's stomach floated in water in a white saucer will show the wings of duns reduced to mere dark shreds, which are strikingly like thin clotted strands of soft hackle. This likeness is not quoted as being directly in point, but as an example of a likeness where no likeness is obviously to be suspected.

Nothing in nature occurs without good reason, and it may well be believed that the taking of nymphs at the fumbling stage of the hatch affords the true explanation for the taking of otherwise unnatural-looking soft hackled flies. It would be interesting to know whether in the early days of fly dressing any deliberate effort were made to represent the natural fly at this stage of partial emergence, or whether such resemblances as have been attained are due to fluke. It is the fact that nowhere in any angling book does one find a direct suggestion that the natural fly should be imitated at this stage – but that is not conclusive – for there can be little doubt that the art of fly dressing has passed through many stages of decadence into the stereotyped, and of renaissance that the origins of its theory may well have been forgotten and buried. (*Side-Lines, Side-Lights and Reflections*)

The evening mist

Skues was never happier than when he was questioning accepted shib-
boleths of fly fishing, in this case the oft-held belief that when the
evening mist comes down it is a waste of time to continue fishing.

THEN I NEVER suspected the dogma that an evening mist puts
the fish down for good, and for years and years I have reeled up
and gone home when the surface began to smoke at night.
Shall I do so again?

On June 16 on the Itchen the blue-winged olive began to
come up in some quantity about eight o'clock, and I expected
to find the fish taking them freely. But the moon was behind
my hand, and I found every fish stopping at once when I began
to cast, and when nine o'clock came the evening rise had
yielded me nothing. Then, creeping round the next bend, I saw
the ominous mist approaching, and I began to despair, as in
duty bound. I was, however, the wrong side of the river for
leaving it to go in, and I had to walk up the bank a mile or so
to reach a bridge. So I moved on to meet the mist. I had not
dismantled my rod, and presently I became aware of a good
trout rising in the middle, and apparently rising quite well,
despite the mist. The size and shape of the ring showed that he
was taking the blue-winged olive. So I gave him my invariable
prescription, the large Orange Quill. In vain. But he went on
rising. He did not appear to be taking flies on the surface. So I
took off the Quill, tied on a Pheasant Tail on No.14 hook,
moistened it in my mouth to make it sink and look like a
nymph, and despatched it to my trout. He was my trout all
right, and the keeper put his weight at two pounds two ounces.

Then I remembered that a bit farther up was a place where I
had seen a good trout as I went by in the morning, and I
approached it gingerly. Yes. Just a little farther out in the stream
than I expected a trout was rising busily. He took my nymph
the first time it reached him, and after a battle royal he joined
No.1 in my bag. The two fish were as like in size and make as
two peas, and they weighed two pounds two ounces each. I was
pleased enough at the moment, but when I think of all the
sport I have probably missed in the past by believing the
authorities, instead of finding out for myself about the behaviour of trout in mist, I refrain from good words. (*Side-Lines,
Side-Lights and Reflections*)

Wind and the evening rise

Skues's constant advice to fellow fly fishermen was never to follow what he called accepted authority without testing it out for yourself. When one considers the veritable avalanche of books on fly fishing and the multitude of fishing magazines with their proliferation of flies, invented and re-invented, available today, it is one of the best pieces of advice that any modern day angler can be given. In this case, Skues is querying the oft-repeated maxim that if there is a wind in the evening there will be no rise.

WHEN I THINK of all the wise things which for years and years I have accepted from authorities and acted upon in sheer innocence, I could swear – swear vehemently. The number of times I have gone in of an evening because of the thoroughly well-established fact that there can be no evening rise unless the wind drops!!

For many years, as many as I can remember during my angling life, I have heard it laid down as the one certain thing in the uncertain sport of fly fishing that with a wind there could be no evening rise. Like a fool, I believed it without testing it, and many an afternoon have I waited in anxiety for the drop of the breeze at sunset, and when the drop has not arrived I have unshipped my rod and turned my steps in disappointment home-along.

It was only in 1916 that, accident having kept me on the river awaiting the return of a friend long after sundown on a gusty June evening, I found that the true proposition probably is that there is no rise to a mere spinner-fall on open water on a gusty evening; but if there be a hatch of fly on a windy evening – and there is no obvious reason why a night-hatching fly should not come out on a rough evening, if a day-hatching fly can come out on a rough morning or afternoon – it should be just as possible to get sport as on a gusty morning.

It enrages me to think of all the good evenings' fishing I have missed through believing the pundits. The moral is 'Never believe a thing you are told about fishing until you have proved it, not only once, but over and over again.'

I had been down to look at the water between my arrival at four o'clock and an early dinner, and I had spotted the blue-winged olive – the first of the season, the keeper said – and had caught a brace with an imitation of the nymph, but they were smallish fish and I returned them.

The wind was then blowing briskly from the south, with a faint shade of east in it, and in gusts. Fortunately, its general trend was upstream, and it served the length I meant to fish fairly well, and I needed nothing more powerful than my five-ounce, nine-footer. My friend, who accompanied me, was very depressed at the strength of the wind and its obvious disinclination to drop spent at sunset. But I recalled my experience of the preceding year (repeated two or three times since) with a view to comforting him, and he decided to stay on, though a very doubting Thomas.

We waited on our separate beats, with such patience as we could muster, from seven to half past eight. The wind certainly moderated a little, but it still blew briskly and gustily, shifting a shade more to the east. About half past eight a small hatch of small pale watery olive, with an admixture of July dun and of spinners, including some jenny spinners, came down, and a quiet protected corner enabled me to identify them.

A fish or two began to take quietly, some clearly taking spinners, others nymphs of the pale watery olive, and occasionally the hatched fly. Soon a big splurging rise said plainly 'blue-winged olive', and, knotting on a nymph pattern with which I had been successful last year, I cast to the fish. He came up at length and missed. In the meantime another fish, two or three yards ahead, had risen somewhat in the same way; but I suspected grayling, and sure enough a few moments later an unmistakable forked tail appeared and sent me on to the next fish. This was rising in a corner, and was, I judged, taking small spinner of some kind. He would not have my Blue-Winged Olive nymph, so I tried him in succession with Tup's Indispensable and Jenny Spinner. He came at both and missed. Then he took a blue-winged olive with the unmistakable swirl, and a few minutes later an Orange Quill was offered him, and had hardly lit on the water before he had it. He put up a gorgeous fight, and proved to be a sixteen-inch fish in excellent condition, and to weigh one pound twelve ounces.

I did not take long to find another fish rising similarly, but I must have made some mistake, for he went down. The next fish, however, accepted the first offer and joined his companion in the creel; he was only one pound six ounces. It was then 9.35 p.m. (*Side-Lines, Side-Lights and Reflections*)

When weeds are adrift

For most of us, weeds adrift in the river, especially if they are coming from someone else's water, are an unmitigated nuisance. Skues points out, however, that the situation can be turned to our advantage if we closely observe just what is happening in the water.

IT IS A misfortune of the length of the Itchen on which I spend most of my weekends during the season, that twice a year, once in the first half of May and once towards the end of July, both that length and the fisheries immediately above are subjected for the miller's sake to a weed cutting which leaves the bottom of the river practically bare. The masses of weed which come floating down from above must carry with them enormous quantities of trout food in the shape of shrimps and nymphs or larvae. But it would seem that insects which are content to harbour in the weeds are not so content to remain in the same weeds when they are detached and floating with the stream; and it has been my observation in previous seasons, as in the present one, that they swarm into quiet eddies, where the trout takes heavy toll of them.

This season, after the May weed cutting on my length was over, I had a weekend and one which was rather instructive in this respect. The general direction of the river is north to south, and during the two days in question there was a strong wind blowing across from the west with a slant towards the easterly, or left bank. For some two hours on the first day there were no fish rising and no weeds were coming down, but as noon drew nigh large masses of fresh-cut weed began to float down and soon fish began to feed. There was no very obvious rise of fly and what upwinged duns we saw were seldom taken by the fish. The trout, however, continued to take something freely under the far (the eastern) bank. As the rises, though generally only making tiny dimples, were often of the head and tail kind usually connected with spinners, we were a little puzzled to make out what the fish were taking. The rise, at the point where we were, was almost entirely close under the far bank and my companion argued, with seemingly irrefutable logic, that this proved that it must be floating fly, probably spinners, that the trout were taking, and accordingly we tried Pheasant Tail and Tup's Indispensable for spinners, and various floating duns. In vain! Presently, however, the invitation of a rather large

Dark Olive Nymph seduced a feeding trout into taking it and a marrow spoon introduced into its belly produced a huge mass of dark olive nymphs.

As it happened all the places down the stream where we saw fish rise, were under the far, or eastern, bank and in every case it was where the water was slack that we saw the trout rising. Usually, i.e., in normal conditions of weed and water, the fish rise best in places where the strength of the current sets. But after weed cutting the nymphs obviously shelter themselves from the current in every little sheltered bay and eddy and there the trout seek them and levy toll.

On the following day, a Saturday, there was no weed cutting above and no push of weeds coming down. On this occasion there was no rise of fish to speak of all day, whether in the slack water or the fast, as there were no nymphs seeking refuge in quiet water from the weeds which, adrift no longer, offered them their usual shelter.

The lesson seems to be that while cut weeds are coming down the chance of getting trout is by no means a hopeless one and one should fish a nymph or appropriate pattern into the quiet bays and eddies, preferably across so as not to line one's trout. (*Side-Lines, Side-Lights and Reflections*)

Loch trout fishing with the fly

This I believe to be a remarkable piece of writing. It has all the attributes associated with Skues: lively prose, tongue-in-cheek humour, and, most notably, a ruthless logic applied to the problems of loch fishing of which he had little practical experience. It was written in 1922 and presaged exactly the developments necessary for stillwater fishing to become more of an exact science, instead of the 'chuck it and chance it' method it was in Skues's day. The small army of investigators called for by Skues was eventually forthcoming, headed by R.C. Bridgett, J.R. Harris, C.F. Walker, Brian Clarke and, above all, by John Goddard, the finest British angler/entomologist of the century.

HAVING DONE NEXT to no loch fishing in my life, I naturally feel qualified to instruct those who have had far more experience than I have had how they should set about the business.

It isn't that I have not read anything about the subjects in books. I have. I have probably read all, or nearly all, the books that have been written on the subject in the English language.

But it is not that which qualifies me to write upon the subject. It is not what is in those books. It is what isn't in them that needs to be written about.

You may find in them long strings, often very long strings, of fancy patterns of flies to be used in lochs. You will be told the rods and gear to be used, how to cast, how to hook and play your fish, how to handle your boat, the size of flask to carry, how much whisky to give your boatman or ghillie, but never anywhere do I recall finding a word about the food of the fish or about why he rises to the fly, natural or artificial. You will be told that certain lochs have certain seasons, differing widely perhaps from those of neighbouring or even adjoining lochs; but it has seemed never to have suggested itself to the writers to inquire why this is so, or to endeavour to correlate the phenomenon with the food supply and other conditions of the lochs in question. Has there ever been any attempt to study the entomology of any loch from the point of view of fish food in its relation to fly fishing? If so, I have failed to notice the work. The names of nearly all the artificial flies tied for loch fishing are fancy names – Hecham Pecham, Green Mantle, Claret and Mallard, and so on. Why? Do not the fish rise to natural flies? If so, why not seek to represent them, either in their surface or their underwater phases, or both? It may be that, on many occasions when the time of the take is on, loch trout are hungry enough and indiscreet enough to take anything moving and remotely suggesting a fly. But is that satisfactory to the genuine angler? Does he want to be ready for the occasions when the trout seem uncatchable and will take none of the garish lures offered to them? I suppose there are such occasions. I dare say they are not absolutely infrequent. On such the right fly might mean a bumper basket. In any case it would be more satisfactory to kill your fish with a fair representation of the flies on which they are feeding.

I am at the wrong end of life to begin; but if I were thirty or forty years younger, and if I could tear myself from running water, or if fate had planted me in the neighbourhood of some loch or lochs providing sizable trout, while there were either no trout streams accessible or only streams infested with fingerlings or troutless, I should (assuming that I had sense enough) endeavour to apply to the study of loch trout fishing with the fly the methods which have made chalk stream fishing, with the wet fly or the dry, so fascinating a study.

I might have to begin with the so-called standard patterns, but from each bank or bay on or in which I took fish on every occasion on which fish were rising I should have autopsies to discover the food which was attracting them. There might be a rise in one little bay of a loch and none to right or left. An autopsy would probably show why. It might prove that the shallows or shoaling deeps of that bay were producing a hatch of flies – duns, caddis, gnats or what not. It might show that a group of land insects, ants, for instance, or grass moths, were blown on to the water there and brought the fish on to feed.

In aid of these investigations I would call the muslin net and the mud-scooping bottle – the latter for the bottom, the former for the surface and mid-water.

These investigations would lead to a study of the various forms of insect life produced by my loch and its surroundings and this again to a determined effort to provide the trout with reasonable representations of the food which they were taking.

Then there is another subject well worthy of study, viz., the judgment of depth of water and the presence of shoals and rocks by observation of wind effect on the surface. In the only week of my life which I devoted to loch fishing in Norway my companion and I devoted not a little attention to this subject, and we found that the depth of the water and the nature of the bottom had a definite effect on the appearance of the wind ruffle on the surface, and from indications presented by these surface effects we were able to follow and fish along the edges of shoals where they dipped to the deep with very gratifying effects on the basket. It is a well-known fact that in shallow seas a much shorter and steeper wave gets up than would be produced in deep water by wind of the same force, and, in miniature, the same thing is true of the waters of a lake.

The great painter, Turner, was asked once with what he mixed his colours, and his unexpected reply was 'Brains'! It may be that some loch anglers bring the same solvent to their problems of fly fishing for trout, but so far I have seen lamentably few indications of the fact in the literature which the sport has produced.

Something needs to be done to lift the entire subject from its slovenly empiricism. There is room on the loch for a small army of investigators of the calibre of a G.S. Marryat, a Halford and a Mosely. (*Side-Lines, Side-Lights and Reflections*)

163

CHAPTER 13

Skues the Humorist

In most of the photographs we have of Skues, mainly taken in later life, he looks rather a grim-faced old man, but lurking behind that stern exterior was a lovable, tolerant and generous person with a sense of humour which was both whimsical and imaginative. For instance, one of the members of his fishing syndicate was a King's Counsel who later became a judge. His name was Lilley and Skues always referred to him in his writings as Fleur de Lys! Many of his humorous pieces were based on incidents in his fishing life and on real individuals. However, as his articles appeared in a variety of publications, he found it necessary to protect his friends and acquaintances by using assumed names.

His articles were written under a variety of pen names, and those involving the Novice were signed Integer Vitae. The phrase crops up in Horace's Odes meaning 'the wholeness of life'.

The Carrot fly

One of Skues's most famous creations was the Novice and his Carrot fly. Dr. Barton, in a note scribbled in the margin of his copy of *Side-Lines, Side-Lights and Reflections*, tells us that the Novice was based on an American named George Benson Stewart, by profession a dentist in Harley Street, and a most inventive man who devised the tiny hand vice which Skues used to tie flies on his train journeys, and who also collaborated with him in producing some of his nymph patterns.

This piece was written in 1912 for the *Flyfishers' Journal* under the pen name of Integer Vitae, and was so popular that Skues followed it with further adventures of the Novice, stretching into the terrible war years of 1914–18 and the Battle of the Somme. No doubt the Club members, many of whom had sons at the front, were cheered by his humour.

The paper referred to in the first paragraph is almost certainly *The Field* and its angling editor, Hugh Sheringham.

I BLAME THE editor of the comic column in the sombre grey weekly journal. It was he who, discarding Bull's Indefensible and other standard flies, was found on the banks of the Itchen using a pattern which (as a tribute, I imagine, to its size and weight) was called the Half Stone; and, what is more, he was catching – and losing – trout with it, and, still more reprehensible, big trout at that. This contemptible parody of insect life was not dressed with a body half primrose silk, half mole's fur, according to the Devonshire prescription. The tail end was a pale orange wool and the shoulders Hare's ear. He offered me one, but, strong in the virtue of my purist upbringing, I declined the subaqueous abomination and went on putting down, and occasionally hooking and losing, and still more occasionally landing moderate sized (some of them excessively moderate sized) trout with orthodox patterns affected by the really good.

It was some months later, on another water, where the trout, running big, can hardly be bothered with the small flies of Itchen and Test, that temptation assailed me. Two days of quite unsuccessful tender to the trout of a variety of small floating flies had induced doubts as to how far it was essential on such waters to maintain the pure faith of the dry fly, and in a moment of absent mindedness, when dressing a few patterns with my angling companion, I found myself building a large insect of the Half-Stone type with conscientious variations. For instance, instead of pale orange-yellow wool I used a yellowish-brown-olive seal's fur, merging much more softly into the hare's ear half of the body. You see the vital distinction. Meanwhile my companion, a novice in the art of fly dressing, had allowed his errant fancy to be seduced by two brightly coloured tags of Berlin wool, secured from our landlady's work basket, one a hot orange and the other a pale orange, and ere I was aware he had produced a vegetable trophy something in this wise:

Whisks:	Two strands of green parrot
Tying silk:	Waxed primrose exposed at head and tail
Body:	In three joints, tapered fat. Tail end, the pale yellow wool; middle, hot orange wool; shoulder end, greenish seal's fur
Hackle:	Short cock's hackle, dyed green olive

With characteristic wit I dubbed that abortion 'the Carrot fly'.

'The trout will be asses, old man,' I said, 'if they take that.'

Over what occurred on the following day, I speak with a decent reticence. I took nothing by my sacrifice of scruple in the interests of open minded experiment. But the Novice with his Carrot fly – I draw a veil over the results achieved – several veils would be required, and one of them would need to be nearly two feet long. What asses trout – I had almost written 'men' are – I am driven to wonder why virtue is so often its own and its only reward. (*Side-Lines, Side-Lights and Reflections*)

Equal to standard – the Bread fly

Here again, the basic idea probably stemmed from a real bridge, namely the one over the Itchen in Winchester, where trout lay under it waiting to be fed bread and other titbits by the locals and their children – and still do!

IF YOU WANT invention or progress in any art or industry, it is to the fresh mind of the comparative beginner that you must go for it. Try the novice. The Novice who was guilty of the atrocity known as the Carrot fly has broken out in a new place. Hitherto the community we visited last year has been in the habit of mitigating its leisure by feeding the trout which occupy – I should say occupied – the broad, bare shallow above its handsome stone bridge with bread. Bread that floated was no good, it had to be new and crumbly, so that it rolled into compact little tapered pellets that would sink readily, but not so rapidly as to prevent the trout wolfing them. The trout at this bridge are always – I mean were always – ready to rush for a pellet. Both Novice and I noticed last year that this was so. My reflections took me no farther. The Novice must have brooded; for on the afternoon of our arrival, he asked me to go with him to an oil and colour merchant, and he betrayed a most curious particularity about the colour of the chamois leather, of which, in the end, he bought a ridiculous little piece. Then we went and paid for our week's licence to fish – with artificial fly only.

Next morning, when the chops and the rolls had been discussed, I said, 'Well, what are you for? Shall we fish the main or the tributary today?'

'Oh,' said he, 'I'll leave it to you. I shall not fish today, I'll gillie you.'

'Not fish?' I said. 'Nonsense.'

'Well, to tell the truth, I can't. Fact is, I've got my limit.'

'Got your limit? Why, bless my soul, there's no fly on before nine.'

'Oh, that doesn't matter. These bridge fish will feed at any time.'

'What, you've been worming them?'

'No. I only gave them what they were accustomed to – or rather what they thought they were accustomed to.'

'Bread?'

'No. Chamois leather.'

Then the diabolical ingenuity of this infamous person broke upon me.

'Let me see this pernicious thing,' I said. He showed it me.

It was the perfect image of a pinch of new bread rolled with a tapering point at both ends, with a hook almost entirely concealed.

'Let's see your fish,' I said, and I rang for Mrs. Tibbs.

'Mr. Novice's trout, please,' I said, when our landlady appeared. She returned with a dish bearing six trout, not one of them under sixteen inches and running to two and a half pounds.

'But this is infamous,' I said.

'I suppose,' he replied meekly, 'it would have made a difference if they had all been small.'

I didn't know what to say to that.

'What do you call this damned thing?' I asked.

'I thought of calling it the "Standard Bread Fly", only "Equal to Standard Bread Fly" would be more accurate, and I know that you are a stickler for accuracy.'

'I should call it the "Underbred Fly" – I consider it most underbred to take this advantage of a confiding township.'

The Novice did not seem to think this at all witty.

'They seem to fancy bread,' he said. 'I might call it the "Fancy Bread Fly".'

'Unleavened bread,' I suggested.

'Oh, no,' he said, 'it does bring about a rise.'

'Anyhow, it's damnable,' I retorted.

'Well, anyhow, you needn't be cross about it. Cross! There's an idea now that I've had on my mind lately. Cross-bred flies. Why not try and improve the breed of artificial fly by careful selection and judicious crossings? For instance, I see great possibilities in a cross between Pope's Nondescript and Gold-Ribbed Hare's Ear,' and he went on, regardless of my studied gloom, to develop this theme, and I heard some remarks about cross-bred flies which he called Flickem's Chancey, the Lariat—

'Suitable for cross lines, I suppose,' I said.

And sure enough, during the six days he gillied me he did provide me with quite a good trio of patterns, one unmistakably by Pope's Nondescript out of Hare's Ear, and I caught some very decent baskets – in the tributary. As for the Novice, he never fished after breakfast, and he ordered a large supply of fishmonger's frails to send away his trout to his friends.

Someone must have seen him at his nefarious work in the early morn and have reported it to the authorities. The inhabitants' recreation was nearly gone. There was a petition of bridge haunters presented to the Association. At the end of the week, when the Novice wished to take out another ticket, his licence was not renewed.

Neither was mine. They were very firm about it, but gave no reasons. The Novice said it didn't matter, for anyone who goes to the bridge will see that the ford above it is empty of the big ones. It was too true. (*Side-Lines, Side-Lights and Reflections*)

Cross fertilization

The Novice has the preposterous idea of cross fertilising fly patterns to improve the breed, and it provides a wonderful opportunity for Skues to indulge his delight in the interplay of words.

ANOTHER SEASON HAS fled since last I recorded in these columns the misdoings of that infernal Novice, and it has been a year full of surprises. I often wish I had never met the chap, but he is so confoundly friendly, I don't know how to get away from him without hurting his feelings; and I hate hurting the feelings of even the most determined poacher. He was busy all this winter, and I saw little of him. When he met me in the Spring and learned that I was off for a jaunt by myself to the Flirt, he said he had never fished in Northumberland, and was coming with me to see how it should be done. I put him on OATH, in capital letters, not to use any more Standard Bread Flies, and he assented with quite surprising readiness. On our journey down he told me he had been working up a stock of flies for the season, and that he was resolved not to use any but flies of his own dressing all through the year. I felt some instinctive misgiving, but I forebore to press the question. Had I known what he had been doing I think I should have turned back and left him to continue his journey alone. It was only after we had arrived at our destination, and had settled into our quarters at Felldown Bridge, that I got an inkling of what he had been up to.

The preposterous fellow had been working all the winter at his absurd idea of improving the breed of artificial flies by judicious crossing. He had numerous small boxes, and, warned no doubt by experience of my disapproval, he only let me see their contents by degrees – one at a time, as he used them.

The first day we were out, the trout were smutting freely, and, using the orthodox patterns, I could do nothing with them. N. put up the first of his abortions. The box was labelled 'The Surprise, by Black Curse, out of Little Chap'. It was, indeed, a surprise. N. brought in eight pounds in eleven fish, quite a good average for the water. He admitted that he had also used a pattern from a second box. It was labelled 'Creme de Menthe, by Corkscrew, out of Green Bottle'. In each of these flies the, if I may call them so, parental characteristics were ingeniously blended, but I told him he might legitimately bow down and worship them, for they were like nothing in heaven above or the earth beneath or the waters that are under the earth. He told me that the jest was not new. I didn't think he would know it. However, there were the eleven trout on one scale and the seven pound weight and the one pound weight and some odd ounces on the other.

Next morning was mild and soft, and I felt justified in predicting a good rise of willow fly. I was quite right. I began with a cast comprising at point Waterhen Bloa, with Brown Owl and Olive Quill as middle and top droppers respectively, and when I met at lunch I felt pretty pleased with myself, for I was able to show three pound or so (eight fish) caught mainly on the point fly under the willows on the mill cauld; N. had only two trout in his basket, though they were both big ones. He did not tell me till after lunch that he had been back to the hotel to empty his twelve pound basket and come out again. I took a look at his fly which he said he had fished unchanged all morning.

'What do you call that monstrosity?' I said.

He handed me a box containing more of them labelled 'The Yell, by Spanish Needle out of the Governor'. It must be confessed that the dog has a whimsical humour in the nomenclature of his atrocities.

'Well,' I said, 'you may safely bow down and worship that, for—'

But he reminded me that he had heard that before. Which was true.

After lunch there was no fly to speak of, and he took off 'The Yell' and opened a box labelled 'The Real Relief, by Fisherman's Curse out of Francis'. It was all over for the day soon after three and we went in, I had one other trout and he turned five out of his basket on to a tray in the kitchen.

'Hello,' I said, 'There is another fisherman in the Inn. Who got that lot?'

'Oh,' said N., 'that's my first lot this morning.'

I said what I was, and he politely begged me not to be it. He said he did not know what he would do if I continued to be that.

'And that reminds me,' he said, 'what do you think of this for a cross,' and he produced another tin box labelled 'Hell-fire, by Downhill into Furnace'.

'Looks it,' I said – I was too discouraged to ask to see any more of his unnatural perversions.

Next day there was a fresh up stream wind, and about eleven there was a nice hatch of large spring olives. I overtook N. at the first ford. He was playing a fish, and the strap of his basket looked uncomfortably tight.

'What have you got on?' I asked incautiously.

'The Broken Tooth,' he replied.

'The what?'

He waded ashore with a fourteen-inch trout in his net, and, handing me a box, proceeded to unhook him. The box was labelled 'The Broken Tooth, by Half Stone, out of Olive'. I groaned and looked at his cast. He had a second fly on.

'And what's this?' I said.

'I call it the Blue Tail,' he replied.

'But it hasn't a blue tail,' I said.

He said, 'Your spelling's at fault. It's "Blue TALE, by Coachman, out of Black Smut".'

'Looks it,' I said. And, by George, it did.

But why pursue this tale of infamy further? And the worst of it is the confounded chap caught fish – lots of them – while I— (*Side-Lines, Side-Lights and Reflections*)

'Some letter'

Mr. Theodore Castwell was one of Skues's most memorable characters. He was probably modelled on the newcomer to Skues's syndicate, who appears to have dominated the other members and introduced various restrictions to the fishery which were very un-popular with Skues.

Heaven but the vision of fulfilled desire – Rubaiyat of Omar Khayyam

MR. THEODORE CASTWELL, having devoted a long, strenuous, and not unenjoyable life to hunting to their doom innumerable salmon, trout and grayling in many quarters of the globe, and having gained much credit among his fellows for his many inge-nious improvements in rods, flies and tackle employed for that end, in the fullness of time died and was taken to his own place.

St. Peter looked up from a draft balance sheet at the entry of the attendant angel.

'A gentleman giving the name of Castwell. Says he is a fisher-man, your Holiness, and has "Flyfishers' Club, London" on his card.'

'Hm-hm,' says St. Peter. 'Fetch me the ledger with his account.'

St. Peter perused it.

'Hm-hm,' said St. Peter. 'Show him in.'

Mr. Castwell entered cheerfully and offered a cordial right hand to St. Peter.

'As a brother of the angle—' he began.

'Hm-hm,' said St. Peter.

'I am sure I shall not appeal to you in vain for special consideration in connection with the quarters to be assigned to me here.'

'Hm-hm,' said St. Peter. 'I have been looking at your account from below.'

'Nothing wrong with it, I hope,' said Mr. Castwell.

'Hm-hm,' said St. Peter. 'I have seen worse. What sort of quarters would you like?'

'Well,' said Mr. Castwell, 'Do you think you could manage something in the way of a country cottage of the Test Valley type, with modern conveniences and say three quarters of a mile of one of those pleasant chalk streams, clear as crystal, which proceed from out the throne, attached?'

'Why, yes,' said St. Peter. 'I think we can manage that for you. Then what about your gear? You must have left your fly rods and tackle down below. I see you prefer a light split cane of nine foot or so, with appropriate fittings. I will indent upon the Works Department for what you require, including a supply of flies. I think you will approve of our dressers' productions. Then you will want a keeper to attend you.'

'Thanks awfully, your Holiness,' said Mr. Castwell. 'That will be first rate. To tell you the truth, from the Revelations I read, I was inclined to fear that I might be just a teeny-weeny bit bored in heaven.'

'In— H-hm-hm,' said St. Peter, checking himself.

It was not long before Mr. Castwell found himself alongside an enchantingly beautiful clear chalk stream, some fifteen yards wide, swarming with fine trout feeding greedily; and presently the attendant angel handed him the daintiest, most exquisite, light split cane rod conceivable – perfectly balanced with reel and line – with a beautifully damped tapered cast of incredible fineness and strength – and a box of flies of such marvellous tying, as to be almost mistakeable for the natural insects they were to simulate.

Mr. Castwell scooped up a natural fly from the water, matched it perfectly from the fly box, and knelt down to cast to a riser putting up just under a tussock ten yards or so above him. The fly lit like gossamer, six inches above the last ring, floated a moment and went under in the next ring; and next moment the rod was making the curve of beauty. Presently, after an exciting battle, the keeper netted out a beauty of about two and a half pounds.

'Heavens,' cried Mr. Castwell. 'This is something like.'

'I am sure his Holiness will be pleased to hear it,' said the keeper.

Mr. Castwell prepared to move up stream to the next riser when he became aware that another trout had taken up the position of that which he had just landed, and was rising. 'Just look at that,' he said, dropping instantaneously to his knee and drawing off some line. A moment later an accurate fly fell just above the neb of the fish, and instantly Mr. Castwell engaged in battle with another lusty fish. All went well, and presently the landing net received its two and a half pounds.

'A very pretty brace,' said Mr. Castwell, preparing to move on to the next of the string of busy nebs which he had observed putting up round the bend. As he approached the tussock, however, he became aware that the place from which he had just extracted so satisfactory a brace was already occupied by another busy feeder.

'Well I'm damned!' cried Mr Castwell. 'Do you see that?'

'Yes, sir,' said the keeper.

The chance of extracting three successive trout from the same spot was too attractive to be foregone, and once more Mr. Castwell knelt down and delivered a perfect cast to the spot. Instantly it was accepted and battle was joined. All held, and presently a third gleaming trout joined his brethren in the creel.

Mr. Castwell turned joyfully to approach the next riser round the bend. Judge, however, his surprise to find that once more the pit beneath the tussock was occupied by rising trout, apparently of much the same size as the others.

'Heavens,' exclaimed Mr. Castwell. 'Was there ever anything like it?'

'No, sir,' said the keeper.

'Look here,' he said to the keeper. 'I think I really must give this chap a miss and pass on to the next.'

'Sorry! It can't be done, sir. His Holiness would not like it.'

'Well, if that's really so,' said Mr. Castwell, and knelt reluctantly to his task.

Several hours later he was still casting to the same tussock.

'How long is this confounding rise going to last?' enquired Mr. Castwell. 'I suppose it will stop soon?'

'No, sir,' said the keeper.

'What, isn't there a slack hour in the afternoon?'

'No afternoon, sir.'

'What? Then what about the evening rise?'

'No evening, sir,' said the keeper.

'Well, I shall knock off, now. I must have had about thirty brace from that corner.'

'Beg pardon, sir, but his Holiness would not like that.'

'What?' said Mr. Castwell. 'Mayn't I even stop at night?'

'No night, here, sir,' said the keeper.

'Then do you mean that I have got to go on catching these damned two and a half pounders at this corner for ever and ever?'

The keeper nodded.

'Hell!' said Mr. Castwell.

'Yes,' said the keeper.

(*Side-Lines, Side-Lights and Reflections*)

Mr. Castwell and the Novice

In 1933, Skues had introduced the awful Novice to the domineering Mr. Castwell. In 1938, he brought them back together again. Once more, Skues culls aspects of his stories from real life, for his friend, Dr. Barton, habitually carried a catapult with him. Barton, in his diary, describes a similar incident to that in this first paragraph.

Castwell has been tramping the river bank, spotting fish for his next day's fishing, and rudely spoiling the fishing for others.

THE NOVICE AND I, concealed behind a big thorn bush near the West bank, had not long to wait before we espied Mr. Castwell creeping up the bank on the far side. A dimple arrested his attention under his bank and he dropped into a kneeling position and waited for the dimple to recur. It did not recur until, noting a rise a few yards higher up, Mr. Castwell began to creep towards it, when there was a recurrence of the dimple almost under his rod point. Hastily he retreated and awaited a further movement before casting. No rise ensuing he made a cast to the indicated spot. Almost as the fly lit the dimple recurred and he struck hastily, but in vain, for the dimple, like the preceding ones, was due to a B.B. shot projected from behind the thorn bush from the catapult of the concealed Novice. Mr. Castwell rose hastily and stamped ferociously on the bank, successfully putting down any trout within thirty or forty yards. Nevertheless, about that distance upstream there was another deceptive dimple which occupied his attention for several moments more.

Meanwhile, the head keeper had gone down to interview the farmer who had the Eastern meadows, and the under keeper, also under instructions, was on his way to the bridge which crossed the top of the water to drive the cattle in the top field into the water. Presently Mr. Castwell became aware of a troop of horses which had been turned into the meadow to graze cantering up behind him along the bank, apparently excited by abnormally early gad flies. He picked up his gear and moved precipitately upstream until he reached a boundary fence a couple of hundred yards up, incidentally tearing his breeches somewhat badly on some barbed wire which had not been there the previous day.

No sooner, however, had he settled down above the fence when a pair of swans, in a state of violent excitement came up behind him, rising suddenly with wings outspread and beating the water with their feet in doing so, successfully to put down anything that might have been rising in their neighbourhood. Could a B.B. shot under their tails have suggested their movements?

Mr. Castwell sat firmly down to wait for the fish to start rising again, meanwhile watching the water for the flies which were hatching. But as he watched the water clouded and in a few minutes it became a thick yellow from the feet of the cattle above. Presently the under keeper hove in sight and Mr. Castwell hailed him. 'I don't think,' he said, 'that I will use my ticket for today.' 'I can't say about that,' said the under keeper. 'You'll have to speak to the head keeper. You have been afishin' two howers.' 'Where shall I find him?' cried Mr. Castwell. 'I expect he's down by the Mill,' said the under keeper. Mr. Castwell turned downstream and turned towards the fence which had torn his breeks to find himself face to face with an aggressive-looking Hereford bull which had led his herd into the meadows above the fence. You bet Mr. Castwell's retreat was precipitate and it was not slowed by the pawings and snortings of the animal behind him. The last few yards of his retreat were still further speeded up by the rush of the animal, and it ended by a not entirely successful attempt of the hunted angler to leap a particularly foul ditch which bounded the meadow. It was a pitifully dirty and bedraggled angler who crawled out on the other side, to watch the bull dealing faithfully with his creel and mackintosh.

Meeting the head keeper on his way home he again said: 'I don't think I will use my ticket today. Can you let me have it back?'

'Well,' said the keeper, 'It be a bit late in the day for that. You've been on the water three hours or more, and besides, I have entered you in the Fishery Record book at the Mill. How many brace can I put you down for?'

The Editor won't print what Mr. Castwell had to say.

(*Flyfishers' Journal*, 1938)

McCaskie's Green Cat

This is not one of Skues's flights of fancy, for the two chief protagonists, McCaskie and his Green Cat, were very real, although the Green Cat was certainly conjured from McCaskie's imaginative fly dressing. Dr. Norman McCaskie was one of Skues's great fishing friends, and fished with him right through to his days on the Nadder.

Here, Skues gently pokes fun at himself and his fellow anglers who must have the correct pattern for the fly on the water, and signs his article, 'Spent Naturalist'.

AMONG MY MOST cherished possessions is a small wad of fine soft fur of a soft but brilliant new-billiard-cloth green which was once worn by McCaskie's cat Tim. I never saw the animal in the flesh – and as green cats are a rarity in this country I am tempted to suspect that the hue may be due to chemical treatment on the part of Tim's owner – on whose mind the activities of the Society for the Prevention of Cruelty to Animals may have made an inadequate impression. However that may be, it is the fact that for years, McCaskie's Green Cat has proved a sort of resort of the destitute for its owner when fly fishing. For on the frequent occasions when he had not a notion what fly was on the water he invariably attached to the end of his cast a hook garnished with a staring dark blue hackle (almost black) and dubbed with the fur of McCaskie's Green Cat. Whether it were due to the fact that the hackle invariably bears a tangled air as of a despairing daddy longlegs in the last throes of dissolution, or to some cryptic virtue in the green feline integument, it has been the fact that these caricatures of the insect tribe have constantly proved fatal to the meticulous trout and grayling of the Itchen when they were refusing the most delicately and accurately dressed flies of the great artists of the fly dressing world.

The first occasion on which I saw McCaskie's Green Cat in action was one October day when McCaskie came down to help me exterminate as many as possible of that pestilent fish the grayling which then swarmed in my water. The fly up appeared to be a pale watery dun. It was up in quantity and the grayling appeared to be taking it freely. Did that deter my guest? Not in the least. He tied on his Green Cat and promptly clawed out a grayling of two pounds nine ounces, the biggest that had been taken on my length during the season – and followed it up with a string of other big fish in the course of the two hours that the rise continued; during which time the fish kept paying the Pale Watery duns tied by me the tribute of a false rise and a miss till I felt like flinging my rod at them in sheer exasperation. It was only after it was all over and I had seen McCaskie's cat and the execution he had done with it that I realized that there had probably been a scanty unnoticed rise of blue-winged olives which the grayling had been taking soundly.

McCaskie's Green Cat accompanied its owner on a visit to my water in the following July, and adorned the end of his line at the close of a Saturday afternoon distinguished by 'nothing doing'. We were just going in for our meal when a trout put up once at the far side of the middle of the stream. He put up a second time to leap violently out of the water with McCaskie's Green Cat clinging firmly to his under jaw. He still weighed over two pounds, after the cat had been detached – a good fish for the water. It was, of course, the blue-winged olive season – but there was no blue-winged olive up, nor anything else for the matter of that. So why this fish, from a length which contains what McCaskie always says are the most discriminating trout he knows, should have taken this emerald abortion, I am at a loss to guess. But when two or three other incidents of the same kind occurred I permitted McCaskie to bestow upon me a wad of the fur and I have taken and lost a good many good fish by its agency – but I have never been able to reproduce with my hackle the action and appearance of a wet and disconsolate daddy longlegs in the throes of dissolution, so I have never been as successful as McCaskie with this particular pattern.

I have, however, found that when in the day time the trout are taking blue-winged olive nymphs (and they never, or almost never, take the blue-winged olive in sub-imago form during the day time), a fly dressed on a No.14 hook with pale orange silk dubbed lightly and loosely with McCaskie's Green Cat and hackled lightly with a soft dark blue henny hackle and glycerined to sink properly is really very effective, even in the hands of an angler who has a prejudice in favour of thinking he knows why he uses any particular pattern rather than another.

It may be that in proclaiming the virtues of McCaskie's Green Cat, I am doing neither the Club members nor McCaskie a kindness. If, as I fear, the breed of green cats or of cats capable of viridity is extinct, I may be merely exposing McCaskie to importunities he has no means of satisfying and the applicants to disappointment. But there 'tis. (*Side-Lines, Side-Lights and Reflections*)

Scaringham

This was a piece of fun poked at another of Skues's fishing friends, Hugh Sheringham, one of the most amusing of all our writers on fishing. Sheringham fished the Itchen regularly by permission of Irwin Cox, the proprietor of *The Field*. How heavy the body was that beat down the bankside herbage can be judged from the fact that Sheringham wrote under the pen name of Piscator Rotundus. He was also renowned on the Itchen for the size of the flies he used, and this gave Skues the model on which he based his own Carrot fly.

WHEN I GET to the waterside I always know quite soon whether my friend Scaringham has been fishing there during the previous month. One reads of the Japanese assaulting Port Arthur, or the Bulgarians advancing on Kirk Kelisse, digging themselves in after a rush before advancing a further stage. That is friend Scaringham's method. At brief intervals along the river bank, after a visit of his, I find a succession of butts, of the size one finds on the grouse moors, but in this case formed by the beating down of flags, reeds and other riverside herbage by a heavy body. I will not further particularise that heavy body.

It is Scaringham's method of digging himself in behind rushes. From the shelter of these embattled ramparts he bombards the trout of that beautiful river with the weird monstrosities which he terms flies, until they are in a state of such abject terror that their nerves do not recover by the time I get down there. Some are so frightened that they surrender. He never catches any, but an extraordinary number of the biggest – those whose nerve has been weakened by luxury and fat feeding – are intimidated and give themselves up.

It is not Scaringham's way to be sparingham, and they are all knocked on the head, scratched somewhere in the mouth with a hook for appearance sake, and consigned to his capacious basket. But those that are left are unapproachable for a week; almost uncatchable for a fortnight; supremely difficult for another week, and timorous for the rest of the month, supposing S. let them alone so long. I tell you this so that you may understand why I never catch any of them. I thought you might like to know. Scaringham goes down at least once a month throughout the season – and oftener at the time of year when I can best get down there myself. I don't think I have mentioned that it is my water. (*Flyfishers' Journal*, Correspondence columns, Winter 1912)

The Member for America and the Surrey fowls

I think that this is one of Skues's most delightful pieces, in which he develops his basic theme to ridiculously funny heights. Once more, the main character is a real person. Walter Durfee Coggeshall was an American who not only introduced Skues to the Leonard rods he used, but was also responsible for developing wonderful silk fly lines. He was popularly known at the Flyfishers' Club as The Member for America, and was renowned for the size of the flies he used which Skues dubbed Surrey fowls.

YOU ALL KNOW those conjurors who produce rabbits and goldfish and other carpenters' tools from mysterious places about their persons. Well, the Member for America is like that, only his hobby is Surrey fowls. How he conceals them about his person is not obvious to the casual observer. I became the casual observer in this wise.

The M.F.A. came down one weekend in early May to cast a line across a little ditch which sniggles through some rather lovely country in Surrey, and for want of a better name is high Thrillingbourne. It was before May-fly time, though the first advance scouts of the army of Eph. Vulgata appeared on that day. The alder, however, in payable quantities, was humming about the banks, and there were red spinners about in number sufficient to interest normal trout. I thought my trout quite normal. I may have to revise my opinion.

I remember an incident being recorded in the eighties in the *St. James's Gazette* in which a fox was drowned by the rising

tide, owing to his tongue being caught between the shells of
the bivalve which closed on it and held him to his doom, 'thus,'
said the narrator, 'posing the interesting question, "Do foxes
eat oysters?"' Next day came a correction, 'Is not the true
question, "Do oysters eat foxes?"'

Similarly I could have conceived of Surrey fowls eating the
trout of the Thrillingbourne; but for the trout of the
Thrillingbourne to – but this is premature. The M.F.A. let me
persuade him to put up a Red Spinner and successfully missed
the first three fish which he tried in the first hundred yards. He
explained that he could not see his fly. I gave him an Alder and
put him on to a riser in the millhead. He missed that once, but
the indefatigable fish was not to be denied and presently
impaled himself on the hook. Then followed a period of ill
success, and the M.F.A. flicked off the Alder and announced his
intention of showing how it was done.

By some feat of legerdemain he produced a receptacle from
about his person and extracted a large Surrey fowl mounted on
a hook which would have intimidated any self-respecting sea
trout. This he knotted on to the end of his line, and raising his
eight foot of stiff split cane he wafted the bird across the brook
to a run in which I had indicated a trout was frequently to be
found. The Thrillingbourne members usually seek to beguile
their fish with flies of 15 and 16 hook sizes, and I anticipated
seeing a huge wake as the three-quarter pounder scuttled incon-
tinent to a place over which the dreadful bird did not hover.
Little did I suspect the spirit of my trout. It rose to the danger
like our men in France and Flanders, and dragged that fearsome
fowl beneath the water, escaping, however, from impalement on
the meat-hook imperfectly concealed among the feathers. His
nerve was, however, unequal to a second attempt, and the
M.F.A. moved on to the next pool. Here two fish were peace-
fully rising, probably at smuts. The first was intimidated and
fled, but the second accepted the challenge and slashed the
Surrey fowl like a big Kennet trout taking a May fly. The
contest was unequal, and very quickly the bird brought the half
pounder ashore.

A little higher up the meat-hook caught in a bush on the far
side, and in the ensuing struggle the bush was nearly rooted up,
bringing with it a length of the farmer's barbed wire fencing;
and visions of juries assessing damages to banks and fences
began to float before my eyes. Fortunately, the tackle gave way,

and the bush remains – to the outward eye – intact, but I misdoubt that its heart is broken.

To proceed. Again the conjuror produced from his store another large Surrey fowl, and with admirable dexterity switched it under bushes on the opposite bank, and floated it down the current regardless of drag. Again and again did the gallant little trout of my ditch vindicate their courage at the expense of their discretion, and, to cut a long story short, during the day no less than nine of them were escorted ashore in the clutch of these fearsome birds. I use the plural, for it must not be supposed that the casualties were all on one side. They were not. The boughs of the overhanging trees are festooned with the bunches of feather which were once the pride of the M.F.A., and I am going down next weekend with waders and a hen coop of suitable size, and where ever I find a broken tree or a damaged fence I shall wade across and rescue the remains of the creature from exposure to the elements. Whether I shall restore them to the M.F.A. is another matter. Rather am I inclined to have them mounted and framed, and exhibit them in my inn with an inscription indicating at once the dauntless courage and the insensate folly of the Thrillingbourne trout. I am also contemplating an epoch making monograph on the question, 'Do trout eat large "Surrey fowls"?' (*Side-Lines, Side-Lights and Reflections*)

Angling as she is wrote

This piece has a particular appeal to me as the present editor of the *Flyfishers' Journal*, and I am thinking of recruiting Skues's advice to stimulate the literary aspirations of my prospective contributors.

As THERE SEEMS to exist among Members of the Flyfishers' Club some backwardness in coming forward with contributions for the *Journal* (due, can it be, to modest doubts of their competence as writers?) the editor has asked me to supply a few hints on how to set about the business.

It must be remembered in the first place that, just as angling with the fly is an art, largely traditional in its nature, so is the writing of angling articles, and anything in the nature of originality should be rigidly eschewed. Study then the work of the best angling authors, take their methods to heart, and all will be well with you. There will be found to be a number of approved gambits, as well-known as the Ruy Lopez or the Muzio in chess.

One of the simplest and most popular goes like this: 'When I arrived at the waterside the trout had already begun to feed. A strong rise of Blue Quills and Gold-ribbed Hare's ears was on, and as the wind blew towards the further bank it was a little difficult to ascertain which of these flies was engaging the attention of the fish. Turning to my fly box I knotted on chance a beautifully tied *Baetis rhodani*, oiled it and dispatched it to the nearest riser, etc.'

There is one difficulty about this gambit which wants watching. When the strong rise happens to be Governors or Coachmen it will be impossible to find the Latin name of its imitation, but this difficulty can be avoided by the selection of some fly other than the Governor or the Coachman to be hatching. The latter indeed seldom hatches satisfactorily until the evening. There is no such difficulty with the Tags. A Latin Tag can be found for almost every occasion, and there are some who do not despise the Greek, but few of the members will be familiar with them. It is well, therefore, to avoid them, for if there is one rule more binding than another, it is the same which guides the popular lecturer. 'Never on any account tell the audience anything they don't know. Then they are able to realize how well informed they really are.' While I remember it, I may mention that this season split infinitives are almost as much in use as the split-winged floater.

Another excellent and much-practised gambit involves the railway journey, the excellence or otherwise of the hotel, the breakfast, the sausages, the kidneys, the eggs and bacon and the home-made marmalade, the laying-in of the sandwiches, the smoking of the after-breakfast pipe. With care this may be spun out so that the angling is not reached at all, or only reached in time to be dismissed in a few lines, not necessarily fishing lines.

In writing an angling article it is always well to begin brightly, so as to attract and rivet attention from the start, like the little boy who began his novel, '"Oh, Hell!" said the Duchess, breaking into the conversation.' A good example of the sort of thing I mean goes like this: 'Pitching my Governor smartly into the river, etc.'

Then there is the chatty method of pretending you are a duffer, and recounting all the disasters which befall duffers. This will be extremely gratifying to all the other members who are duffers. (This sentence may be read in two ways. Readers should be careful to select the right one.)

The rich vein of sentiment may be entered into with advantage, but to attempt that of humour is fatal.

Here is a graceful way of illustrating sportsmanlike self denial. 'The biggest trout I ever caught took a piece of bread when roach fishing, which was duly returned to the river, being the close season.'

Another class of article is more pretentious. It describes terrific battles with strong fish hooked under unusual circumstances – circumstances, if one may put it so, 'different to' the usual. What a picture, for instance, is conveyed in the following words: 'Passing the rod from the right hand to the left while climbing the fence, the trout tore violently down stream.' I have often wondered how he did it.

But there are still more marvellous and tragic events chronicled in angling. Here is an example. 'The now exhausted fish came floating belly upwards to my feet when I deftly slipped the net under and was killed.' (*Flyfishers' Journal*, 1916)

Narrow escape of prominent angler

Here is one of Skues's classic tales of the duffer with pretensions to be an expert.

EVERYONE WHO HAS had the privilege of reading *Fly Lines and Sly Lines* by the distinguished angler-author, Arnold Ougher, a work which is generally admitted to have inaugurated a new epoch in the art of trout fishing in the Dampshire rivers, will learn with sympathy and joy of his escape from a totally unexpected and undeserved disaster which nearly overtook him on the very last day of the season, and would have wrecked a unique record.

He had had a more than usually strenuous and remarkable season, fishing the Doubting Club water on the Quest from the morning of the opening day, the 1st April, till the 29th September, and spending by the waterside some hours at least in every twenty four – Sunday sometimes, but by no means always, excepted – and during the season it is not too much to say that he had besieged and succeeded in putting down not only every sizeable trout in the water, but most of the unsizeable ones, not once only but many times, and that without ever hooking or even rising one of them.

Whether it was due to fatigue induced by the season's exertions or to the unexpected warmth of the day, or to both of these causes, the fact remains that at about three o'clock on the 30th September, while resting on the bank, with his line trailing in the water so as to keep limber while waiting for a trout to rise, the distinguished author fell into a doze. From that he was suddenly awakened by the accident above referred to. A trout had seized his fly.

The angler sprang to his feet and hastily grasped the rod – immediately realizing that the trout was quite sizable. He is as all his readers know from his work, a man of infinite resource. His luck did not entirely desert him, for within a minute the trout had twisted off, and the great angler was thus able to go in with an absolutely unbroken record. (*Side-Lines, Side-Lights and Reflections*)

The stuffed pike

Typical of Skues's dry sense of humour is a tale he tells in his reminiscences which were never published.

THERE USED TO be a huge stuffed pike in a case placed over the entrance to the Flyfishers' Club and Punch had a picture which might have been suggested by that pike with an elderly, well-dined, gentleman looking up at it and saying, 'The man that caught that fish is a damned liar.' (*Trivialities of a Long Life*)

CHAPTER 14

Famous Fly Fishermen

Skues was born not long after the Crimean War and the famous charge of the Light Brigade commemorated in Tennyson's poem. Before he died he had seen the ultimate in warfare, the dropping of the atom bomb. It was a huge life span, during which he met and fished with most of the great fly fishermen and writers of the time.

George Selwyn Marryat

Marryat was one of the few renowned fly fishermen whom Skues did not meet, though he recollected seeing him wearing his famous tam'o shanter at the annual Winchester v Eton cricket match. Although Halford freely acknowledged Marryat's help in his great works, *Floating Flies and How to Dress Them* and *Dry-Fly Fishing in Theory and Practice*, there has been much discussion over the past hundred years as to just how much Marryat contributed to the books. Simon Ward, a fly fishing instructor, fly dresser and river keeper from Hampshire, has been researching Marryat for eight years, and claims that he has unearthed hard evidence that without Marryat's genius Halford would have been very hard pressed to have produced the work he did. His opinion is that Halford would have been lost without Marryat. This is extremely controversial, and we shall await the publication of his findings with interest. Meanwhile, we should note

that Ward has tracked down Marryat's descendants in South Africa
and discovered that they possess a fly box full of Marryat's exquisitely
dressed split-winged floaters.

Sadly, the fly book discussed here by Skues has disappeared from
the possession of the Flyfishers' Club. However, his conjecture, made
75 years ago, that Marryat probably had a separate fly box for chalk
streams has now been proved correct.

ON FEBRUARY 14, 1896, the world in general and that of fly
fishing in particular became the poorer for the passing of
George Selwyn Marryat. He died leaving behind him probably
the most uncontested reputation ever enjoyed in the history of
fly fishing for supremacy as a practitioner of that art and having,
on the confession of F.M. Halford, exercised upon that writer
the predominating influence which gave us the body of his
great work on the dry fly and its entomology.

It is in the work of his friend, 'Detached Badger' (*Halford's
pen name*), that G.S. Marryat's record is to be found, apart
from the memories of the few survivors among his friends (of
whom, I cannot, alas, claim to have been one); for he wrote no
book, and so far as I am aware, he contributed no articles to
the Angling Press.

Marryat's 'portmanteau' or fly book

Looking back over the collection one cannot help being
impressed with the enormous predominance of patterns better
calculated to fish wet than dry, and it seems impossible to
doubt that at one stage of his angling career, and that not sepa-
rated much from the period of Marryat's collaboration with
Halford, indeed overlapping more or less, the great man must
have been content either on chalk streams or on other waters to
fish 'wet as Niagara'.

Of the quadumvirate who fished the Ramsbury length of the
Kennet – Halford is dead, Basil Field is dead, Orchardson is
dead, and Nat Lloyd gave up fishing for golf years ago, and has
passed out of my ken. There may, however, be members of the
Club or others who occasionally or possibly frequently fished
with Marryat in those great days – and it would be of immense
interest to angling history if any of them would recall for the
benefit of posterity whether Marryat continued to rely on the
book under review to the end, or whether he latterly carried a

fly box for chalk streams and used the book for the rough water fishing of other rivers. (*Side-Lines, Side-Lights and Reflections*)

Four Field *angling editors*

In the last two decades of the past century and the first three of this one, *The Field* had a succession of superb fishing editors, all distinguished writers and expert fishermen. Skues was in a unique position to meet them as his stretch of the River Itchen was leased at that time by Irwin E.B. Cox, one of the proprietors of *The Field*, who, naturally, gave his angling editors permission to fish there. Here are memorable portraits of three of them: Francis Francis, with his 14-foot rod dubbed a weaver's beam by Skues; William Senior, fated to be dogged by bad weather; and H.T. Sheringham, who took concealment when fishing to the ultimate and, incidentally, launched Skues's career as an author with his advice and encouragement in the writing of *Minor Tactics of the Chalk Stream*.

IN THE TWO and forty years during which I have been fishing the same water on the Itchen, it has been my privilege to know, and occasionally to meet upon it, the four great angling editors of *The Field*; Francis Francis, William Senior, C.H. Cook (John Bickerdyke) and H.T. Sheringham (Piscator Rotundus) who have covered the last half century.

It was probably practical wisdom on the part of the proprietors of that paper which dictated that each of these occupants of the Angling Editorial chair should be an accomplished all-round Angler, and it perhaps ill becomes one whose freshwater angling has been almost entirely confined to fly fishing for trout and grayling, with a rare excursion among chub and dace, to write of these distinguished editors, save in their relation to the branch of angling art with which he is most familiar. But having had the honour of fishing with all of them on that stretch of Itchen so long rented by the late Mr. Irwin E.B. Cox – one of the proprietors of *The Field* – I should like to put on record a few memories of each of them, as an angler, on that most difficult water.

It was I think in late May or early June of 1883 that I first met Francis Francis. He was fishing the length of the main river, from the west bank, in a meadow called 'Winnal Moor' while I was negotiating the length above the Duck's Nest Spinney. The wind (from the N.W.) set across both lengths and several times,

on looking over to him from my own preoccupations, I saw
him manoeuvring up and down the bank, with his fourteen- or
fifteen-footer describing the curve of beauty and more than
once he was stamping furiously upon the bank to emphasize his
dissatisfaction with whatever it was that caused the gut to break
off on the strike and leave the fly to the trout. He was not the
only angler to fish a long double handed rod in those days. Mr.
Irwin Cox had a fourteen-foot split cane, by Hardy, which was
still in his possession when he died in 1922, and it was sold to
an angler who purposed using it as a light salmon rod. The use
of these weaver's beams seems strange to modern anglers, who
can cover the same length at least as cleanly, if not as effectually,
with a five-ounce nine-footer. When we assembled at the hut at
lunch time, Francis Francis had three beautiful two pounders,
and I only rivalled him in having left flies in several fish.

At the hut at the same time, I found William Senior, with
whom this also was my first meeting. I forget his score, but it
was not equal to that of Francis Francis.

I only met Francis Francis once again. It was, I believe, in the
May fly season of 1884, on the same water, and he then was
under the shadow of the malady which brought about his death
in 1885. He had, however, taken several trout on the May fly,
and he gave me a pattern, which to my lasting regret, I
promptly left in the jaw of a trout in the side stream below the
single railway arch.

It came to my knowledge recently that before Mr. Cox
became lessee of this water, it had been rented by Francis
Francis jointly with George Selwyn Marryat from
1879 to 1882, the pike and most of the big cannibal trout
netted out, and fresh stock turned in, which might account for
the fine head of fish I saw there when I arrived in 1883.

William Senior it was my good fortune to meet again, many a
time. In 1893, he joined with F.M. Halford in putting me up
for membership of the Flyfishers' Club, a favour for which I am
eternally grateful to them.

It was, however, on the Winnal water that prior to my
election I most frequently met him. And much as I liked and
admired him, I did not like finding him fishing on Winnal
water, not because I grudged him bank space, but because, for
some reason known only to the powers above, poor Senior was
pursued by a vindictive fate which decreed that whenever he
came down to fish there he was buffeted by violent storms of

wind and rain – and the skies, of course, made no invidious distinctions between him and me on these occasions. I recall that it is recorded in one of Halford's books or articles that Francis Francis made somewhat the same complaint of his own luck in weather on the Test. And it really seemed as if Senior's ascent to the angling editorial chair had involved the descent on him of the mantle of Francis Francis's desperate luck in weather.

Poor Senior's luck lasted to the very end. On the last occasion when he fished that water, before he put by for good the Fairy fly rod which was such a joy to him, he brought down a parson whose hat was plucked from his head by a specially violent gust, and next moment was whirling along under the tussocks of the opposite bank while its unfortunate owner was making desperate but ineffectual casts to retrieve it. And as he reached me he cried, 'Here am I, a Clergyman of the Church of England, and there's not an appropriate word that I am allowed to say.'

Senior always used to say that the water in question was the most difficult water he knew, and I believe his experience was very wide. I often wondered why, with his wide experience and casting the neat line which he cast, William Senior was not more fortunate on the Itchen, and ultimately I came to the conclusion that it was due to an increasing unwillingness to take the reverential attitude necessary if one is to keep out of sight of the wary trout of that river.

Senior became full editor of *The Field* in 1900 or thereabout (near the outbreak of the South African War), and for a time he attempted to continue to act as angling editor also – but he found it too much for him. So in 1901 C.H.Cook (John Bickerdyke of the *Book of the All-Round Angler* fame) took the sub-editorial chair, and, like his predecessors, was dowered by Mr. Irwin Cox with standing leave to fish the Itchen. I had known Cook at the Flyfishers' Club, since 1894 – but came into closer contact with him as a contributor to the angling columns edited by him; particularly in connection with the somewhat strenuous controversy excited by the light rod question. It was not, however, my fortune to see much of him on the Itchen, and I recall no particular impression of his style or success beyond a general impression of competence.

Cook ceased to be angling editor towards the end of 1903, and Senior made me known soon after to Cook's successor, H.T. Sheringham, since so widely known as the author of a series of delightful books on angling, and for his charming articles in his own columns and elsewhere, notably in the *Morning Post* under the pseudonym of 'Piscator Rotundus'. Like his predecessors, H.T. Sheringham was provided with the standing leave to fish Mr. Irwin Cox's length of the Itchen – and I met him there on several occasions. I was then engaged in my effort to work out the resuscitation of the legitimate wet fly method on the chalk stream, and on more than one occasion, I found Sheringham fishing frankly wet – once with a sort of variant of the Half Stone, tied with hare's ear instead of mole and rough orange wool instead of yellow silk for the better half of the body on quite a large hook and taking good fish. Out of this pattern was evolved by my friend, 'the Novice', and myself, the pattern known as the Carrot fly which figured in a series of papers in the *Flyfishers' Journal*.

In one respect Sheringham was not like Senior. Far from failing to adopt the proper reverential attitude for concealment when fishing, Sheringham used to dig himself in and I used chaffingly to compare the semi circle of battered down flags surrounded by a screen of waterside herbage, which marked the scenes of his operations, with a fortress from which H.T. Sheringham hurled flies known, as a tribute to their size and weight, as Half Stones, at the trout with the intention of stunning them. Catch them he certainly did. I never fished so closely with him as to have any chance of mastering the secret of his method. It is betraying no secret to say that but for his advice and encouragement it is improbable that the papers collected in *Minor Tactics of the Chalk Stream* would ever have seen the light in book form, and the same is true of *The Way of a Trout with a Fly*.

After Mr. Cox gave up the water in 1920, Sheringham might have continued to fish it and would have been gladly welcomed by the small group of Mr. Cox's successors – but for various reasons, partly, I am sorry to know, ill-health due to overwork for the country during the war, and partly the distance at which he lived, he never let himself be persuaded to do so. (*Side-Lines, Side-Lights and Reflections*)

'Coggie' – the Member for America

Skues had a number of American friends and correspondents. Coggeshall was a fellow member of the Flyfishers' Club and a man of some ingenuity. He was instrumental in introducing Skues to

Leonard rods. Shortly afterwards Skues acquired one, and from then on never fished with anything else. His fly lines were the envy of his fellow members and, indeed, of professional tackle makers, and Dr. Barton records that when Skues lost the landing net which Coggeshall had made for him, he never saw Skues more distressed. They searched for it all the evening and part of the next day but it was never found. The fishing rod bequeathed to the Flyfishers' Club by Mrs. Coggeshall was also ill-fated as it was destroyed when the Club's premises were blitzed during the Second World War. To complete the chapter of accidents, Skues records elsewhere that after Coggeshall's death he was given the last six of his precious lines by Mrs. Coggeshall. They were in a parcel which he inadvertently left on a bus or train or taxi, and they were never seen again.

Dr. Barton, in his personal copy of *Side-Lines, Side-Lights and Reflections,* made the following note: '"Coggie" would never kneel when fishing. He declared to me he never knelt to any fish. He was an R.C. and a bit superstitious.'

TWO YEARS HAVE passed away since that May 6th when our good old friend Walter Durfee Coggeshall was taken from us; and, though an appreciation of his mind and character appeared in the *Flyfishers' Journal* and there were affectionate obituary notices in *The Times, The Field* and elsewhere, no attempt appears to have been made to put on record for posterity any impression to the effect which his life and activities had on the art of trout fishing in this country. That he made a very definite mark I shall endeavour to show; indeed, I doubt whether there have been many individuals in this generation who have made a greater mark upon the art than he did though he seldom wrote a line on the subject.

To him and to his activities may, I think, be attributed the evolution of the light rod, though he took but a slight overt part in the press controversy of 1902. It was in the early stages of that correspondence that I first made his acquaintance, visiting him in his Upper Phillimore Gardens home somewhat hesitatingly in response to an invitation to call and see his Leonard rods. He then owned two, one being the old fashioned whippy type, possessing as much backbone to all appearance as a piece of string, but stiffening up wonderfully when a line was passed through the rings and pressure was applied. The other was an early, perhaps the first, attempt of the house of William Mills and Son, of New York, to incorporate the special features of the

Leonard split cane, viz., high courage and resilience, steely
spring and light weight, in a rod of the English dry fly type.
The latter rod may be seen at this day in the Flyfishers' Club,
having been presented by Mrs. Coggeshall to the Club after her
husband's death. It is ten feet long and weighs six and a quarter
ounces; and, having handled many fly rods, I can truly say I
never handled a more exquisite piece of the rod-maker's art
than that. The date it bears is 1901.

Coggeshall passed a line through the rings and bade me pull
as hard and roughly as I chose and defied me to break it. I was
amazed at its courage and resilience. A few days later we met at
Mitcham to give the rod a trial on the Wandle. I am not much
of a caster and never was (having sprained both my wrists
severely at football in 1878 and having never really recovered
from the injury) but I put out twenty four yards of heavy
Halford line with that rod against a stiffish breeze and a friend
with a good wrist put out twenty six yards.

The press controversy went on, the advocates of the light rod
owing much to Coggeshall's help and encouragement. It eventually died out, but not until Coggeshall's ideas had made their
mark. His press cuttings on the subject fill some four thick
volumes. Light rods were built in increasing numbers, and the
rod makers, when they had sold out their stocks of the old
wrist-breakers, began to keep more adequate stocks of the light
type of weapon, and Coggeshall's battle was won against a
dogged weight of opposition which would have daunted most
men.

In memory of the controversy Coggeshall very generously
gave me the 1901 rod some years before his death, but it was
so beautiful that I could not bring myself to expose it to the
rough usage of the waterside, and after his death I returned it
to Mrs. Coggeshall, who presented it, as a rod of historic interest, to the Club, while to me she gave his pet nine-footer,
which dates back to near the same time.

For Coggeshall's mind was not standing still. From the ten-
footer he went on to the nine-footer, the eight-footer and
even shorter rods. In 1904 occurred the Fly-casting
Tournament at the Crystal Palace, and I believe I am right in
saying that it was his inducement which brought over Mr.
William Bates Mills and his son to take a hand in the fly-
casting contests and to show what his light rods could do.
They made a great impression.

Along with Coggeshall's interest in the light rod developed his interest in the line which it needed to bring out its high qualities, and after numberless experiments he had developed by 1903 a prescription for dressing fly lines which made them the envy of the professional fishing tackle makers. He was most generous of them, as many members of the Flyfishers' Club have good reason to recall with gratitude. He gave me one in 1903, the dressing of which after much hard wear was still almost intact twenty years later. Unfortunately the application of the dressing involved so much 'elbow grease' as to render it impossible to market the finished line at such a price as the ordinary angler would be prepared to pay, and, therefore, though latterly Coggeshall imparted the secret of his prescription to a firm of fishing tackle makers, the lines which they made with it were not equal to Coggeshall's, possibly for lack of the innumerable rubbings down, re-coatings and re-polishings which Coggeshall found necessary for his works of art. Among his belongings when he died there were to be found numerous bottles and cans of oils, gums, varnishes, etc. used by him in his experiments.

With the same prescription, Coggeshall would dress landing nets and I used one he gave me in 1906 hard until 1923, when I had the misfortune to lay it down by Itchenside and leave it for a few moments and never found it again. It was then still perfectly sound and had to all appearances years of wear in it.

In trout flies, as representations of particular insects, Coggeshall never took the interest which one would have expected of his active and ingenious mind. Brought up in the United States to fish with a large fly, he never could reconcile himself to fishing with flies dressed on small hooks, and his collection contained relatively few flies smaller than a May fly. Duns on No.8 or 9 hooks, Sedges on even larger wires, Jenny spinners on No.11's were commonplace with him, and though he was chaffed about them as 'Coggie's Surrey fowls', it is the fact that he caught numbers of trout with the enormous patterns.

Members who frequented the Club after Coggie's death will remember the black tin of 'Surrey fowls' from which all were at liberty on Mrs. Coggeshall's invitation to help themselves to memorials of our old friend.

But though he was no precisian in the matter of exact imitation, and no fly dresser, he was acutely interested in the mechanics of the tools of the art, and he illustrated this fact in 1907 by presenting me and the Club each with a Farlow cam-lever vice. Then in the year 1921 or 1922 he induced a dealer to put upon the market a most ingenious little vice known as 'The Coggie', the feature of which was the adjustment of the stem to any angle by means of the ball to which it was attached being jammed by a screw, impinging on and fixing the ball in its cup.

The items which I have mentioned include only such of Coggeshall's interests as had a special appeal for me, but probably every member of the Club with special interests who had to do with him could testify to his acute and stimulating contributions to the special subject in hand, be it barbless hooks, line dressing, casting records, reel making or what not. (*Side-Lines, Side-Lights and Reflections*)

Theodore Gordon

Theodore Gordon, the father of the dry fly in the United States, corresponded with Frederic Halford who sent him his folio of flies. *Minor Tactics of the Chalk Stream* introduced nymph fishing to the States, and Gordon also exchanged letters and ideas with Skues. Schwiebert tells us in his book, *Nymphs*, that Gordon also fished nymph-like forms when the fish were taking below the surface. By 1943, when Skues was in his mid-80s and was living at the Nadder Vale Hotel, he began to dispose of some of his countless fishing treasures. These included flies and feathers sent to him by Gordon. Skues had for many years had links with the Anglers' Club of New York, and had written articles for its *Bulletin*, and so he felt that the two flies he possessed which had been tied by Gordon would find an appropriate home at their headquarters.

I HAVE LATELY found among my oddments two trout flies tied by the late distinguished American angler Theodore Gordon and sent by him to me in the course of our correspondence about the last decade of the 19th century. One is a Mayfly tied to gut with a cork body and summer duck wings. The other is a small upwinged fly also dressed with Summer duck wings but with the fibres bunched in the modern manner. If the New York Anglers would care to have them I will with pleasure post them to you or send them to any representative of the Club over here, as the Committee may determine. (Letter to L.K. Moreshead, Secretary of the New York Anglers' Club, 24th July, 1943)

Because of the war, the letter took three months to arrive.

> I AM GLAD to learn that the N.Y.A. will accept the custody of
> Theodore Gordon's flies and have pleasure in sending them,
> hooked into the paper in which they reached me. Gordon's
> correspondence was a great pleasure to me and I greatly regret-
> ted his passing. He sent me a copy of the picture of him and his
> dog which was reproduced in the *Bulletin*. (Letter to
> Moreshead, 14th October, 1943)

George M. L. La Branche

La Branche had speculated about nymphs in his classic, *The Dry Fly
and Fast Water,* which appeared four years after *Minor Tactics of the
Chalk Stream*. He appears to have accepted an invitation from Skues
to fish the Itchen which, despite its reputation for yielding fish to
small flies only, was suitably beguiled by La Branche's large fore-and-
aft patterns.

> THE SEASON WAS also distinguished by a visit from a hitherto
> rare Trans-Atlantic migrant, whose appearance however in this
> country is likely to become annual. I refer to Mr. George M. L.
> La Branche, who tried on these classic waters the large fore-
> and-aft patterns with which he beguiles the trout of God's Own
> Country. He could not have made the experiment under more
> hopeful conditions, for the wind was persistently violent – and
> he brought up and killed in the first short length he fished a
> trout approximating two pounds to one of these large patterns.
> (*Flyfishers' Journal*, Summer 1928)

J. W. Dunne

Dunne was a most remarkable man who combined great originality
and imagination with mathematical precision. He was an early
pioneer in aircraft design, evolving a monoplane shaped like an
arrow-head with its wings swept back which was fifty years before its
time. His book, *An Experiment in Time,* which appeared in 1927,
was a philosophical speculation on the nature of time, which caused
a considerable stir. However, he had already created large ripples in
the fly fishing world three years earlier with his *Sunshine and the Dry
Fly*. Not only did he endeavour to achieve translucency in a fly in a
different way by dipping his hooks into a tin of quick-drying white

enamel, covering them with artificial silk and touching the result with oil, but he held the naturals back uppermost on glass held in the sun's rays, looking at them from beneath. This constituted a direct attack on Halford's method, which looked down on the flies on their backs in a white saucer. Dunne contended, therefore, that Halford saw them under the wrong conditions which invalidated his record. Dunne had corresponded with Skues before his book was published, and Skues had invited him down to the Itchen. In this letter to his young American correspondent, Foster, Skues tells what ensued. His reference to cut hackles is an interesting one, as he once told his friend Dr. Barton that a man who would cut a hackle would cut your throat!

J.W. DUNNE I met before he published *Sunshine and the Dry Fly*. He was a friend of Dr. N.J. McCaskie who introduced us. I had a correspondence with Dunne about his theories while his book was still on the stocks and I have his letters somewhere still. I had long been impressed with the value of translucency in trout flies.

It was not until the early twenties that I met Dunne. In the meanwhile I had tried other methods to achieve translucency, the most successful being the use of seal's fur for spinners . . . I was impressed by his theory and got him down for a weekend at Winchester. He only got one trout (a two pounder) and that was on his idea of a B.W.O. nymph. But I got his book when it came out, also a set of his silks and cellulite and I bought all his patterns except the Green Drakes. I never, however, could do any good with them, possibly because I hated the look of his cut hackles. McCaskie, however, did well with one of his patterns. But I still thought I could make something of Dunne's central idea of cellulite over a white enamelled hook, and disregarding his blending of cellulite I tied several flies with ordinary starling wings and ordinary dyed olive hackles but with bodies of cellulite to my own fancy, and I found that when these flies came over a trout without drag they were generally taken at the first offer. But I also found that the cellulite cut and frayed and went fluffy with the least excuse, and that once it got fluffy it was of no attraction to the trout. The least touch of the serrated edge of a sedge ruined it as readily as did the teeth of a trout and one trout was fatal to the fly's future usefulness. These patterns took much longer to tie and were so readily ruined that I gave them up. (Letter to Foster, 3rd January, 1942)

Earl Grey

Grey was the British Foreign Secretary at the outbreak of the First World War, remembered for his declaration, 'The lamps are going out all over Europe. We shall not see them lit again in our lifetime.' He would probably have much preferred to have been fly fishing, and his book, *Flyfishing*, published in 1899, is regarded rightly as one of the classics. Skues pays tribute to him and recalls him as a fellow pupil at Winchester School.

IN THE PERSON of Viscount Grey, known in his younger days, and indeed through the greater part of his career (and especially to fly fishers), as Sir Edward Grey, the Club lost by his death on the 7th September last a distinguished and loyal member, though one who had not been able for many years past to give the members as much of his company as they would have liked; so that most of them had to be content with the pleasure derived from his classic volume on *Fly Fishing*, also *The Charm of Birds*, *Fallodon Papers* and others. Though he had served the country in the most difficult and exacting offices of State, fly fishing was probably nearer his heart than any mundane ambitions; indeed, Mr. Gladstone said of him: 'Edward Grey might be anything he liked in public life but he prefers to go afishing'; and although the part he took in the Great War of 1914–1918 will undoubtedly not let his name drop out of history like the names of so many temporarily eminent public servants, it is as a fly fisherman and as author of the books above-mentioned that his memory will continue green while his volumes and the new editions of them hold together.

The year 1876–7 was my last year at the School, and in 1877 I had to give up to preparation for examinations the fly fishing at which I had been making inadequate efforts in the summers of 1875 and 1876 – but I remember Grey as a small boy in Eton jacket, grey trousers, and a straw hat with the distinguishing ribbon of Du Boulay's House, being pointed out to me in Meads. But, being absent from the riverside in 1877, I did not make his acquaintance while he was at the School, but I recall his representing the School in racquets – I think in 1880. He was also a distinguished tennis player, and the qualities of hand and eye which enabled him to excel at racquets and tennis no doubt contributed not a little to his success as a fly fisherman.

In the same article, Grey on Marryat:

> 'ONE COULD NOT say which was the more instructive, to watch
> his fishing or to listen to his talk; no one had more information
> to give; no one was more gracious in giving it; his knowledge
> seemed to result not only from observation and experience but
> of some peculiar insight into the ways of trout. In the manage-
> ment of rod and tackle he displayed not only skill but genius.'
> (*Flyfishers' Journal*, Autumn 1933)

H.S. Hall

Henry Sinclair Hall was one of the triumvirate, together with Halford
and Marryat, who initiated the dry fly revolution. He was also one of
the four original members of the Flyfishers' Club and lived to see its
fiftieth year, dying in 1934 aged 86. He got in touch with W.H.
Aldam, the author of *A Quaint Treatise on Flees and the Art a'
Artyfichall Flee Making*, published in 1876, having noticed that the
two mayfly patterns in that book were tied on eyed hooks. Aldam
supplied him with a number of Japaned Limericks, down to number
17. For the rest of the story and Hall's other accomplishments, Skues
takes up the tale.

> TO MEN INNUMERABLE outside fly fishing circles H.S. Hall must
> be known as joint author of probably the most widely used
> school text book on Algebra. But his enduring fame will be in
> the memory of trout fishers with the fly in that he was not only
> the inventor who first made practicable the eyed hook for trout
> flies, but that he also worked out, with the aid of George
> Selwyn Marryat, the still unsurpassed method of dressing split-
> winged trout flies on his hooks so that they would not only
> float but cock.
>   The invention of Hall's Snecky Limerick bend of eyed hook
> with upturned eye begun in 1878, was perfected by March
> 1879, and has never been superseded, being for upwinged
> floaters to this day the most successful bend of eyed trout fly
> hook. For this section of his work Hall received due credit, but
> the credit to which he is entitled for evolving the dressing on
> his hooks of the split-winged floater has been seriously over-
> shadowed by the fame of F.M. Halford's *Floating Flies and How
> to Dress Them* which could hardly have been written but for
> Hall's previous work, as the worldwide development and

dominance of the dry fly which followed could hardly have been achieved. It is also apt to be forgotten that before *Floating Flies* was published in 1886 Hall had published earlier in the same year, a chapter in the Badminton Library on *Chalk Stream Fishing with the Floating Fly* which gives him priority over Halford.

In 1883 Hall was instructing George Holland in his method of fly dressing which brought the double dressed split winged floater to a perfection never since surpassed.

Hall was probably the first in permanent angling literature to call specific notice by name to the blue-winged olive. He described it in his Badminton Chapter and had previously described it in *The Field* and, possibly, in *The Fishing Gazette*. Hall also evolved and described in the same chapter the detached body for trout flies, from which Halford took his pen name of Detached Badger. (*Flyfishers' Journal*, Summer 1934)

Izaak Walton

In his last years, Skues corresponded regularly with W.H. Lawrie, the author of *A Reference Book of English Trout Flies* and several other books. Sadly, most of the correspondence was lost during a Trans-Atlantic crossing. Perhaps we reveal ourselves more frankly in letters which are never intended for publication, and this certainly seems the case in Skues's forthright demolition of the saintly Izaak.

FRANKLY AND UNFORTUNATELY I confess I have never under-stood or shared in the enthusiasm evoked by the *Compleat Angler*. Izaak Walton was to my mind a tedious old gentleman and I suspect him of being something of a humbug. (Fragment of a letter to W.H. Lawrie)

CHAPTER 15

Dry Fly; Wet Fly: Halford, Skues and the Nymph

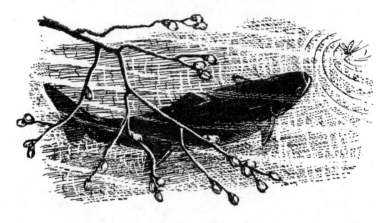

It has been said that one of the less attractive attributes of Skues was his continual criticism of Frederic Halford. In one respect, Skues had an enormous advantage; he lived for 35 years after his protagonist had died and could therefore not answer back. Sadly, Halford, on his way back from North Africa in 1914 and looking forward to the coming fishing season, died before his liner reached Southampton.

In order to put the debate into a proper perspective, it seems to me necessary to divide it into three phases. The first is Skues's personal relationship with Halford and assessment of his work. The second is Skues's ever-expanding vision of the role of the nymph and its relationship to the dry fly and Halford. The third is the reaction against nymph fishing which appears to have taken place in the 1930s, necessitating Skues's vigorous defence against the dry fly purists whose arguments were based on Halford's doctrines.

Shocks and a lesson – Halford

The first thing to remember about Skues's account of this encounter is that it was written 60 years after it took place, and the memory could be somewhat coloured by subsequent events. However sceptical Skues may have been at this time, there is no doubt they were on friendly terms, Halford generously offering to put Skues up for membership of the Flyfishers' Club. Though Skues declined, he subsequently became a member three years later, Halford proposing him and William Senior seconding.

IN EARLY SEPTEMBER 1891, having gone through a pretty strenuous time, I was badly run down when I started with an angling friend from the British Museum to spend ten days of my three weeks' annual holiday on the upper waters of the Yore; and at the expiration of that ten days I was not a little surprised to find that, thanks to the bracing moorland air and the good feeding provided by the good natured landlady of the inn at which we stayed, I had put on 13lb in weight. From there we planned to proceed to Winchester and to spend the remainder of our three weeks upon the Abbots Barton stretch of the Itchen immediately above Winchester by the kind permission of the client who was the lessee of the water. I had been presented in 1887 with a copy of Halford's *Floating Flies and How to Dress Them*, and in 1889 with Halford's first edition of *Dry Fly Fishing in Theory and Practice*, and both of us, relatively inexperienced, looked on these immortal works as revelation from on high with all the authority of gospel truth.

We had heard on the day of our arrival in Winchester that the great man was putting up at The George and was nightly welcoming his worshippers at that hotel to hear him expound the pure and authentic gospel of the dry fly – which no one would dream of questioning. So that evening found us, after our meal, among the humble listeners. It came to our ears on that occasion that we were to have the great man's company on the Abbots Barton water, the lessee having invited him for a week. With becoming reverence we listened to his words of wisdom until it became necessary that the session be broken up.

On the following day we were on the water a quarter of an hour or so before our mentor's arrival – taking the side stream, my friend above in the Ducks' Nest Spinney, I a couple of hundred yards further downstream, thus leaving the main river, the fishing of which was reputed the better, to the great man. He was not long behind us and presently we saw him casting on Winnal Water, the main river. Soon afterwards he crossed the meadow which divided the two streams and accosted me from the left bank of the side stream to advise us kindly on the fly to put up, and to make his advice clearer he cast his fly to light on the right bank of the side stream, having first ascertained that I had mounted a fly of George Holland's dressing, known as the Quill Marryat. He insisted that his fly, which was an India-Rubber Olive, was the right fly. My selection was based on little pale duns seen on the water. I took a look at his fly and was not a little shocked to see how coarse was the gut on which his fly was tied, but I was also too polite or timid to venture on such a comment.

We met at lunchtime and he inquired how I had done. I said two and a half brace. He had one trout only, but congratulated me civilly and offered to put me up for the Flyfishers' Club, then recently formed. Not expecting, despite my additional 13lb in ten days, to live long enough to make it worthwhile, I declined and did not in fact seek membership till the autumn of 1893, when a voyage to the Cape and back had gone a long way to re-establishing my health.

Halford only fished the Abbots Barton length for three more days of this week, but just as I had been profoundly shocked to do better than the great master did on the first day, I was fated to be similarly shocked on each of his three other days. Yet it encouraged me to rely most on my own observations and not to attach undue importance to authority. My friend, by the way, caught the biggest fish of the week (1lb 13oz), but it was his only catch.

At this period I had little Itchen experience – perhaps three or four days each year since 1883, but for years afterwards I looked back on those four days whenever I was faced with the alternative of letting myself be guided by authority or going on my own wilful way, and I have seldom had grounds for regretting the lesson of September 1891. (*Itchen Memories*)

Writing to Sir Tom Eastham in 1945 Skues gives a more revealing glimpse into their relationship which illustrates his rather competitive nature. Halford's becoming 'nasty' must have taken place some years later, as in 1891 Skues was not yet into fishing the wet fly to any extent.

IN SEPTEMBER 1891 I fished the Itchen with him (Halford) for a six-day week and wiped his eye every day, and he was quite pleasant about it and wanted to put me up for the Flyfishers' Club and, later on, asked me to contribute a fly dressing chapter to his *Dry Fly Entomology*. It was only on the use of the sunk fly that he became nasty. (Letter to Sir Tom Eastham, 27th November, 1945)

F.M. Halford

In 1929, Skues gave a considered assessment of Halford for the *Salmon and Trout Magazine* which I have had to abridge somewhat for the purpose of this book. It rightly accords Halford his supreme place as the prophet of the dry fly, yet there are niggling inferences that perhaps Marryat played a bigger part in the writing of Halford's first two books than he is given credit for.

THE DAYS WHEN Frederic Maurice Halford bestrode the fly fishing world like a giant with none to say him 'nay' are no more. Time has brought its inevitable revenges – and, with the questioning of some of his doctrine, there has obtruded of late a disposition to belittle the essential service which he did to fly fishing and his place in the hierarchy of great anglers. This is not as it should be – and it is the purpose of this chapter to examine and set forth, now that he is some fifteen years gone from us and while there yet remains a generation which remembers him, the true nature of his achievement.

In his circumstances, gifted with ample means to ensure abundant leisure for the study and practice of his art by the side of his beloved chalk streams, with a mind acute and powerful, great powers of observation and unwearying industry, he came withal to the business at a singularly fortunate time in the history of fly fishing for the accomplishment of his mission in life, for it brought him into close association with a group of exceptional men – a group such as has probably never before or since in the history of fly fishing been equalled for fly fishing ability, interest and accomplishment.

First and foremost we have George Selwyn Marryat, universally regarded as the prince of fly fishers, fly dressers and waterside naturalists; Francis Francis, then angling editor of *The Field* and an all-round angler of great versatility and experience; H.S. Hall, who, with the aid and stimulation of G.S. Marryat not only evolved and made practicable the eyed hook which made modern dry fly fishing a practical proposition, but converted to the use of the dry fly the method of upwinged fly dressing which is described in Walton's time, and trained the incomparable George Holland to dress his patterns to perfection. There were also Major Carlisle (South West), Major Turle (of the famous knot), Dr. Wickham (inventor of Wickham's Fancy), W.H. Pope (of Pope's Nondescript fame), H.P. Hawksley (the double tapered oiled silk line) and a number of others.

Before he came into contact with them Halford had had apprenticeship of a sort on the Gloucestershire Coln and the Wandle – but it was in April 1879, that he met and made the acquaintance of G.S. Marryat in John Hammond's shop at Winchester. Marryat and Francis were at that time lessees of a stretch of the Itchen above Winchester and H.S. Hall was at that time in Winchester itself, busy (with every encouragement from Marryat) upon the development of the hook which, under the title of 'Hall's Up-eyed Snecky Limerick', was to revolutionise the art.

It was about this time, or possibly a little earlier, that the oiled silk line came from America, and with it the six-piece split cane rod. Messrs. Eaton and Deller, and simultaneously, or not long after, Messrs. Hardy Bros., catching at the possibilities of the situation were soon adapting the method of rod building to English conditions of fly fishing, not only wet but dry, with the result that rods to carry the weight of oiled silk lines and to project them into the wind became an accomplished fact. H.P. Hawksley (surgical instrument maker), one of the group, bettered American instruction and produced double tapered oiled silk lines of a beauty and finish never since surpassed and only perhaps equalled later on by the amateur work of the late Walter Durfee Coggeshall.

Dr. Wickham had recently acquired a stretch of the Test and had formed the Houghton Fly Fishing Club (not that which originally bore and has since resumed that place name), and, joining this association of distinguished anglers, Halford found himself in an ideal position for the work that lay before him.

The enthusiasm which Halford put into his pursuit may be gauged by the fact that before the end of 1880 he had decided to try and write a full treatise on the theory and practice of the dry fly, and 'with Marryat's assistance the work of collating the necessary materials was seriously taken in hand.' It has been suggested that Halford himself was not an originator or inventor, and that at best he was a recorder of other men's methods and discoveries. It is not a fair criticism, for it might be said of almost any man. If all that any writer owed to his predecessors and contemporaries were eliminated from his credit, there are few to whom any credit worth speaking of would remain. The fact stands, that of all that group of angling supermen, Halford was the one upon whom the genius of Marryat fastened for the performance of the great work.

It was not, however, the book on *Dry Fly Fishing in Theory and Practice* which first made its appearance, but the work which took the fly fishing world by storm in 1886 under the title of *Floating Flies and How to Dress Them*. The distance of the date from the year (1880) when the plan of writing a book on the subject was formed, is sufficient evidence of the long and laborious apprenticeship which Halford underwent by way of preparation before publishing. The book had an instant and a well deserved success. The only regrettable feature of it was, to use an Irishism, one which was not there. There were no illus- trations of the natural insects which the dressings purported to simulate – such as gave Ronalds' work such a special value; and, for some reason undisclosed, the lack was never made good in any subsequent volume.

In 1889 after two more years of incubation, the work on which, in the judgment of the present writer, Halford's fame stands solidly based, was given to the world, dedicated appro- priately to G.S. Marryat.

Looking back on that work after some forty years of further experience, and making due allowance for the advance of mechanical achievement in the manufacture of gear, for the forming of the light rod, for the discovery of the use of paraf- fin, and for the fact that Halford had not, as he records in his autobiography, learnt his fly fishing on the rough streams devoted to the wet fly, it is fair to say that in its near on three hundred pages there is practically nothing on the positive side which the writer need, if living at this day, feel any occasion to recall or qualify. This is I think a testimony to the book which could hardly be repeated of any other work in the literature of fly fishing, and a magnificent justification of Marryat's choice of Halford to be the prophet of the new cult.

If Halford had never written a line after the 1889 edition of *Dry Fly Fishing in Theory and Practice*, his title to a supreme place in the Anglers' Valhalla would still rest secure. He did a great work in that volume, and produced an effect on methods of angling for trout which will probably never be wholly lost.

In the Spring of 1914 he went to his rest. May the turf lie lightly over him. (*Side-Lines, Side-Lights and Reflections*)

What made the dry fly possible?

By 1921, Skues had had a further 11 years' experience of fishing the nymph since his first book. Now, in *The Way of a Trout with a Fly*, he examined all aspects of trout behaviour which he said would lead up to 'an understanding of the true theory of trout-fly dressing.' The second part of the book, entitled *Some Further Minor Tactical Studies*, consisted of articles he had written for various journals on different aspects of fly fishing, and those pieces on dry and wet fly fishing inevitably brought him back to Halford.

In this passage, he explains the advances in fishing technology which made it possible for the cult of the dry fly to emerge.

THE USE OF the dry fly connotes the ability of the angler to fish upstream whatever the state of the wind. The clearness of the chalk stream required the casting of a longer line than was necessary on rough streams. The silk and hair lines which, prior to the coming of the American braided oiled silk lines, were the best that could be produced could not be cast into an adverse wind. They could be cast upstream with the wind, across stream with the wind, and downstream with the wind, but, as a general proposition, casting against the wind was beyond them. A fly cast upstream or across with the wind might very well float or sink – in either case it might be taken by the trout – but a fly cast downstream was *bound* to sink. And as any violence in striking when the fly is downstream is apt to be visited with a smash, rods, though built long to fish far off, had to be floppy in the top to ensure gentle striking. The result was also the keeping light of the reel line, and thus was produced a combination which, exquisite in its way, was the very worst that could be conceived for dry fly fishing. Stewart preached the stiff rod and the upstream cast, but his was necessarily a short cast.

The things which made the dry fly generally possible were the coming of the heavy American braided oiled silk line and the split cane rod. I remember buying my first length of oiled silk line in 1877, but I knew so little of its purpose that I used it for sea fishing, and it was, I think, in the eighties that, stimulated by American progress in the building of split canes, our makers began to build split canes suitable for carrying these heavy lines. The heavy line was needed to deliver the fly dry and to put it into the wind, the split cane, or a wood rod on the same lines, was necessary to deliver the heavy line.

With the hour came the men, Mr. H.S. Hall, Mr. G.S. Marryat and Mr. F.M. Halford, who evolved from the poor feeble types of dry fly of the seventies the efficient dry fly of the eighties and the present day. (*The Way of a Trout with a Fly*)

The excommunication of the wet fly

Skues examines why the wet fly became anathema on the chalk streams. In doing so, he refers to Halford's 'fair mindedness and intellectual honesty which characterises everything that came from his pen.' He does not criticise Halford, but points out that he was wrong when he said that the wet fly did not pay, largely because he did not associate it with fishing upstream. Skues points out that nowhere did Halford say that use of the wet fly was wicked, and the inference is that this came from his dry fly purist disciples.

I HAVE BEEN trying for some time past – but hitherto in vain – to discover the precise moment of time when the theory that it was not sportsmanlike, and therefore not permissible, to fish with the wet fly upon chalk streams was given to a reverently awaiting world, and who was the prophet from whose lips the words of wisdom fell. I recall some years ago seeing it propounded in the press – I believe in *The Fishing Gazette* – it was a rule upon chalk streams that the dry fly only must be employed, and I remember being not a little amused, for up to that time, though fishing quite a noted length of a crack chalk stream, and meeting upon it many excellent fishers with the fly, I had never heard the theory propounded by any one of them. True that almost without exception, as I myself at the time, they fished dry, but that was because they believed that thus they were more likely to be successful. Frequently, and perhaps more often than not, that would be so; but they made the error of mistaking the particular – the frequent particular, the pretty general, if you will – for the universal and I believe that, if once they had been convinced that it was not always the dry fly that paid best, but that on parts of most days the wet fly, properly applied, was the more attractive, they were open minded enough to be ready to reconsider their practice on its merits, and would still be so but for the edict that the wet fly was anathema on chalk streams. Yet, though I laughed, the writer was right and I was wrong. So perhaps I may be forgiven if I take up a little space in examining the question historically, to see just what it all means, and to discover, if possible, how it came about.

Whatever may be the present state of chalk stream opinion on the subject, there can be little doubt that, in its inception the dry fly was not adopted for any other reason than that it was found to pay – that is, to kill trout which would not yield to the seductions of the wet fly as then practised. Francis Francis was a broad minded angler, with ample experience of wet fly fishing, whose period comprised the early days of the dry fly, and, writing with a knowledge of both, he used, in his *Book on Angling*, these wise words: 'The judicious and perfect application of dry, wet and mid-water fishing stamps the finished fly fisher with the hallmark of efficiency.' What was it that led chalk stream angling opinion so far from these ideals?

The words quoted by me are quoted with approval by Mr. F.M. Halford in chapter 11 of *Dry Fly Fishing in Theory and Practice*, headed, 'Floating Flies and Sunk Flies'. That chapter is written with the fair mindedness and intellectual honesty which characterizes everything that came from his pen. And yet I think I detect in that chapter, and in that volume, much that has lent support to the tendency of thought which we are inquiring into. It was there argued at considerable length and with much acuteness that *on chalk streams the wet fly does not pay*, that the dry fly is successful on these streams when the sunk fly is utterly hopeless. It is not suggested that it is wicked to use the wet fly, only that it is ineffectual. But, in order to test this argument, it is necessary to see what Mr. F.M. Halford meant by the wet fly. Let me quote his exact words:

'The sunk or wet fly he (the angler) casts to a likely place, whether he has or has not seen a rise there (more frequently he has not), and, in fact, his judgment would tend to tell him where, from his knowledge of the habits of the fish, they are most likely to be found in position or likely to feed. Thus wet fly fishing is often termed *fishing the water* in contradistinction to the expression *fishing the rise*, which is applied to the method of the dry fly fisherman.'

Mr. Halford, therefore, understood wet fly fishing as fishing at large all over the water as against fishing the rise. Would he at that time have objected (had it occurred to him to do so) to a wet fly fisherman confining himself to fishing the rise, or the located fish, with the wet fly? I can hardly think so. He was more open minded than that. He said in the same chapter which I have quoted:

'Some dry fly fishermen are such purists that they will not, under any circumstances whatever, make a single cast except over rising fish, and prefer to remain idle the entire day rather than attempt to persuade the wary inhabitants of the stream to rise at an artificial fly, unless they have previously seen a natural one taken in the same position. Although respecting their scruples, this is, in my humble opinion, riding the hobby to death, and I for one am a strong advocate for floating a cocked fly over a likely place, even if no movement of a feeding fish has been seen there . . . There is no doubt that an angler catching sight of a trout or grayling lying near the surface, or in position for feeding, can often tempt him with a good imitation of the fly on the water floated accurately over him at the first cast.'

Would he have denied to the wet fly man – had he believed that the wet fly paid – the same privilege as he would accord to the dry fly man? I see no reason to suppose so. But it will have been seen from these quotations that at that time at any rate the idea of the wet fly being used much as the dry fly, and cast only to rising fish, to fish seen 'hovering' in position to feed, and to likely places carefully chosen, had apparently not occurred to him. In fact, the comparison which he has made is between the dry fly practice of chalk streams and the unintelligent wet fly practice of rough rivers, applied, if you like, to chalk streams, and not between dry fly practice and wet fly practice deliberately thought out and adapted to use on chalk streams.

He says of the wet fly, it is true, 'It is said that there are days when, even in the clearest of them, the sunk fly is found more killing than the floating one. This may possibly be true, but in many years' experience such days have not fallen to my lot, and I should be inclined to consider them as *happening one*, or, in other words, as the rare exceptions which go to prove the rule.'

I propose to give later on my reasons for doubting whether, with his special dry fly equipment, Mr. F. M. Halford often made the whole-hearted experiments essential to bring this comparison to a real test. He never believed the wet fly on a chalk stream would pay.

Now, where in the writings of any angling authority do we get it laid down that the wet fly is wicked, and that the high-

and-dry school are entitled to look down from a height of ethical superiority upon those who can, and do, alternate wet with dry? I have looked in vain.

The fact, however, remains that there *is* or *was* a body of opinion hostile to any use of the wet fly upon chalk streams, and apt to claim a higher ethical standard than is enough for those who do not object to fish these rivers on suitable occasions with a wet fly; and it would be interesting to see how it came into being. I suspect the evolution was much as follows:

The necessity of casting upstream in all weathers evolved the heavy tapered line, and that again seemed to necessitate, and did in fact evolve, the heavy rod and the double-dressed floater. This equipment was quite unsuited to wet fly fishing, and so employed was quite as likely to result in scaring the fish as in catching them. Then wet fly fishing, in the sense of casting across or across and down stream a dragging fly, was apt to attract small fish, and to result in their being hooked, or pricked and scared. This was undoubtedly bad for the water. *Ergo*, wet fly fishing is bad for the water, and ought to be barred.

This opinion became firmly rooted in many minds, and no doubt it was easier to make a rule of no wet fly, especially as the wet fly was not believed to pay, than to make a distinction between wet fly according to knowledge and mere wet fly. It was, no doubt, suggested and believed that even a wet fly cast upstream to bulging fish was apt to line them and scare them. (I believe this is quite incorrect, for the trout must constantly be having weeds and other matter brought downstream quite as likely to touch and scare it as the line, and would think nothing of a touch from a line merely carried by the current). So the wet fly became anathema with some folk. In brief, it did not pay, and it did harm.

But when it has come to be shown that, rightly fished in the right conditions, it does pay, and does no harm, unless adding to the angler's sport and the weight of his basket be harm, the ground of objection is changed. It is too deadly. It is as bad as worm fishing or the use of an Alexandra. It is not fly fishing at all. These violences defeat themselves. I am quite willing to admit that whatever is unfair to the brother angler or damaging to the water is rightly to be barred, but to say that it is fair to cast a dry fly persistently over a bulging trout with no genuine hope of getting him, and is unfair to cast a sunk fly to him with a good chance of getting him, seems to me absurd.

If I am right, the opponents of the wet fly fairly used seem to
be driven upon the argument that it is not fly fishing. This is a
mere verbal distinction culled *ad hoc*, and as an argument it
leaves me cold. For generations wet fly fishing was the only fly
fishing – on waters, too, where the dry fly now reigns supreme
– and in those days, if records do not lie, baskets were not inferior to the best of the present day. And if a method of wet fly
fishing, which, in the sense only of its giving one an added
chance of trout, and no other, is detrimental to the water, is a
sin, then I am quite content to remain in my iniquity with
Kingsley and Francis Francis, and a host of other good anglers,
and I deny the right of users of Wickham's Fancy, Gold-Ribbed
Hare's ears, Pope's Nondescripts, Red Tags, Macaw Tags and
Bumbles and fancy flies generally, to cast the first stone at me.
The light rod, casting a medium line, available for either dry fly
or wet, and a supply of a few patterns, specially dressed for sinking, in addition to one's floater, render it possible for the angler
to cast upstream to his trout, dry fly or wet, as he may judge
best, with no more fear of injuring the young stock in the one
case than the other, and with an added chance of sport by a
method no whit less difficult or fascinating than the dry fly.
(*The Way of a Trout with a Fly*)

Halford and the wet fly

In 1935, Skues again returns to Halford's misunderstanding of the
wet fly, and how Halford, and other anglers who fished the dry fly,
never realised that trout which broke the surface were often feeding
on hatching nymphs, and that it was not solely when they were on
the bottom or bulging in weeds. Skues's own conclusion that nymphs
on the point of hatching are practically inert has been disputed by
Sawyer, who said that he had never seen a live nymph floating in the
film without seeing some movement of legs and body, and that
Skues's success was probably because his flies were sparsely hackled
which produced a certain movement of the fibres. However, Peter
Lapsley reminds me that if you watch ephemerid nymphs in an aquar-
ium their movement generally, and their progress to the surface,
consists of short bursts of energetic swimming followed by (usually
longer) periods spent hanging, completely inert.

IT IS NOT seldom both useful and interesting to re-read, in the
light of interim experience, books which have made a great

impression on one in the past. This observation is due to the fact that, accident having driven me to a re-reading of Halford's *Dry Fly Fishing in Theory and Practice*, I find myself understanding, as I have never hitherto done, the reasons which led him to take up such a die-hard attitude on the subject of the dry fly.

Reading that remarkable volume from end to end, I find that apart from his misunderstandings of the use of the wet fly, and his belief that it was necessarily a chuck and chance it matter, he believed that times when the trout were bulging or feeding at the bottom were the only times that they were nymphing, and that his observation, generally so sound, never served to make him understand (1) that trout, lying under banks in particular, are constantly feeding on nymphs as quietly as they do on floating fly and with as little rushing about; and (2) that on such occasions the nymphs (with their skins inflated, as he recognises, in readiness for hatching) are not darting about and lively, but practically inert, as they drift slowly upwards with the current towards the surface.

Halford was not the man to go back and continually to revise his opinions and to bring them up to date in the light of later experience. Once having established a proposition to his satisfaction it became fact. And so we find that in the later editions of *Dry Fly Fishing in Theory and Practice* and in his other volumes, while he broke out in other directions, and in particular into an attempt to standardise patterns of floating fly for all time, he went on building his argument on the subject of the use of the wet fly in chalk streams on the insufficiently observed data brought to the production of his first magnum opus. It is the more remarkable inasmuch as again and again throughout his writings he insists that the great bulk of the food of the chalk stream trout is subaqueous. So that in the end he was driven into the extreme position of having to maintain that trout must not be fished for on chalk streams with representations of what they most fed on, but with what they fed least on, namely, the hatched and floating fly.

Another strange feature of the case is that, so far as may be judged from Halford's writings, and from contemporary literature in the press and in book form, neither he nor the multitude of anglers who fished the dry fly, ever showed the slightest consciousness that a vast proportion of the rises of trout in position, whether under a bank or not, which broke the surface (quite apart from occasions of bulging) were cases of the taking of the hatching nymph, and not the hatched fly. And I think it is safe to say that most dry fly anglers must have gone on, year after year, in this unconsciousness, casting carefully dried flies to trout which were exclusively busy with subaqueous food. If such anglers were using, as they often must have been, one or other of the patterns which seem to have an attraction for subaqueous feeding fish, such as the Red Quill, the Gold-Ribbed Hare's Ear and Pope's Green Nondescript, the success brought by such patterns may, with the odd occasions when a subaqueous feeder would take a floater and the not infrequent occasions when trout are taking a floater and the not infrequent occasions when trout are taking both hatched and hatching fly indifferently, have served to keep them from discovering the truth which, had their flies been persistently and invariably refused, must in the end have broken in upon them.

There is no use in saying, and I do not suggest, that to ascertain whether a trout rising under a far bank is taking duns on the surface or under water is not a matter of extreme difficulty. Even now, after years of concentration on the subject, I am often deceived, and my own conversion came about through my approaching the question from quite a different angle, as described in *Minor Tactics of the Chalk Stream*. For many years it never occurred to me that F.M. Halford and his distinguished associates could be wrong, and it was not until after that volume was published that I began to realise, increasingly as the years went on, what an immense proportion of the food taken *at the surface* was nymphal, and that much of the trout's subaqueous food was taken there and not at the bottom or in bulging in the weeds as Halford clearly believed.

In view of my own slowness to deduce the true facts it would ill become me to cast a stone at any brother angler. But I cannot help thinking what a difference it would have made to the last half century of fly fishing if Halford and his friends had realised the truth as it has latterly appeared. It might have availed, to quote his own words in *Dry Fly Fishing in Theory and Practice*, 'to revolutionise the whole art of fly fishing as practised in Hampshire.' (*Flyfishers' Journal*, Winter 1935)

The nymph debate

It does seem that in the years before the 1939–45 war, and almost 30 years after *Minor Tactics of the Chalk Stream*, Skues's many articles and other books, and the advocacy of other nymph fishermen, there was a strong reaction towards dry fly purism and renewed efforts to impose a rigid dry fly only code on the southern chalk streams. Skues was forced into a robust defence of his methods, and this entailed a rebutting of Halford's theories on which the dry fly lobby stood. However, as far as I can ascertain, it was directed only at what Skues considered were Halford's misconceived ideas about the wet fly and was never intended to reflect on his great works as a whole or on him as a person.

This is amply illustrated by a debate held at the Flyfishers' Club in 1938 when, despite Skues ably defending his principles and theories, in which he was supported by John Waller Hills, he was attacked in the debate by a majority of those present.

Skues must have felt bitter that after 30 years during which he had made enormous contributions to the Club, including being the mainstay of the Club Journal, his theories and practice were being disparaged by some fishermen whose inexperience and ignorance of his methods were self-evident in what they said. He seems to have been especially disturbed by the remarks of Dr. Mottram who, in his book, *Fly Fishing: some New Arts and Mysteries*, published in 1915, had so ably expounded his own research into the nymph. Now, Mottram appeared to have deserted to the other side.

It must have seemed to Skues that the ghost of Halford, who had died 24 years previously, continued to haunt him. Certainly, it is clear that after the debate he resolved to set out his views once and for all in another book, which became *Nymph Fishing for Chalk Stream Trout*, which was published in 1939 on the eve of the Second World War. Ernest Schwiebert, commenting on this book in his own volume, *Nymphs: a Complete Guide to Naturals and Imitations*, says, 'the book is somewhat flawed with a detailed and critical analysis of the fallacies in Halford, sustaining an argument won thirty-odd years before with a theoretical adversary who had died twenty five years earlier.' However, the question might be asked, had it been won with the majority of chalk stream fly fishers at that time and, indeed, has it been won to this very day? John Goddard tells me that when he was a member of the Piscatorial Society in the late fifties and early sixties they had a number of debates on nymph versus dry fly, and even at that time a big majority of the members were still what can only be termed dry fly purists, and were violently opposed to any form of nymph fishing. He formed the conclusion that the main reason they were opposed to this form of fishing was due more to their inability to spot trout beneath the surface and so become a competent nymph fisher than any other reason. A similar debate was held at the Flyfishers' Club only four or five years ago in which the same prejudice was evident.

Reaction

Skues himself, in his final defence in book form of the practice of nymph fishing, came to rather similar conclusions.

IN THE LAST year or so I have, somewhat to my surprise, seen signs of a movement on the part of some chalk stream anglers to try to re-rivet upon their brethren the fetters of the exclusive dry fly, from which I had hoped that time, experience and common sense had enabled anglers to shake themselves free. But whenever I have come across anglers who wish to re-establish the exclusive dominance of the dry fly, I have almost invariably found that they ranged themselves under one or more of the following heads:

1   Men who do not understand and will not take the trouble to learn the art of fishing with the nymph.

2   Men who find the whole fascination of chalk stream fishing in seeing the fly taken on the surface – a good enough reason for their own practice, but none for intolerance nor for restricting the practice of anglers who find an even subtler charm in taking subaqueously trout which, while feeding at or near the surface, are not taking the floating natural insect.

3   Men who suppose it to be a 'chuck and chance it' method of fishing the water. These are radically and ignorantly wrong, for it is nothing of the sort.

4   Men who think it an unduly deadly method. It is too difficult an art to be that, even if the charge were true. After all, the dry fly came in as an improved and more deadly method, enabling the angler to catch trout untakable in light or calm weather by the wet fly as then understood. Why then should an art which gives the angler a chance of taking trout for the time being untakable by the dry fly be barred?

5   Finally (and these are the great majority), men who do not
know what a nymph is like and assume that the objects
commonly sold by tackle dealers as such – most of which bear
no resemblance to the real insect and have whatever success
they obtain simply as lures, illegitimate on chalk streams – are
what is meant by nymphs. This class are justified in their objections to the use of such objects under the name of nymph or
any other name, but are not justified in objecting to the use of
proper representations of the natural nymph. (*Nymph Fishing
for Chalk Stream Trout*)

In the same chapter, he emphasises that fishing the nymph is complementary to fishing the dry fly.

DR. MOTTRAM, ONCE an advocate of the nymph, but in his later
days a protagonist of the attack on nymph fishing, cannot put
his case higher than that nymph fishing on streams where the
trout can be easily caught out with the dry fly alone, ought not
to be allowed. On such streams, who would want to fish the
nymph at times when the simplest and more obvious method of
the floating fly is available? (*Nymph Fishing for Chalk Stream
Trout*)

It is interesting to contemplate what the subsequent history of fly
fishing would have been but for Skues's 50-year advocacy of the
upstream wet fly and nymph. Would the practice of dry fly fishing
have become even more universal and rigid? It may have done for a
time, but we all know that history decrees that all fashions and movements have their day, and are then supplanted or modified by new
ideas. The most dramatic modern-day example of this is the over-
throw of Communism after its holding sway for 70 years over large
parts of the world. The practice of upstream wet fly fishing in the
north of England and in Scotland was deep-rooted and was bound to
influence southern anglers, as it did Skues. Although readily acknowledging their debt to Skues, original thinkers such as Sawyer, Kite and
Schwiebert would inevitably have surfaced and modified our sport on
the lines with which we are familiar today.

CHAPTER 16

Skues and the Itchen

The River Itchen and the River Test are regarded world-wide as the two great classic chalk streams. The Itchen rises some miles north west of Petersfield and flows via Winchester into Southampton Water at Southampton. In Skues's time, the Abbots Barton stretch of the water to the north of Winchester consisted of about two miles of main river stretching from the southern edge of Kingsworthy to the recreation ground on the outskirts of the city, together with around two miles of carriers or sidestreams. Skues fished it for 56 years and it is associated uniquely with his name. He was not, however, the first famous fisherman to cast a fly there. Before Skues fished the water in 1883, by permission of the lessee, Irwin B. Cox, one of the proprietors of *The Field*, the previous tenants had been no less than the great George Selwyn Marryat and the equally renowned Francis Francis, author of one of the best-read books of the nineteenth century, *A Book of Angling*.

After Irwin B. Cox gave up the lease of Abbots Barton in 1919, the water was taken over by a small syndicate of which Skues was a founder member. The water had been neglected during the war, and varied in quality from year to year, as Skues was never tired of telling us, but, generally speaking, the sport available to a very small band of anglers was of the highest quality. Indeed, in his book, *Angling Letters of G.E.M. Skues*, Walker points out that Skues was born (piscatorially speaking) with a silver spoon in his mouth, and knew little of the weariness of fishing hard-flogged hotel or association waters. However, John Goddard tells me that he had regular access for nearly 15 years to the Abbots Barton stretch of the Itchen which was the same water that Skues had fished for most of his life, and he considers that because of its extreme clarity and rather slow flow it is one of the most demanding stretches of fly water that he has fished anywhere in the world.

This, then, was the scene of Skues's countless fishing days through every kind of weather from perishing Aprils of wind and rain on the exposed Abbots Barton water, through to the hot summer sun and

217

dreaming meadows. Throughout the years and the conditions, there is Skues, his enthusiasm undimmed, his dedication unfailing, observing, hypothesising – and always catching fish.

Most of the following extracts are taken from *Itchen Memories* which was published posthumously, and, though it is marred by a number of misprints caused in part by Skues's handwriting which became smaller and more spidery in his old age, it gives a picture of the many happy years he spent on that river.

Two blank days

This is an account by Skues of his fishing the Itchen in the later years of the nineteenth century. It is the story of two blank days, but what blank days! On the first he took 20 trout and on the second 24, but they were all under the takeable length. They are not the kind of blank days that most of us ordinary mortals experience.

NOT A VERY interesting subject? Perhaps not. But if you feel like that about it, pass on. I found it a bit intriguing. I could not fix the date of either of these days with any exactitude – not even the years.

The first, however, could not have been earlier than 1887 for I recall I was using a 10ft Greenheart of Farlow's painted a heron blue, which had been presented to me by a client of my firm in that year. It must also have been after 1888 (probably several years after), as I only began fly dressing in that year and I was casting a Little Red Sedge tied with a rolled landrail wing of which I did not discover the merit in my first year or two of fly dressing.

On the occasion in question I had been on the Itchen above Winchester all day without seeing any hatch of fly or rising trout either on the main or the side stream, and seven o'clock found me on the right bank of a straight stretch of a length of the side stream. I resolved to try a few chance casts with one of my Little Red Sedges before going back to my lodging; regardless of the non-existence of any hatch of fly or rise of trout, and as a beginning, I cast over my bank so that the fly only, with about 18 inches of gut, lit on the water. Almost as it lit the fly was grabbed by a trout, which I turned down and promptly netted out, and, as it was under the 12-inch limit of those days on that water, it went back into the river a few steps behind my stance. I dried my fly and made a fresh cast close to the bank a

219

few feet higher upstream. That, too, was taken, but again by a trout below the 12-inch limit, which in due course I returned to the water downstream. Cast after cast in the 200 yards or so up to the Cow Bridge (which crossed the stream about its middle), all delivered close to the bank, elicited rise after rise of trout, all of which took firmly, and all of which, being below the size limit, were promptly returned to the river, so that by the time I came within casting distance of the Cow Bridge I had had out and returned no fewer than nineteen unsizeable trout.

The bridge, however, presented a more hopeful prospect, for past experience had led me to hope for much better fish on the far side of the span. Not a bit of it. The fly was grabbed as promptly as ever, but again the trout proved unsuitable. So, after turning him in again, I reeled up in disgust and took the path across the meadow to return to my lodging to record a blank day.

The second occasion I have to record occurred some years later – a bright, fresh, hopeful sort of midsummer's day. Yet hour by hour went by without any hatch of fly or any sign on the surface to tempt me to cast, and by five o'clock I had got to the corner of the first bend below the railway arch. That corner usually held two or three decent trout, and I approached it cautiously so as not to scare them. There was no rise there, however, and after waiting a few minutes I dropped my fly – a Red Spinner with a claret seal's fur body and a sharp blue cock's hackle – at the point where I had hoped to find a takeable fish. At the second or third offer it was firmly grabbed – but by a trout of disappointing size, which had to go back. Two or three more took the fly below the railway arch – but again were unsizeable. So I turned to the sidestream which at this point approached the main. Here again trout after trout (though here they *were* rising) took my Red Spinner gaily and had to go back for the same unsatisfactory reason, until I had brought the number caught and returned to twenty four, and then, in despair, I reeled up and went in to record another blank day.

Now why on both occasions were only unsizeable fish willing to feed? (*Itchen Memories*)

Diary of an Itchen week

I have selected two days from this diary. The first is a Sunday, a non-fishing day. Skues, nonetheless, was down on the river, and describes the river plants and wild flowers he found there in the height of summer. The next day he is on the river betimes. Like the good all-round angler he is, he takes fish on sedge patterns, tries dry flies, catches fish on nymph patterns, uses spinners in the evening, and finally, on the advent of the blue-winged olive, kills a brace on Orange Quill.

Sunday 16th July, 1911

OUT AT EIGHT. Strolled round to the sawmill and found trout already busy in the head, lining up along the edge of the bend where the strength of the stream runs. Watched intently through Goerz Trieder monocular for twenty minutes, but never fly on the water, though the fish were rising regularly several times a minute. Every now and then the upper limb of the trout's tail peeped through the widening ring as he descended. This suggested spinners, but a careful study of the surface showed no sign of a spinner. Sunday being a dies non, went and sat on slope commanding higher reaches, and saw more fortunately placed anglers setting out with their rods.

This near the end of second week of drought. Very hot and sunny. River low, weeds high, and giant rushes so grown as to be a nuisance in places. This is a great year for mullein; tall spikes in great clusters. Ragwort also in huge patches; toad-flax, both yellow and lilac, in great profusion. Never saw so many green-veined white butterflies; they seem to have meeting and mating places in damp spots; could have covered two dozen in one spot with landing net. Cows up to their middles in river, or capering round with dinky little kinks in their tails. Horses, too, pestered with flies. But for a brisk breeze from west to south west mitigating the heat, it would be unendurable. Glad I had foresight to order in large supply of syphons. After lunch, trout still busy in mill-head. Still no sign of fly, but one rod's gillie said his master had done well enough with No.14 Whitchurch. Royal sunset. Dispute whether red enough to ensure fine tomorrow; wind prescribed.

Monday 17th July

COULD NOT SLEEP; up at five and out in meadows. Took rod, in case. Fine and sunny, but air close; no dew on grass. Trout already under banks, but mostly in places where weeds prevented flow of water, and quite unapproachable. Broad banks of ribbon weed for 15 to 20 feet on either side, often loaded with piles of cut weed sent on from upper waters. Found one trout in running water and got him with a small Landrail and Hare's Ear Sedge.

After breakfast met Keeper Humfry, who says lower end of side stream has been cut, and that I was in for week of weed cutting. Used expression designed to meet the case. Just my luck! Sun hot and high, wind veering west to south west, enough to temper extreme of heat but not put up much ruffle.

Found trout rising steadily in main, putting up noses as if taking surface food. But no fly to be seen. One fish came short to small No.1 Whitchurch, and was pricked with Pope's Nondescript 16. No spinners or fly on water. Used small-meshed fly net and caught pale-brown nymph. Matched it from my nymph box, and tackled trout rising in bays on opposite bank. In course of morning killed two brace and lost three others, besides mistiming one or two; delivered nymph wet by means of switch cast. Not a winged fly in any fish killed. Returned one trout. Evening rise in two parts. First, small fly or spinner (could not get on to the right pattern, and continued trying too long). Then blue-winged olive. At length awoke to situation, and put up Orange Quill on No.14 hook and killed brace of bankers. Home to interview syphon. (*Itchen Memories*)

A curious contrast

Skues ponders why, on two successive days of similar weather conditions, his catch on the first day was almost exclusively grayling, and the next day trout. Here he makes judicious use of both wet and dry fly.

IT IS ONE of the charms of fly fishing that no two days are exactly alike, however closely the weather conditions may seem to correspond. This is an account of two consecutive spring days on the Itchen which presented a remarkable contrast.

I have long had an affection for the large dark olive, and as it is seldom seen on the Itchen after mid-April I determined, in

spite of a keeper's warning that the trout had not yet begun to
get under the banks, to snap a couple of days by the waterside,
and I chose Wednesday and Thursday, April 9th and 10th.
Tuesday the 8th did not give me much encouragement, for it
was a bitter day of north-east wind, and, indeed, that wind had
been prevailing for nigh a week. It was therefore more for the
pleasure of stretching a line against the wind with my ten-foot
Leonard than with any expectation of sport that I strolled into
the meadows at about 10.30, fortified by waders and a mackintosh against the icy wind which blew dead down-stream. But by
the time I had assembled my rod and had passed the line
through the rings I saw, to my astonishment, a large dark olive
skating along the surface, propelled by the wind at more than
the natural pace of the stream, and before eleven o'clock the
first rise was in evidence; and very soon I was aware of no less
than three trout on the feed in the short stretch which was in
sight. I watched them carefully to see if they were taking the
surface duns, and soon made up my mind that they were not.
So I knotted on a wet pattern of the large dark olive, and began
with No.1. He, however, was 'not taking any', and the same
was true of No.2. The light, indeed, was a bad light – a sort of
dull leaden colour in sky and on the water, but everything
looked preternaturally clear. The third fish was an inexperienced
person, an inch under regulation length, and he was returned to
the water to gain his inch and wisdom. Then there came a
break in the clouds and a brief gleam of sun, but the large dark
olives, which had been growing more numerous, began to
slacken, and I could find no more rising trout. On a little bare
patch, however, under the far bank, just where a small meadow
runnel discharged into the stream, I made sure I spied a sizable
trout, and after an ineffectual shot or two I got my fly over
him. He looked at it and turned away. The next shot got it in
the mouth of the runnel. An underwater turn towards the bank
brought the fly into his, as I rightly judged, and I shortly had
the pleasure of netting out my first keepable trout of 1913 – a
well conditioned fish of fifteen inches. Before I had consigned
him to my bag the cathedral clock struck noon. From that time
on I did not see another large dark olive.

I had opened on the side-stream, but now I migrated to the
main. For a while there was a lull. Then I became aware of a
scattering rise of small palish olives. I cast over a number of
rising fish with but little success, for though I rose several of

them they all came short except four, and I was convinced that they were all grayling, like the two brace I caught. Since grayling were, as the chemists put it, 'in excess' in the water, and as the standing rule is to kill all you take, I knocked my two brace on the head. Presently I turned downstream again, and seeing another grayling put up I cast down to him and let the fly swing over him. In a second he took firmly and was fast. Another followed, and another, almost as fast as I could cast. Fish which came short at a fly floating loose struck firmly and hooked themselves on a taut down-stream line. By degrees ere five o'clock I raised my two brace of grayling to nine and a half brace, and thought I had done good service to the water in doing so. All this time I had not seen another trout put up. Returning to the side-stream I found nothing moving, a fact which did not surprise me at the time of day at that time of the year; but presently I spied a hovering fish of good size over a pale gravel patch. I despatched my dark Greenwell's Glory to him, and at the fourth offer he took it gaily. He proved to be the duplicate of my first trout of the day, both in length and condition. Finding no other fish showing, and feeling disinclined to return to my inn, I strolled back to the main, and between 5.30 and 6.15 I killed another brace of grayling. The startling thing, however, was that the trout were beginning to line up along each bank, as if preparing for an evening rise. I even brought up (and missed) two. I did not, however, wait for the evening rise to materialize, showing thus most commendable restraint.

The following day opened rather milder than its predecessor, with the wind from the north veering to the north-west. I was by the water-side punctually at a quarter to eleven, but in spite of the milder weather I saw no fly and no movement of a fish till 11.30. Soon after that hour chimed I saw, about a hundred yards up, a trout of two pounds if he was an ounce show half out of water as he swirled half across the stream to take a nymph. I crawled up into position, but he never showed again, and after waiting a quarter of an hour and making a couple of chancy casts I moved on. Two more fish broke the water, but I failed in much the same way to place them. I now came to a little spinney, just above which there is a sure find for a good fish. There is a little nook in the bank at the far side which is seldom untenanted when any rise is towards. Today was no exception, for hardly had my wet Rough Olive reached the holt ere my rod was a hoop and I was battling with a big fish. Alas! he elected to go down, and the spinney and its barbed-wire fence forbade any following. I had to hold and chance losing him, and in a few moments he had kicked off. Two or three minutes later the same fly tempted a very bright fish, just over one pound, and he went into the basket. A few yards farther on, over a bright-green weed patch, a big fish was cruising, and alternating bulging rushes with soft, tiny little rises. I suspected him of an occasional dry fly, and watching him I found him guilty. Accordingly I put up a small Pope's Nondescript, tied with hare's ear legs, and was about to approach him, when another trout broke the surface a little nearer. He had the first offer, and must have followed the fly down, for I was lifting the fly for the next cast when he slashed it and missed. I lost no time in covering the larger fish beyond. He came up promptly and was hooked, but got off after a flounder or two on the surface.

I had now reached a broad shallow in which there were several fish in position, and, selecting a good one, I put the same fly over him several times. Presently, just as I was about to lift it for another cast, the fly was taken by a smaller fish lying below him and to the far side. He was, however, a nice pounder, who looked as if he had not spawned, he was so fat and bright. His struggles, however, put off all the other fish on the shallow and I moved on.

I now came to a place where a long belt of trees protected the water from the north-west wind and left it absolutely unruf-fled. Under the far bank there were one or two fish rising at intervals to a very small pale dun, which began to hatch out in nice quantity. I missed the first fish, which I covered with a No.1 Whitchurch tied with honey-dun cock's hackle on a No.16 hook; but the second fish, making an almost invisible ring, and putting up a single bubble as he sucked in the fly, proved to be a sixteen inch fish in beautiful fettle. He scaled two pounds one ounce when weighed in the evening.

The next fish was taking in a similar place and in similar style. After being covered several times he came up and fastened, and after an extraordinarily brilliant fight came to net – one pound four ounces. The next fish I rose and missed – entirely my own fault. Then, almost in the spot where I had taken my second trout the previous day, I saw what looked to me like an excep-tionally fine trout move across an open patch. I changed my fly and put on an Ogden's Hare's Ear. While I was doing so he rose. He put up a second time within a couple of inches of my fly, and a third time a couple of casts later to take it. He weighed one and a half pounds that evening when I got in. Here the river bent so as to receive the full force of the north-wester up the next stretch, and I turned down again to get to the main. On my way I found one trout only rising, but he was willing, and made up my three brace as the clock struck two. I walked some way up the main, but did not see another fish rise, whether trout or grayling.

A curious contrast these two days! The first, the colder of the two, the rise began earlier and went on till after six, and the grayling were on all the time. The second, the milder day, was entirely a trout day, and the rise beginning at 11.30 was all over by two o'clock. The same flies were on both days. Why this contrast? (*The Way of a Trout with a Fly*)

A curious Itchen experience

Here is a prime example of Skues's powers of observation and deduc-tion. It is also the only time, as far as I can discover, that Skues mentions that he possesses marrow scoops of two different sizes to extract a trout's stomach contents. The friend Skues was fishing with was Dr. Norman McCaskie, who comments in his diary for the 27th June, 1930, 'It is a question how far this kind of fishing is fair or not. Carried a step further, with a close imitation of a toad, it would be too deadly.'

THE HEAVY RAINS of the Winter of 1929–30 and of the Spring of 1930 filled up the marshy fields which adjoin the Itchen on one side so full that the bank broke down in several places; and at one time, when the mill at the bottom of our length holds up the water a bit, it will be streaming into the marsh from the river and when again the water is let off at the mill the overflow of the marsh will come pouring back into the river through the same gaps. The result is that this year no angler, so far as I have seen, has fished from the marshy side.

In drier years it has often proved a very attractive side from which to fish, especially of an evening, enabling me to get behind good trout otherwise not very accessible and to look up the light on the water to the last moment of the blue-winged olive rise. I remember one July a number of years back finding the bank of that side so swarming with minute toads that it was hardly possible to move a step without crushing four or five.

In the present year of grace I was fishing from the other bank of the river (the west bank) with a friend on the evening of June 26th; it was about the time of the small spinner fall and the accompanying hatch of small pale watery duns, but to my surprise I noticed not only one but several trout making rises of extraordinary violence and obviously taking something much bigger than spinners or pale wateries. I wasted some time on a nymph of the blue-winged olive and again on that fly (so deadly when it is on) the blue-winged pale watery, but in vain. Then suddenly I had a brainwave.

Could the trout be taking tiny toads swept into the river from the bank where it let the water through? I, of course, had no toad nor anything like it to try, but it struck me that if the trout were taking under water anything so big as a baby toad they might be tempted by a big fly. I accordingly knotted on a Sedge fly (tied to sink) of a pattern given to me by Dr. Arthur Holmes and since used with success on the Test, and I put it across to the next rising fish. As it reached him there was a faint hump in the water and I was into him.

In due course I wetted my marrow spoon and passed it down the dead trout's gullet, and to my gratification, though not to my surprise, I found no less than four little toads among the contents brought up. *Toads*, if you please, not *frogs*.

To cut a long story short, in the next three quarters of an hour I caught four more trout with the same fly, and my friend to whom I communicated the discovery and gave a pattern of the fly, caught another. Each trout after being killed had his contents brought up in the marrow spoon, and every one had at least three little toads in it.

That marrow spoon with scoops of two different sizes is an enormous find. It should be put down the trout's throat wet, and it will, if turned in the stomach, bring up the entire contents in a wonderful way. A small enamelled basin should be carried to enable the angler to spread out the contents of his fish in water without the horrid and sanguinary mess of an autopsy. Thus he may find, as I did on this occasion, how the trout 'larn 'em to be twoads'. (*Itchen Memories*)

The swan's sense of decency

Skues describes his encounters with the swans who habitually nested at a point opposite McCaskie's Corner, one of the best fishing places on the river. In an introduction to Dr. Norman McCaskie's book, *Fishing: my Life's Hobby*, published posthumously, Skues says that for some reason which he never fathomed, shortly after a visit by McCaskie, the corner became known as McCaskie's Corner. I have read McCaskie's diaries and they offer no clue.

AT MCCASKIE'S CORNER, where my friend McCaskie has lured some excellent trout to their doom, the Itchen comes down in a straight run of say, 300 yards from the north, turning at McCaskie's Corner, at a right angle, and running due east for a hundred yards or more to the paddock abutting on the church-yard of Winnal St. Magdalen and then turning south again for maybe another hundred yards to the most northerly buildings of Winchester. The land on the east side of the river was marsh land, the haunt of coot, moorhen, mallard, teal and tufted duck, and at the point opposite to McCaskie's Corner a pair of swans had established a huge nest, barring passage to anyone along the east bank. Upstream, just around the corner above their nest, is a spot under the east bank which for all the years I have known the water has been the haunt of good trout – just a longish cast from the west bank.

Well, as I came up the west bank on that May morning a trout put up in the expected spot, and I prepared to cast. I had seen and passed the cob swan rooting weeds from the river bed some yards below, but, being on the far side from his nest, I felt no reason to apprehend his interference. Yet no sooner had I let out nearly enough line to reach my fish (note the word 'my') than I became aware that the bird was surging upstream under forced draught and had almost reached a point directly between me and the fish.

There was just time, I thought, for one cast. But as my Tup's Indispensable alighted I perceived that the line had fallen across the swan's back between his neck and wings. I saw also that the trout had risen, and, striking quietly, I hooked it. The rush of the fish straightened across the swan's back, lifting it, but not high enough to escape ruffling the bird's neck plumage. He turned and cursed me, and for several minutes I played the fish with the swan surging to and fro between it and me.

228

The moment came when the trout seemed ready for the net, but first the swan had to be fended off. I picked up a handy clod of earth with grass growing in it and lobbed it luckily into the middle of the swan's back. It drove him off for the necessary moment, and I dipped out the trout (2lb 6oz) while the swan sheered off, still raging and swearing.

That, however, was not the end of the matter. The following weekend, coming up the meadows on the west bank I reached a point just downstream of the southerly corner of the paddock above mentioned, when I thought I spotted a suspicious movement under a willow on the east bank. I had put on experimentally a newly devised pattern of the iron-blue nymph, and after several offers thought I spotted another suspicious movement under the willow. The next moment I was battling with some trout, and felt quite happy.

Not so happy, however, when a moment later I espied the cob swan surging downstream again under forced draught, obviously bent on intervention. I played the trout as hard as I dared and actually had it under my rod point when the swan arrived. He stood on his tail on the water within striking distance of the fish, and flapped his wings and cursed me savagely by all the gods in the swanny Pantheon without ever repeating himself. I was afraid from his behaviour that he would strike the line with his wings or the fish off the 17 hook with his beak. Just in time I espied a loose half brick and with a second lucky shot lobbed it on to the swan's back. Snarling with rage, he drew off, long enough to let me get my net under the fish and hoist it ashore – three and a quarter pounds. The swan was left cursing.

You would have thought that after that relations would be strained between the swan and me. Not a bit of it! Within a few weeks he and his wife with a team of cygnets were, as boldly and persistently as a swarm of Neapolitan beggars, impudently demanding to share my sandwiches. No, I do not consider the swan a self-respecting bird. (*Itchen Memories*)

Disagreement with colleagues

Skues's syndicate which leased the Itchen consisted of four members at the time he resigned. Their relationships seem to have been very happy until a new member came along who suggested various restrictions with which Skues disagreed. That member later resigned. Two members with whom Skues appears to have been on excellent terms were Judge Lilley, fondly referred to by Skues as Fleur de Lys, and Bostock, who was connected with the Lotus shoe firm. Abbots Barton seems to have been owned at this time by the Simonds family, and Sir Gavin Simonds was the fourth member of the syndicate. Skues records with disapproval that in 1937 Sir Gavin installed a stew in a small side stream from which 160 fish were turned into the main and 40 into the side stream. It may well be that Skues's disagreements were largely with Sir Gavin. However, there seems no doubt that members of the syndicate generally were not happy with Skues's fishing of the nymph, as his letter to his friend, John Evans, shows.

I SEE SYMPTOMS (one in the last number of the *Flyfishers' Club Journal*) of a recrudescence of dry fly purism. I do not recall whether I told you in the last year that I had one of our syndicate tackling me on the subject of nymph fishing and objecting that it was not fly fishing within the meaning of our agreement with the landlord of our length of the Itchen, and I found the other members of our little crowd so much in sympathy with him that I agreed not to fish nymph for the rest of the season, and had it not been for the fact that, with our stock of trout so low as it proved to be, it would have been difficult for them to get a new member to replace me, I would have resigned and looked for another rod elsewhere. As it is I have agreed not to resign for 1937 or, if I am still a going concern, for 1938.
(Letter to John Evans, 28th December, 1936)

Despite a growing disillusionment, Skues did not appear to have too bad a 1937 season. He killed 21 fish, of which only one was below one and a half pounds, and one was 3lb 5oz. Furthermore, he also caught his record Itchen trout, needless to say on a nymph pattern. Twenty one may not seem many, but one must remember that he only fished weekends and finished in August.

I DARESAY YOU remember being smashed by a violent trout in the straight above McCaskie's corner. Well, on Saturday last, just opposite that spot, I hooked, on a nymph, a trout so strong that I had fought him down nearly to the corner before I even got him to my side of the river. At that point, however, he decided to go back, and that helped me by side strain to get him under my bank and eventually to net him out just above the upper hatch. He weighed 3lb 14oz, a disappointment as the spring balance when I lifted him out went down to 4lb 2 or 3oz, but still the biggest trout by over half a pound I ever had out of the Itchen. (Letter to Wauton, 26th July, 1937)

McCaskie's last day

Skues's grievances against the syndicate are summarised in this piece about the last time he fished the Itchen with his great friend, Dr. Norman McCaskie. Some writers have stated that Skues was hounded from the Itchen because of his nymph fishing. This is plainly nonsense. Certainly, we have seen that his colleagues were unhappy with his nymph fishing, and this may well have involved a degree of jealousy because he caught more fish than they did. The restocking plainly irked him and the rod-sharing with guests was probably the final straw, as, over the years, he had entertained a succession of famous and not so famous anglers on the water.

His last day with his old friend was particularly pleasing because, for the first time, McCaskie got the knack of fishing a nymph.

ON JUNE 8TH, 1938 (in my eightieth year and very last on my dearly loved Itchen) my good friend, Dr. Norman McCaskie – yes, McCaskie of the Green Cat – was to have his birthday on that length which I had been fishing every season since May 1883.

For a string of years previous to 1938 conditions on that water had not been entirely happy. It was not only that my experimental and pioneer work in establishing the use of the artificial nymph as a fair and legitimate method of taking chalk stream trout was not approved by all the other members of the little syndicate which rented the Abbots Barton fishery, but several years earlier a new member had been elected whose activities from the first had not been conducive to the maintenance of the happy spirit which had hitherto prevailed among the members; and though he had resigned his membership several years previously (dying shortly after), that happy spirit had never been recovered and the uncomfortable spirit which has been brought into the whole functions and proceedings of the syndicate persisted among the members years after that member had resigned and died.

Although his introduction to the water should have satisfied him that that water was well stocked, yet he never missed an opportunity of proposing some fresh restriction upon the privileges of members, and for some reason which I never succeeded in comprehending he invariably succeeded in persuading the other members that the restriction he was for the moment proposing was demanded by the circumstances of the water; and as invariably I found myself in a minority of one, he also led the other members into voting expenditure on restocking, the only effect of which was to send down into the city waters shoals of little fish to be caught in scores by the city anglers in the Weir with maggots and worms. The number of days on which a member might have a guest on the water was more and more narrowly restricted, until in the previous year, though the number of members of the syndicate had declined from six to four, the only terms on which a member might have a guest to fish with him were that he must either share his rod with his guest or let the guest do all the fishing. In either case the number of fish that might be taken was one member's quota. More and more I resented these restrictions, and I would have resigned in 1937 if I could have found another water approximately as good and as accessible, but I had not done so, and had paid my subscription for the season of 1938 in June, and only in the ensuing April did I find myself able to secure for that and the two following years a rod on the Nadder with the privilege of having a friend to fish with me.

Thus it came about that on the last occasion when I would have the pleasure and privilege of entertaining my friend McCaskie on the Itchen we were confined to one rod between us. That rod, however, was that little 9-foot miracle of split cane from the U.S.A. which had been the joy of my life since it was given to me by a lifelong friend in 1905.

As July was at hand, I had tied an ample stock of nymph of the July dun, and I may say at once that it proved an entirely correct solution. Having come down to Winchester overnight, and having no need to spend any part of the morning on fly dressing, I was able to make an early start.

It was a lovely morning, more like July than June, and it was not long after ten o'clock when the Nuns' Walk, alongside the little Hyde brook, took us to the keeper's hut on the side stream. I took McCaskie there, because on two or three previous occasions I had spotted a handsome two pounder under the west bank of the side stream just above the weed rack and, having on each occasion risen him without succeeding in hooking him, I wished to give my friend the chance of seeing whether he could do any better. His luck, however, was out, for though, like me, he rose the fish, he failed to hook him, and he handed back my little Leonard to me. A cast upstream under the east bank brought me a trout of one and a half pounds, and then we made our way across the meadows eastward to the main stream, reaching it just above the clump of tall trees on the far side of the river. Thence we crept slowly up to the railway arch (which was now the top limit of the water) without finding a feeding trout, thence slowly down again to the clump, still finding nothing doing; then McCaskie insisted on my taking the rod, and just above the clump I caught another one and a half pounder but returned it in the hope of better fish.

McCaskie found nothing doing opposite the clump and handed back the rod. Nothing was rising under the east bank alongside of the tussock paddock on the downstream side of the clump, but the bright sun enabled me to spot a good fish lying deep on the clay-coloured bottom and, when I saw him move out just as my nymph was approaching, and then turn back to resume his position under the bank, I tightened and, as I fully expected, hooked the trout, and presently McCaskie netted him out for me – two and a half pounds. The rest of the water under the tussock bank was undisturbed – and McCaskie had not fished many yards down it before he had hooked another fish which put up a prolonged fight but came unstuck at the net. Bad luck. I will not recount our further experiences of that day in detail. But for the first time McCaskie got the knack of rising and hooking the trout on a nymph, and though several of his fish had to go back we took in two and a half brace – best fish two and a half pounds. His getting the knack was a great pleasure to me, and my only regret was that we were to have no more of the Itchen together. (*Itchen Memories*)

CHAPTER 17

End Pieces

The Nadder and the end of fishing

Skues was to see out the remainder of his fishing days on the River Nadder where he took a rod in 1938 on the Wilton to Barford St. Martin length. Fishing on the Nadder was never going to measure up to his experiences on the Itchen, so in some ways the last years were an anticlimax after the glories of the Itchen.

Writing to Wauton he says:

> THE NADDER HAS been a great disappointment to me. It contains, or contained, a few (very few) biggish fish, not at all free risers, a very few medium sized fish and apart from stock turned in this year very few other trout at all.
>
> I took a fortnight off for May fly and never saw a trout take a May fly. There was never a sufficient hatch to hang the trout in, though every weekend from 12th May to the end of August there was never a day that I did not see at least one in the air, and on the 31st July I twice saw as many as five in the air simultaneously.
>
> The general direction of the stream is west to east so that the wind is nearly always downstream. Unfortunately when it is easterly there are few parts which are fishable by reason of trees and other obstructions. (Letter to Wauton, 12th September, 1939)

234

In 1940, Skues finally retired from his London law practice and went to live beside the river at the Nadder Vale Hotel. The late Peggy Baring, who became the Countess of Malmesbury, recalled an incident which occurred during Skues's sojourn at the hotel. Whilst staying at the Nadder Vale for a weekend, she came down to breakfast one morning to be confronted by a furious Skues who said, 'You are in my seat.' Later, they became friends and he took her and her consort to his room and tied some flies for them.

Now that he was living permanently at the hotel, he had more time to spend on the river and, despite more gloomy reports to his correspondents, he started the 1941 season very well.

THE SEASON BEGAN on the 13th April with quite a strong rise of grannom for one day and a sporadic appearance for several days after. My first trout was two and a quarter pound. Soon after C.E. Sykes, as my guest, got one of 2lb 6oz. I had several others from one and a half pounds to two and a quarter pounds before the May fly began to hatch. It was a week before the trout began to take them but in the week I had two of 2lb 9oz each and one of 2lb 2oz and was broken in weeds by a big fish on Iron Blue. Then on a Friday the trout came on to the May fly and I hooked 2 two pounders, landing one two and a quarter pounds and losing the other at the net. In the afternoon of the same day in a stretch where I had only seen one trout rise this season I found six other risers and got another 2lb 9oz on Iron Blue. Next day I got another two and a quarter pounder on the same stretch on May fly and lost another in weeds. Then the deluge came and next day the Nadder was a brown flood and when that had subsided all interest in the M.F. had departed. (Letter to Wauton, 12th July, 1941)

By the end of the season, the River Catchment Board, as it was then, was tearing out the river bed and piling it in unsightly mounds which were slippery and dangerous for an 83-year-old. Skues was bitter about the activities of the Catchment Board and, worse still, his fishing landlord gave up his lease and the new owner had no vacancy to spare for him. He was reduced to membership of the Club fishing the Bemerton stretch damaged by the Catchment Board which gave him only 30 days fishing out of 153 in the trout season.

He lamented to Wauton that the 1942 season was very poor, but 1943 was even worse. 1944 was mediocre and in 1945 he failed to land a single fish over the size limit. The end was now in sight. He wrote to Sir Tom Eastham:

> I FEAR I must give up fishing as recently I have been troubled with fits of giddiness and if one should overtake me on one of these treacherous banks engineered by the Catchment Board or when wading and I should fall in the water I should not get up again. (Letter to Sir Tom Eastham, 24th September, 1945)

'As pants the heart'

The end of our fishing days is an acute reminder that the termination of our own personal season is not too far away. Skues had contemplated this long before 1945, and this piece was written when he was 64. It contains literary references to fishing and other topics, humour and that lightness of touch which endeared him to so many people.

> TO THOSE OF us who have worn out a long lifetime under the sky there must come one day a realization that we are at last on the home stretch and that, though this is in many respects an interesting old world, we are not sorry for it, if only we were not, like King Charles II, such an intolerable time a-dying; and to such it will fall at times to wonder what will be the sphere to which we shall be translated when the great promotion comes.
>
> The tastes of the fisher with the fly are simple and homely. No curious eye is his to measure the pearl gate and the jasper wall. Not for him the choirs of swan-winged angels in white surplices nor the jewelled glories tabulated in the Revelation of St. John the Divine. Some few of us even may be in secret sympathy with the small American boy who asked wistfully, 'Did anyone seed it 'sides John?' There is, however, one touch in that outpouring which has its appeal, the 'river of pure water which proceedeth out of the throne.' Did not a keen Scots angler look forward to whipping it with a fly busked with the hackle from Gabriel's wing?
>
> The notion of creating one's own heaven is no new one in the history of man, and perhaps St. John created his.
>
> If Edward Fitzgerald may be believed, his Persian singer of the eleventh century, Omar Khayyam, had a glimpse of the same idea in another shape:

I sent my soul through the invisible
Some letter of that after-life to spell
And presently my soul returned to me
And answered 'Thou thyself are heaven – or Hell'

while the Red Indian of North America passes in faith that he will re-awake in the Happy Hunting Grounds.

So, maybe, the members of the Club, if they came to formulate consciously their wishes for a hereafter, would fain find it in a well-watered country – beside such streams as they loved in the days of youth and strength and never ceased loving till the end.

Some of us would pass our time beside – or haply waist deep in – great rocky rivers haunted of salmon or sea trout, boiling in torrent or moving in swift solid might like molten glass. Others would choose the checkered little torrents of the moors with trout lurking in pools and eddying corners. But for me whose angling days have been spent in the main in the water meadows of Southern England the desire of the chalk stream persists, and I would fain find my happiness once more beside those gin-clear waters – 'rivers rustling o'er green grail of beryl' – to which I have so often gone for solace and refreshment in the years that have been taken from me, and in the company of good anglers, my friends who have been or are to be, who have gone before or are to come after.

Gently to chip old Izaak on his cribbing his fly dressing from Mascall when he had a real authority to hand in his friend Cotton; to find from Mascall why it was necessary to convey his fly dressing from Dame Juliana; to learn from that wise and devout and gentle lady, who understood so well the true spirit of angling, the far off sources from which she drew her lore. To seek in Cotton's memories the earliest hints of the dry fly. To discuss flies and fly-making with Ronalds and Aldam. To debate with Kingsley of Alder and Caperer and the small fly which he despised. To penetrate, perhaps, the secret of G.S. Marryat, and to learn the ruder lore of Francis Francis, and to meet once more with Carlisle and Turle and all the giants of the golden age of the dry fly renaissance. To catch in solitary moments shy glimpses of Pan and Syrinx peering through the reeds. And withal to bask in the exquisite sunlight of spring, to drink in the glory of grass and leaf and blossom – and to rest. (*Flyfishers' Journal*, 1924)

'Go softly. . .'

Four years later, Skues wrote this piece which goes a long way to explain his eternal enthusiasm for his fishing right through to his last days. It includes a wonderful quote from Rudyard Kipling.

ONE OF THE wisest of the sayings of wise Mr. George Herbert, author of so many wise sayings, was, 'He begins to die who quits his desires.' And true! Though it may possibly be not always wise to be too true. But of all the desires which persist in man, commend me to the desire of the fly fisher for the water brooks, which may perhaps explain why so few fishers with the fly die in their youth, though they be of those whom the Gods love; for while they may live many years, to them it is given that they never live to grow old. Yet I imagine that in the bosom of every fly fisher the desire for the water brooks, though general, is not so general as to preclude a special passion for some one of them, which to him is the archetype and crown of them all, which signifies to him in particular all that the 'happy hunting grounds' signified to the Red Indian, ere the white men came in to disturb him; and more, for it signifies loveliness beyond and above all sport and all desire of sport. To each some special loveliness not to be found otherwhere, and in every season, from the days when the first young grasses begin to push greenly through and above the sere brown berries of yesteryear and the jasper studded sproutings of the burdock remind one where its huge rhubarb-shaped leaves shall provide shelter for approach in later months, through the glory and the burgeoning of the later Spring and early Summer to those after days of regret and looking back when the rod is taken down and put away till – when? Therefore, did some angler poet (Kipling) write:

> *Go softly by that river's side*
> *Or when you would depart*
> *You'll find its every winding tied*
> *And knotted round your heart*

Go softly, brother angler. And again go softly, when it is time to go. (*Flyfishers' Journal*, 1928)

To Incognita
From a letter

'Ah, then I see Queen Mab hath been with you'

From all his writings and the comments and recollections of his friends, Skues appears to have been a confirmed bachelor all his life. He would seem to have been immune to the tugging of heartstrings by the fair sex that most men experience in their lifetimes. However, there is one extraordinary outpouring in a piece he wrote for *The Fishing Gazette* when he was only 32 years old. He includes it in his *Side-Lines, Side-Lights and Reflections,* and it is further illuminated by some comments which his friend, Dr. Barton, wrote in his own personal copy.

The most interesting revelation is that Incognita, the disguised person to whom the letter was addressed, is identified by Dr. Barton as the daughter of Dean Kitchin of Winchester Cathedral. The Reverend Doctor George William Kitchin was Dean from 1883 to 1895, and was the author of a book, *Winchester*, a local history. Barton pens a note at the foot of the letter, 'sunt lachryme rerum!' – a matter for tears. On Skues's visits to the cathedral he obviously worshipped this lady from afar.

As he takes her through a vision of fairies and the mating dances of May flies and other creatures of the night, the setting is Abbots Barton Farm, and the 'stately avenue of elms beneath which the saintly sisterhood walked of old' the Nun's Walk which leads to the fishery.

DEAR LADY,
Forgive the liberty I take in writing to you. You do not know who I am. You are never likely to know, nor need you care. It eases me to write to you; to think that in your mercy you may spare some gentle thought of pity for me. It need not make you angry, for I shall not presume. If I were rich, if I had anything to offer, I might come to you in other guise. If—

I was hot and restless and miserable, and I could not settle to anything. I went out into the open, and – I would you had been with me, for I have been in fairyland.

Outside the old farm steading, under the grey flint wall, the uneven tussocky turf lounges eastward to the water meadows. Here and there irregular spreading rings of brighter green mark the dancing schools of the fairies. But no fairy, sprite, or pixie

ever dares flip wing within the grey gloom of the farmyard. For
the farm was of old time a convent – consecrated walls, within
whose hallowed precincts no pagan presence may intrude.

To the north stretches a stately avenue of elms, beneath
which the saintly sisterhood walked of old, conning their beads
and meditating the vanity of earthly wishes, an avenue now
given over by the irony of fate to the wooings of men and
maidens of the city, and above to the cawing of a dean and
chapter of innumerable rooks.

As the sun sinks slowly westward the flaming petals of his
setting envelop the western hill tops and the motionless upper
branches of the elms in their soft pinky blaze. Eastward, the
level meadow stretching down to the riverside will soon be
wrapt in a mellow golden glory.

Try and fancy you are with me, and that I am your friend.

The level rays stretch out our shadows, long and distorted,
many yards before us. For a while a hush has come upon the
birds. Only to the northward a string of mallards with out-
stretched necks and vigorous wing hurtle through the upper air.

The corncrake thinks he has cause to complain of us, and
goes his grumbling way. Here and there from the tussocky side
of some ditch, or from some clump of meadowsweet, the
brown sedge warbler starts his querulous complaint. The swal-
lows are resting for a moment – for a moment the peewit ceases
his lament. The two kingfishers are resting poised on yonder
bush by the carrier. The swift has left us for the south, and one
misses his eerie skreeling cry.

But, look! the sun has laid his chin upon the hill top, and
the whole basin of the river is flooded with a magical golden
radiance. The air is shot with sunshine, and sparkles like a
delicate champagne.

The wind has dropped at the approach of night. In ten
minutes the sun will be off the water. In these ten minutes will
be packed glimpses of all that is loveliest in fairyland.

As we approach the river dainty groups of exquisite beings
throng the air in advance of us, all around us. Beings with
wings of filmiest gossamer texture and of rainbow radiance,
dancing rapturously in the expiring sunbeams. Madrigal and
minuet, serpentine or mazurka – to what exquisite strains,
unheard of mortal ears, are they dancing. Some of them with
bodies of a glassy clarity, decked at shoulder and at tail with
hues of orange, olive, or port wine hue. Some with great cock-

ling eyes of brilliant orange, all with long waving threadlike tails. Some glowing in the mellow sunlight like little animated red-hot needles, or dainty flagons of red wine. Others again of sherry hue glistening filmy fair tightropes, each served by its little brown attendant, link the blades of grass together in a fantastic network.

Here indeed is fairyland.

But the ten minutes are gone. As the sun sinks below the rolling westward down, the dancers magically vanish, leaving not a trace behind. The pink fades slowly in the sky, and as we move softly up the river bank, silent dimples break the water here and there close by the brink, and the widening rings tell us that the trout are taking down our beautiful dancers to the place where the good fairies go.

But think not that all is over yet. There is more fairyland to be seen. As the evening grows on, little fawn-coloured dames come fluttering abroad – tripping daintily up the sedges, running anxiously along my sleeve and over my shoulder and neck, wrapping their dove-hues or dappled cloaks around them with a grace no lady, save my lady, shall excel. The moths, their humble servitors, in dusky liveries, steal out from among the stems of grass, and come buzzing mysteriously and busily from flower to flower.

And so, hour after hour, the night through, host follows countless host, short-lived miracles of God's handicraft, going each swiftly to his inexorable doom. Lives of a day, an hour, yet not so short as to escape the horror of a violent death. To think that you and I hold our lives by a tenure scarcely less frail.

> *When you and I behind the veil are past,*
> *Oh what a long, long time the world shall last,*
> *Which of our coming and our going heeds*
> *As the sea's self might heed a pebble-cast.*

(The quotation is from Fitzgerald, author of the *Rubaiyat of Omar Khayyam*.)

We, too, must go. *Cras ingens iterabumus aequor.*

(Another of Skues's quotations from the Latin of Horace – Tomorrow we sail on the great sea or Tomorrow we begin a great journey.)

Beloved – let me call you so this once – I have no fear of death
for myself, but for you, for you—

But see the moon is topping the eastern slope, and shows us
a wet silver mist rising dank and chilly, knee high over the
pastures, and I must take you in. Let me wrap your cloak
around you. And so in silence to your home. And tomorrow,
when you sit enthroned in the cathedral, you shall never guess
who among the worshippers is he who opened to you the gates
of fairyland. Good-bye. (*Side-Lines, Side-Lights and Reflections*)

Matrimony

I have been able to discover only one other glimpse into Skues's
attitude to the other sex in a fragment of a letter which he wrote to
W.H. Lawrie the year before he died.

I WILL NOT pursue the argument beyond saying that in putting
it and parentage behind me, I entertain no doubt that I have
missed the best part of a man's life. (Letter to W.H. Lawrie,
26th March, 1948)

The last cast

In 1946, the new proprietors of a magazine called *Game and Gun*
changed its name to *Country Sportsman*, and re-launched it in
January 1947, inviting notable writers to contribute, including Skues.
Though in his 88th year, Skues wrote this delightful article which not
only gives an account of the last fish he ever caught, but reveals that
it was on a fly tied with winging materials sent to him over 50 years
before by the great American fly fisher, Theodore Gordon.

AT THE BEGINNING of the present century and maybe for several
of the last years of the nineteenth, I contributed a good many
articles, mainly on trout flies and their dressings, to *The Fishing
Gazette* over the *nom de guerre* of 'Val Conson'. In those days
The Fishing Gazette had an American correspondent or contributor named Theodore Gordon, who, though he died comparatively young, lived long enough to establish a great name
among American anglers and to have a standard American
pattern of trout fly called after him; and our contributions to
The Fishing Gazette led to a longish correspondence between
him and me. Nearly every one of his numerous letters to me

contained samples of American fly dressing materials (feathers and dubbing mostly) some of which remain among the materials recently presented by me to the Flyfishers' Club. Among the feathers sent me were a few Summer duck feathers, the best of all in my opinion for winging May flies or for hackling Straddlebug patterns of that insect. My letters from Gordon, on my becoming an Honorary Member of the Anglers' Club of New York in 1927, I presented to the Club.

The fishing which has chiefly engaged my attention was a stretch of the Itchen, where the May fly died out about 1900. So it came about that I did very little May fly fishing for the rest of my life, and Theodore Gordon's Summer duck feathers remained unused until some years after I had retired from business in 1940 when I took a rod on the Bemerton Club length of the Nadder, where the May fly have the unusual habit of dribbling on through the trout season and on to mid-November. I amused myself during my leisure by tying two or three Straddlebug patterns with Summer duck feathers of Gordon's giving, but somehow I seldom used them on the Nadder and I had one specimen left after age and infirmity had led to my resigning my rod on the Nadder and giving up fly fishing and fly dressing for good.

It was after this that a kind friend sent me a ticket for a day on the Wylye, and said that if I did not feel equal to using it myself I might pass it on to a friend. A brother, some seventeen years my junior, was to visit me in July, and was both able and willing to make use of the ticket. We drove together some two or three miles up the Wylye from Wilton and got on to the river on a day not far from August, at a place just above a mill, where, when the mill was not working, the surplus water was let off over a series of cement terraces into a small stream which joined the main channel below the mill. As we came to the tumbling water I thought I glimpsed a trout flash into the shelter of the white water at the foot of the fall.

We went down a few hundred yards to near the junction of the main stream with the let-off, and worked slowly and steadily up the let-off till we neared the terraces of tumbling water where my brother called a halt, complaining of fatigue aggravated by lumbago, and begged me to take his Leonard rod for a few minutes while he rested. I took off his fly, and, despite the lateness of the season – as I said, it was near August – I tied on the last of my Summer duck Straddlebugs. I picked the whitest patch of white water at the foot of the fall, and at the very first cast I thought I saw a dark body turn under the foam, and, raising the rod top, was at once attached to a trout, which my brother, refusing the rod, presently netted out. It was only 1lb 13oz, but we did not see another trout rise all day, nor a single May fly either in the air or on the water. So I owed the very last trout of a long life, with over sixty years of fly fishing, to a correspondence of some fifty years ago with a kindly American, long since dead, whom I never met. (*Angling Letters of G.E.M. Skues*)

Afterword

The importance of G.E.M. Skues, an angler-writer for today

G.E.M. Skues may be drifting from our ken; this is not as it should be for the most important fly fishing writer of the twentieth century. This essay sets out his fundamental importance to fly fishing for trout at the end of the century.

In 1947, Skues was corresponding with a French angler and wanted to send an experimental beetle pattern to him. Skues delayed replying while he combed the meadows along the River Nadder, where he was then living, hoping to find a specimen of the actual beetle to send along with his imitation. He noted at that time of year, the small thistles with pale pinkish flowers which bloom in the meadows should be covered with the insects, but he thought that cold weather must have killed them off at an earlier stage. 'For I have hunted the meadows for six days since the thistles were in bloom and have not found a single specimen.' Skues was then a month short of his eighty-ninth birthday. The anecdote reveals the man: the observant eye, the persistence, the inquiring mind, the experimental angler. Though no longer able to fish or tie flies, he was still searching for a better way and trying to aid another angler.

In 1883, when Skues began fishing the River Itchen, the dry fly was already established there since the 1870s and probably the 1860s. In 1885, H.S. Hall wrote about the dry fly for the Badminton Library, and Frederic Halford published his first two books in 1886 and 1889, 'after which,' Skues wrote, 'the dry fly on chalk streams became at first a rage and then a religion.' John Waller Hills said in his fine autobiography, *My Sporting Life* (1934), that he bought Halford's *Floating Flies* in 1886: 'I do not know how often I read it. I believe I knew it by heart. So clear was the writing, so unimpassioned, so convincing that I, like most others, took it as gospel.' Hills added 'no angler of this age can realize the effect Halford's books had upon our generation.' Of Halford's 1886 book, he said it 'was a revolution and a revelation.' Skues wrote of Halford's second, 1889 book, *Dry Fly Fishing*: 'I think I was at one with most anglers of the day in feeling that the last word had been written on the art of chalk stream fishing.'

Skues later lamented that 'one result of the triumph of the dry fly . . . was the obliteration from the minds of men . . . of all the wet-fly lore which had served many generations of chalk stream anglers well.' Anglers thought that only the dry fly could be effectively used on chalk streams 'or that the wet fly was ever used there.' Halford asserted that the wet fly was not successful on chalk streams and that it was hopeless on hot, bright, calm days. He believed that the wet fly angler who fished the chalk streams with an open mind would become a convert to the dry fly. Skues thought that Halford did more than anyone to discredit the wet fly on chalk streams.

But Skues had two advantages over Halford. As a young angler, he had spent much of his off-season time in the British Museum reading the fly fishing literature and was aware of the wet fly history on the chalk streams. In *Way of a Trout*, he said there is 'scarcely a book on trout-fly dressing and trout fishing which I have not studied and analyzed.' Also Skues had fished the wet fly on British north-country rivers (as had Hills). Halford began his fly fishing directly with the dry fly and, as Skues observed, there is 'no evidence Halford made any study of the older writers on fly dressing.'

Skues also had conversations with one of the last of the old wet fly men on the Itchen. He learned how they filled good baskets fishing downstream with long thirteen or fourteen foot rods, keeping their light hair lines off the water as much as possible, and drifting their wet flies over trout lying at the tails of the weed beds.

The method didn't appeal to Skues. A downstream wind was needed, since the line was too light to cast into the wind, and without a wind ripple on the super-clear chalk stream water, the downstream angler was exposed to the trout. Skues couldn't pick his days so when he could get to the Itchen, it might be bright, calm and the water glassy-smooth.

Skues's first wet fly experience on the Itchen came by accident. In 1892, he wrote, 'after some patient years of dry-fly practice, I had my first experience of the efficacy of the wet fly on the Itchen.' His wet fly success occurred when dry flies with inadequate hackles were immediately seized by trout when they sank after having been refused when floating. Several years later, after another accidental success with the wet fly on a difficult German limestone river, Skues began to think seriously about the systematic use of the wet fly on chalk streams.

Skues reasoned that if he were to succeed with the wet fly, and having eschewed the old downstream technique, it must be by a wet fly modification of the dry fly method of upstream casting to individual fish. He began with the bulgers.

For many years, Skues wrote, bulgers were the despair of his life. The trout would be seen actively feeding under the surface, swirling left and right, thereby making a boil or bulge in the surface. Skues cited a letter written to *The Fishing Gazette* where the writer complained that if the 'trout were bulging you might as well chuck your hat at them' as a fly. Halford had advised dry fly anglers to leave bulging fish alone. But Skues had fished the Tweed where the trout bulged all the time and the Tweed wet fly men had success with them. So Skues showed the Itchen trout an old Tweed wet pattern, the Greenwell's Glory, well soaked, cast upstream to the feeding fish 'like a floating fly' but sunk, and had success with it.

Skues sent a short article to *The Field* in 1899 which he regarded as the 'first public statement of the modern theory of wet-fly fishing on Chalk streams . . .' The article, modestly titled 'A Wet-Fly Suggestion,' described his antidote to the bitter complaints of dry fly men that the trout are bulging more each year, taking nymphs as they come up to hatch. So Skues asked, 'What is the moral for the dry-fly man? . . . When your fish are bulging give it to them wet.' In the past, he observed, 'anglers used to get good baskets on Itchen and Test with the wet-fly. They will have to come back to it again. Someday they will learn to combine . . . wet-fly science and dry-fly art . . .'

In the same year as Skues's article, Sir Edward Grey published his classic book, *Fly Fishing*, and opined that north-country wet fly tactics will not work on the southern chalk streams, and in any case, he knew the wet fly well enough to be sure that it had 'very narrow limits' on a chalk stream. Grey was wrong.

In 1900, Skues began fishing a fly that later became famous, the Tup's Indispensable. While the originator of the fly intended it for a spinner (it was a wingless, cock's hackled pattern) Skues discovered that dressed with a shorter, softer hackle and fished wet, it worked better with the bulgers than his winged wet Greenwells. When soaked, 'it was a remarkable imitation of a nymph he got from a trout's mouth.' It became the foundation of a small number of nymph patterns. In his early experiments, Skues thought his wet flies were taken for hatching nymphs. But then he found nymphs in trouts' mouths 'with no show of wings.' This led him to experiment with short-hackled, wingless patterns dressed to imitate nymphs.

Skues always found 'that pernicious insect,' the blue-winged olive hatch to be difficult. Dry flies didn't work for him. He tied his first specific nymph imitation for this hatch. With a dubbed body of olive seal's and bear's furs and a turn of a tiny blue hackle, he had immediate success with it after the trout, as usual, declined his floaters. But 'on this subject,' he noted, 'I am only at the beginning of inquiry.'

Other anglers had not 'suspected the propensity of chalk stream trout,' Skues observed, 'to feed largely on nymphs (outside the practice of bulging).' Most chalk stream anglers were unaware that 'for hours and days at a time the trout were feeding on nymphs and were letting the natural hatched-out insect go by.' These anglers kept casting dry flies at 'trout which were seen to be breaking the surface.' Skues's observations of the overwhelming propensity of trout to feed on nymphs were confirmed by his analyses of stomach contents. 'Up to the present,' he wrote in a 1930 article, 'I do not think there has been a trout whose stomach has yielded two percent of winged duns. Nymphs, nymphs, nymphs, all nymphs.'

He thought that the vast majority of even highly experienced anglers were ignorant of the nymph's existence, its form and character. Halford, however, was not one of them. Skues noted that Halford's analyses of stomach contents revealed to him that the vast bulk of the trout's food was underwater. But Halford ignored the implication because he believed the nymph could not be imitated. In his 1886 book, *Floating Flies*, Halford advised the dry fly angler to avoid trout feeding on larvae, shrimp and snail. And in his 1889 book, *Dry Fly Fishing*, he pronounced that head and tail rises of trout were a bad sign because it indicated that the trout were feeding on larvae close to the surface. He came to warn dry fly anglers off bulgers and tailers too.

John Waller Hills remembers in *My Sporting Life*, that when he first started to fish the Ramsbury water on the Kennet in 1902, the purist 'reigned a despot: nothing was admitted but the dry fly. Nymphs were not dreamed of.' Hills continued: 'Halford's very real invention and advance had reached its limit and had run itself out. We went to sleep over our oars. We became set and inflexible and it was not until we read Mr. Skues's *Minor Tactics* in 1910 that we woke up.' After describing recent changes in dry flies: the introduction of the spent spinner and new dry fly designs for duns, he turned back to Skues. 'But the greatest change of all was started by Mr. Skues's book. I was fascinated by it. . . .' But he noted that Skues's reform made way slowly. And Halford did not yield an inch.

In his last book, *The Dry Fly Man's Handbook* of 1913 (he was dead the next year), Halford gave what amounts to a reply to *Minor Tactics*. 'I am told, however, that there is a school of fly fishermen who only fish the sunk fly over a feeding fish or one in position if it will not take a floating fly. This . . . is a third method of wet-fly fishing, the other two being the more ordinary of *fishing the water* with sunk fly either upstream or downstream. Candidly, I have never seen this method in practice, and I have grave doubts as to its efficacy.'

Skues had no doubt as to the nymph's efficacy. In 1939 he reflected that his method of nymph fishing 'constitutes as real if not as great an advance in the art of fly fishing as the dry fly indubitably did. It has the merit of superseding or getting over serious difficulties and limitations of the dry fly . . .'

Skues's great insight was that trout in chalk streams mainly eat nymphs, including during hatches, and not the adult, emerged flies. He developed the flies and the fishing method to implement that insight. Halford's dry flies were a final flowering of the Victorian dry fly, which was essentially the old winged wet fly made 'vertical'. But nymphs tied specifically as imitations of larvae were new and radical. No one else did this before Skues with the exception of George Selwyn Marryat, the grey eminence behind Halford, who had tied nymph imitations in 1883 but soon abandoned them. Marryat probably fished them downstream in the old wet fly style. (George Holland, the renowned professional fly tier in Winchester, who dressed the nymphs for Marryat according to his specifications, told Skues that Marryat never caught any trout with them.) Skues had a truly modern mind, and he saw, generations ahead, what is becoming the predominant approach today in fishing hatches on fertile, insect-rich streams on either side of the Atlantic. The combination of low-floating dry flies, so-called emergers or nymphs fished in the surface or fractionally below it, and in the upstream style to rising fish owes its origin to Skues.

As with many profound innovations, Skues's discovery and development of nymphs and his method of fishing them seems simple in retrospect, but it wasn't. The great Marryat didn't do it, Halford couldn't do it, Skues did. He had his own early failure. Skues remembered that as early as 1888 he 'was already intrigued by the idea of representing the nymph artificially,' but like Marryat, Skues also abandoned it 'for a long time, discouraged no doubt by the failure of G.S. Marryat and Holland . . . ' But Skues returned to the idea, persisted, and changed the world of fly fishing for trout.

Skues thought that his nymph fishing was a new art or perhaps, he thought it was 'fairer to say, a new phase of an old and largely forgotten art.' John Waller Hills was right that Skues led a counter-reformation of the wet fly against the dry fly, but only partly right, for the fully aware and deliberate representation (Skues always preferred that word to imitation) of the nymph was new. So it was a counter-reformation with a new theology and not just a revival of the old faith.

Skues had always maintained that the nymph was supplemental to the dry fly. At the early time of *Minor Tactics*, I think he believed it, but by his later writings my judgement is that he no longer did, but maintained the assertion as a defensive position. Later in life my reading is that he saw the nymph as the central method of chalk stream fishing. In the fourth 1949 edition of *Way of a Trout*, he added a chapter called 'The Constant Nymph', referring to the predilection of trout to feed on nymphs over duns – 'the strong attraction of the constant nymph.' It was 'nymphs, nymphs, nymphs, all nymphs' as he declared in his 1930 article. In the posthumously published *Itchen Memories* (1951) Skues said in the preface that 'for several years past, therefore, I have only fished the floating fly when I was definitely convinced that that was what the trout were taking . . .' In 'The Constant Nymph', Skues summed up: '. . . the angler who offers his trout a proper pattern of nymph stands a better chance of sport than does one who offers it a floating fly.' He never abandoned the dry fly, of course; there were times it fished best when the trout actually were on the emerged duns (and, of course, spinners) and he still enjoyed fishing dry flies. So he came then, I believe, to feel that the nymph was the major method on chalk streams, not an auxiliary to the dry fly. So why did he not say so explicitly? Because he knew he was holding a red flag in his hands and he did not want to wave it, too, at the dry fly men. So he maintained his deflationary title in 1921 when he sub-titled his book *And Some Further Studies In Minor Tactics*; and he maintained his deflationary position in the 1939 statement cited earlier, so as to try to turn away wrath with a soft word. He knew that the statement quoted from the preface to *Itchen Memories* would not be published until after his death.

Halford was long gone, but his followers remained and they were still a problem for Skues. The members of the Abbots Barton syndicate on the Itchen which he belonged to came to disapprove of his use of the nymph; then Skues was 'a minority of one,' as he put it, against re-stocking the water; and guest days were gradually restricted until he was required to share a rod with a guest or let the guest do all the fishing. Skues wrote 'more and more I resented these restrictions,' and he resigned his rod on the Itchen in 1938 where he had fished for 56 years.

Also in 1938, Skues took part in a 'star chamber' of a debate (as Donald Overfield has described it) at the Flyfishers' Club, which essentially put on trial his life's work in establishing the nymph as an effective and ethical method on chalk streams. Opinion at the debate went against Skues. To then make a claim for the nymph as the central technique of chalk stream fishing, and the demotion of the dry fly to second rank, would have only intensified Skues's problems and brought them on earlier.

Skues kept other things to himself.

• Gordon Mackie wrote in *Trout and Salmon* magazine some years ago that Skues knew the 'induced take' (moving the nymph slightly as it comes close to a trout to stimulate a take), but avoided writing about it for fear that any intentional movement of the fly would have aroused cries of his using the old downstream and dragging wet fly.

• Skues had corresponded extensively with James Leisenring, and probably was aware of the 'lift' technique, but if so, he again refrained from writing of it.

• Frank Sawyer, in his 1958 book, *Nymphs and the Trout*, had criticised Skues for writing that nymphs floated inertly in the surface. Sawyer argued that there is always some movement in the nymph. But Sawyer's statement is only partly true: periods of vigorous movement to break from the shuck alternate with inert rest. The struggle to escape the shuck is not continuous. This is certainly true of the nymphs of the *baetis* and *ephemerella* genera in insect-rich, flat-water spring creeks in the U.S. These genera also would have been the two most important to Skues and the chalk streams. Henrik Thomsen, the Danish fly tier, made the same observation of alternating struggle and inert drift in his excellent 1981 paper, 'GEM Skues, the Conservative Rebel.'

Skues was too close an observer not to have been aware of any characteristic movement of nymphs as they drifted in or just below the surface. His assertion of a comprehensive inertia may have been debate-tactical. If Skues had admitted that nymphs move as they drift under the surface he would have yielded the argument over the effectiveness of nymph fishing to Halford, who, of course, asserted that nymphs could not be imitated because of their vigorous wiggling movement. Skues needed to maintain his no movement assertion or his counter-argument to Halford would have been severely weakened – as a debating matter, not in actuality.

Vincent Marinaro criticised Skues for not 'emancipating' the dry fly as he did the wet. I do not know whether Skues could have done so, but he was not likely to focus on it after 1921 or so when the dry fly became less and less important to his thinking. The dry fly wasn't central to him or to his estimation of generally effective chalk stream fishing anymore. His awareness of 'the constant nymph' pushed aside the dry fly's importance.

Skues thought that many dry flies, winged floating patterns, were only taken by the trout because of their resemblance to nymphs anyway, the wings being ignored. He believed that nymphs were far more precise imitations than wet flies and 'probably more exact than floating artificial flies are of the floating natural duns or spinners.' He was convinced that it was more important to offer the right nymph to the trout than the right dry fly 'for the trout gets a clearer view of its subaqueous food than it does of its surface prey.' These are not the considerations of a man who believes the dry fly to be central to chalk stream fishing and the nymph its auxiliary.

John Waller Hills described how the trout beat him one evening on the Test, with Skues as his guest, in the blue-winged olive hatch. Skues saw that the 'trout were taking not the hatched fly, but the hatching nymph, on or just below the surface. A difficult thing to spot: fish are not moving about as when bulging, but stationary, apparently rising. He had seen this, I had not. He had caught fish, I had not.' Skues was a master at reading the message of the rise form.

He wrote in 1939: 'The due appreciation of *how* a trout is rising forms the very essence of fishing, whether it be with floating fly or artificial nymph – and it is often no easy matter.' Prior to Skues there had been '*no systematic attempt* [my emphasis] to differentiate the varying forms of the rise of trout' in angling literature. In *Way of a Trout*, Skues analysed the types of rises, because he believed that 'close study of the form of the rise may often give the observant angler a clue, otherwise lacking, to the type of fly which the trout is taking, and to the stage and condition in which he is taking it.'

Norman McCaskie described 'Skues's differentiation of the rise forms of trout as the greatest feat of pure observation in the annals of fishing.' Even given that McCaskie, no mean angler or writer himself, was a friend of Skues, this high praise still stands. Skues's differentiation of rise forms was a direct influence on Vincent Marinaro, who thought that recognising the various rise forms by the trout fisherman 'is as important as a fingerprint or footprint in human affairs.'

Skues was a great fly fishing tactician, probably the best ever for the kind of fishing he loved: the fertile, insect-rich, flat-water streams of the chalk valleys. Reading Skues on tactics today is like going fishing on a great and challenging trout stream with a friend who is the best angler you have ever met. Whether it's Skues showing you why the left bank, for a right-handed angler, with his rod-hand on the in-shore side, is the bank of advantage, not a handicap; or joining his adventures with the alder fly on a German limestone river; or why a day blowing a gale, and a large dry fly, is the recipe for catching a big trout if you know where one lies; reading him on tactics is a delight, never dated, and absorbingly interesting.

Skues gave the nymph its myth, as Datus Proper said Vincent Marinaro did for terrestrials. But Skues was much concerned with terrestrials, too: he had a floating red ant imitation that would have satisfied Marinaro's criteria even though Marinaro said he could find none in the American literature and nothing acceptable in the British. Halford's ant, a whimsical Victorian version, looked like an upwinged mayfly imitation. (That may explain why Theodore Gordon thought the Royal Coachman was an ant imitation.) Skues was also much taken with beetles, he used and devised several imitations, fished both dry and wet. He ignored grasshoppers, but they are a hot-summer insect, not a usual event in Britain, but ants and beetles flourish everywhere.

As terrestrials have assumed large importance in modern fly fishing for trout, especially in the U.S., so has the soft hackle fly. Soft hackles are prominent now in fishing hatches by both dry fly and nymph fishermen. Skues pointed out that 'the hackle provides flotation and imitates wings and legs. The soft tips of the hackles make a far less alarming drag than does a cock's hackle.' Datus Proper said that 'Skues deserves much of the credit for bringing the soft-hackle design to the attention of modern dry-fly and nymph fishers.'

In Colonel E.W. Harding's 'splendid treatise', as Marinaro called it, entitled *The Flyfisher and The Trout's Point of View* (1931), Harding noted that Skues was the first to discuss the trout's point of view systematically: that is, what the trout sees and how it sees it. Harding said that Skues's *Way of a Trout* was the primary inspiration for his own book. He added that 'I doubt whether the value of *The Way of a Trout with a Fly* is realized even yet, nor how it must eventually affect the form of fly fishing literature.'

Skues's writings on nymphs, rise forms, and the trout's point of view have directly and indirectly influenced the mainstream of writing about imitative fly fishing for trout in the twentieth century from Harding to Marinaro, Datus Proper, Clarke and Goddard, Gary Borger, and Gary LaFontaine. Harding was thought a crank on the chalk streams and his book languished until after World War Two, when Marinaro picked it up and began the dry fly revolution of our time. Datus Proper, after acknowledging the personal influence of Marinaro and his writings, said that 'only G.E.M. Skues has made a comparable impact on my thinking.' Proper was referring to his own landmark book, *What the Trout Said.*

The Way of a Trout, in addition to the profound insights it provides (Gary Borger said that it 'can never age because it provides so many basic insights into trout fishing'), became so influential because it laid out an agenda for future studies in imitative trout fishing. That was a great thing to have done.

Alfred North Whitehead, in a famous remark, said that the safest, general characterisation of European philosophy is that it consists of a series of footnotes to Plato. In many fundamental respects, modern studies in imitative fly fishing for trout are a series of footnotes to Skues.

Robert H. Berls
March 1998

Bibliography

Skues's books

Minor Tactics of the Chalk Stream (A & C Black, 1910)
The Way of a Trout with a Fly (A & C Black, 1921)
Side-Lines, Side-Lights and Reflections (Seeley, Service & Co, 1932)
Nymph Fishing for Chalk Stream Trout (A & C Black, 1939)

Posthumous
Itchen Memories (Herbert Jenkins, 1951)
Trivialities of a Long Life (An unpublished manuscript of Skues's reminiscences)

Collections

Silk, Fur and Feather, a collection of Skues's articles published in *The Fishing Gazette* (*The Fishing Gazette,* 1950)
Angling Letters of G.E.M. Skues, edited by Commander C.F. Walker (A & C Black, 1956)
The Way of a Man with a Trout, a collection by T. Donald Overfield of Skues's articles published in the *Flyfishers' Journal* (Ernest Benn, 1977)
Barton, E.A. *Diaries,* 1920–1938
Clarke, B. & Goddard, J. *The Trout and the Fly* (Ernest Benn, 1980)
Dunne, J.W. *Sunshine & the Dry Fly* (A & C Black, 1924)
Francis Francis, *A Book on Angling* (London, 1867)
Goddard, J. *Trout Fly Recognition* (A & C Black, 1966)
Stewart, W.C. *The Practical Angler* (Edinburgh, 1857)
Halford, F.M. *Floating Flies and How to Dress Them* (London, 1886)
  Dry Fly Fishing in Theory and Practice (Sampson Low, 1889)
  Dry Fly Entomology (London, 1897)
  Modern Development of the Dry Fly (Routledge, 1910)
  The Dry Fly Man's Handbook (Routledge, 1913)
Harris, J.R. *An Angler's Entomology* (Collins, 1952)

255

Hills, J.W. *A History of Fly Fishing for Trout* (Barry Sherlock, 1973)

Lawrie, W.H. *A Reference Book of English Trout Flies* (Pelham Books, 1967)

McCaskie, N. *Fishing: My Life's Hobby* (Falcon, 1950)

McCaskie, N. *Diary, 1924–32*

Mottram, J.C. *Fly Fishing: some New Arts and Mysteries* (Seeley Service, 1915)

Sawyer, F. *Nymphs and the Trout* (A & C Black, 1958)

Schwiebert, E. *Nymphs* (Winchester Press, 1973)

Stewart, W.C. *The Practical Angler* (Edinburgh, 1857)

Vines, S. *Frank Sawyer, Man of the Riverside* (Allen & Unwin, 1984)

Voss Bark, C. *A History of Fly Fishing* (Merlin Unwin Books, 1992)

Ward, F. *Animal Life Under Water* (1919)

Williams, A.C. *A Dictionary of Trout Flies* (A & C Black, 1949)

Index